5024 E. McDowell

A Man's Journey Into Culinary Exploration

A Story Cookbook

To Eileen
Thank you
Best wishes

Credits:

Typesetting/design/layout by Debra N. Ross, DNRoss & Associates, Phoenix, Arizona.

I would like to thank Debra Ross for assisting me with the editing of the original manuscript.

I also would like to thank my daughter, Lisa Ligidakis, for helping me with the editing of this immense project.

A special thank you to everyone who believed in this project and who's support enabled me to complete my work.

Printed in the United States of America

Printed by Biltmore Pro•Print, Phoenix, Arizona

Other works by Nick Ligidakis:

"Nick's Creative Cooking Made Easy," © 1987 ISBN 0-9615418-4-9
"My Golden Collection of Original Desserts," © 1993 ISBN 0-9658158-1-1

Published by:
Inkwell Productions
P.O. Box 388
Phoenix, Arizona 85001
Contact above address to order any of Nick's books.

Coming soon:

"The Heroes of my Thoughts"
   True heroes will make you believe in yourself. They will inspire your mind with the confidence to be the best that you can be. And through their examples will infuse your heart with courage to overcome the difficulties in your life.

CONTENTS

The story of how the restaurant has started, how the recipes were developed and how the inspiration for the charity work began.

This story begins on page 1 and continues throughout the book.

CHAPTERS OF THE STORY

THE AGING OF THE MIND

We go through stages in our lives thinking we have done and accomplished so much. Then a time comes that one's mind is overflowing with memories and events. When we sit back and take a break, we begin to think of our accomplishments and find only emptiness. We ask the question, "What have we done with our lives that will create a legacy when we are gone?" Most of us are unable to answer this question. All that comes to mind are stories, adventures, relationships, friendships, satisfactions and disappointments. We are searching for one thing we have done with substance and value. We look through the pages and everything we saw as great accomplishments now seem meaningless. The glories and the triumphs, the defeats and disappointments, the celebrations, separations, laughter, sadness, the happiness and the loneliness all seem a faded memory of yesteryear.

Just as everything else will fade and disappear, physical beauty is unforgiving. However, the beauty of the mind is eternal and everlasting for generations to come. You sit back and try to figure out what happened to the beliefs of your heart, the same beliefs that brought tears to your eyes when you watched your heroes win and the bad guys lose. What happened to the emotions you felt when you heard about the hungry stomachs or the laughter on the children's faces? What happened to the songs of freedom that made you proud? Why have you let your heroes down by forgetting their beliefs and ideas? When we sit back and analyze our lives, everything seems like a giant puzzle – pieces of different colors scattered around and we are desperate to assemble them. Is life worth it? Like thousands of pieces thrown around without meaning; pieces with faded numbers, others with bright colors or just black and white? Where do we begin and where do we end with this impossible puzzle? The best place to begin is within ourselves.

It was at the beginning of 1984 on one of my trips back from California to Phoenix that I had time to sit back and collect my thoughts. Through fifty years of my life there were a few times I thought I had everything: strength, confidence, charm, courage to dare, health and vitality and the ability to survive. But what did all this really mean? All of those qualifies can be self destructive if not used properly. They can be used to blossom into maturity. Maturity usually comes without warning and is impossible to miss. I used to believe that some people never matured. However, the truth is everyone comes of age though some choose to ignore it. They choose to live their lives without commitment or take responsibility for their own self. I am a firm believer that taking responsibility will make your life easier in the long run. Assuming that one's life becomes more convenient without responsibility, this attitude affects our society in a negative way.

I remember the exact year of my maturity – it was 1984. I grabbed the opportunity and held it like the most precious possession in my life. Time had come for me to practice what I had learned from life, and to look up to my heroes for inspiration because the road to self peace was filled with obstacles. There were people who looked up to me as an example. The people who knew me then could not believe the changes and the people who know me now cannot imagine my life any other way. Lifestyle is a reflection of your beliefs.

I had stood on the lines to demonstrate human rights and spoken out against corrupt governments and useless monarchs. I refused to be a product of society, a society I did not like. I was proud to see our heroes decorated, and cried when they died. I felt sad when wars killed our children and destroyed our future generations, and I watched helplessly the hunger of children and the abuse of elders. We all say we're compassionate for the unfortunate, yet we do nothing. We continue with our lives and worry only for ourselves. I believe this attitude will come to hurt us one day in our life. Then we will not be able to handle rejection by society. By then society will no longer need us for we will have nothing of substance to offer.

Maturity of mind and soul will always be needed in our society, now and after we are gone.

DEDICATION TO MY CHILDREN

Lisa Nicole
Steven Michael
Joseph Nicholas

Without them none of this could have happened.

*A*t about age 38 I had a serious conversation with myself. One of those conversations that I like to have with people who are interested in analyzing life and human behavior. The conversation lasted several hours. I asked myself two questions: one was about direction and the other was about selfishness.

I believe that our direction of thinking changes if it is for someone or something you love a great deal. This love will also make you less selfish. If the direction that my life is moving is to please me, then I have been selfish. By human nature we do not always listen to our inner voice. We allow others to influence us. When the time comes in our lives to listen to our inner voice and follow the path we are given, this is a sign of maturity. The point is that after we have matured we are the only ones that know who we are. To know our capacity and our limitations has its benefits, but to get there takes lots of hard work. Only when you reach a time in your life when you can say to yourself that you know who you are and believe it, can you trust your decisions without outside influences and without favoritism toward yourself.

So at the age of 38 and after many adventures in my life, I had come full circle. Only the characters in my life change throughout the years. I have taken the place of my father and my children have taken my place. Different people, same roles. I told myself I had to be the best example I could for my children.

My children have been raised to be independent thinkers and to form their own opinions. None of my children are easily influenced by someone else's lifestyle or beliefs, even mine. So I knew my efforts to influence their lives had to be something spectacular and maybe I could draw their respect which would blossom into love for life. It was time to become an example, and the cause of that change of direction made hard work easy to handle. When you have a mission to accomplish, the difficulties along the way do not matter. Everything can and will be overcome.

FOR THE LOVE OF AN ART

*P*erhaps Lisa Schnebly Heidiger describes it best (see page 301): "The restaurant is here because Nick wants it to be. His restaurant is his mission…Nick creates dishes the way Mozart made music, all in his head, able to picture the final result without writing it down or tasting it first."

The restaurant was a way for me to express the art of cooking. I had imagined in my head and nothing was going to stand in the way of accomplishing it. Along the way there were difficulties and along with the difficulties came advertity.

I was not trying to be a martyr or prove a point that in order to complete your art you must go through prosecutions. In life it just happens that way! What was success in my mind was failure in other people's eyes. I struggled and succeeded in things that were important to me but I failed at things which were unimportant for my life. This is not a justification, but an expression of the satisfaction I felt in doing that which was important to me.

But let me say one thing. What people thought was hard work was not difficult for me. It was only an effort to complete what began in my mind years ago to develop the picture I had envisioned. What others thought perceived as tremendous suffering with its accompanied difficulties, to me it was just another challenge which would build my character and the character of my restaurant and eventually bring us both to maturity. That maturity reenforced the determination of my mind and the beliefs of my heart.

Perhaps Lisa wrote it the best.

"You've got to sing like you don't need the money,
love like you will never get hurt,
dance like nobody is watching.
It's gotta come from the heart,
if you want it to work."

A TRIP TO THE PORT OF HOPE

*A*t every turn there was a breathtaking picture of beauty. Driving down the narrow, twisted roads of the island of Thassos, every sharp turn brought sounds of worry from my passengers. I wanted to stop and enjoy the beauty of the island, but was forced to concentrate on the road ahead. Looking at my watch there was little time to get to the Port. A voice from the back seat said, "We should never have come this way." Another person responded, "Yes, we should have gone the way we knew." Yet another added, "We chose this way because when we looked at the map it seemed shorter." We had to drive up and over a mountain to get to the other side of the island.

As we climbed the mountain, to the right of us was the deep drop to the crystal clear blue water. Every turn in the car brought a new picture of natural coves formed by trees and rocks. On the left were the mountains in all their beauty full of green trees. I had a hard time concentrating on the turns between the trees and the sea. I was driving fast to get to the Port on time. "Slow down!" I heard many times. "Careful!" I heard more times than ever. By now everyone was convinced that we had missed the last ferry back to the mainland; however, I had no doubt that we would make it.

On our way through the tiny villages, we had to pass people on the narrow streets who were moving very slowly, enjoying life. Other times we were forced to stop because large busses would block the roads. Everyone in the car became anxious trying to rush life and the slow-moving people. The villagers were full of peace. Looking back now I envy those people. We work a lifetime to find inner peace and in those remote villages they had peace in their everyday life. Finally we passed the bus, more turns, and more sounds from the back seat. We were passing the beauty and serene nature too fast as we were leaving the peaceful people behind us too soon. With agony in our hearts and all eyes on our watches we finally made it to the Port. We made it just in time for the last ferry. I've always wanted to go back and take that road again. But the next time I will slow down and enjoy the beauty of the land and keep that picture in my mind forever. Once we made it to the Port we were still rushed to make it to the ship and to move on to a different place.

I compare that story to my life now. How many beautiful moments have gone by because I had to catch a train or a ship to move me to a different place. I've thought a lot about my restaurant life over the past 13 years. Accomplishments and disappointments were many. In fact, some go through a lifetime without accomplishing as much as I have in such a short time. But what does all this really mean? What is more important? Rushing to the port to catch a ferry or avoiding the disappointment by taking time to enjoy the view?

Just like that trip I took with Sofia, Stavros, Tasos and Teressa, the restaurant was on a similar trip: full of twists, heartbreaking moments, turns of disbelief. Every day a new experience. Every turn a new event.

Regardless, all I had to do was reach the Port. But the road there was difficult yet gratifying. Another question asked was: Would I ever get there? But I had no doubt in my mind that I would.

Klima is on the Island of Milos, and it is our favorite vacation place.

WE MUST DARE TO BE DIFFERENT

I remember the day vividly. It was early afternoon as I pulled in front of that little restaurant. I stopped the car and sat for a few minutes looking at the storefront window. There was a picture of a large pizza and another picture of a chicken, both badly drawn and with bright colors that would catch your attention. The words "pizza" and "chicken wings" were written under them. I leaned back in the seat of the car hesitating whether to open the door or not. So many thoughts went through my mind. This was the second time I parked in front of "Golden Pizza." The first time I drove away without getting out. I do not know if I wanted anything to do with that place, but my friend John kept telling me about this little pizza place which the owners wanted to sell and it would be a good opportunity for me to start all over again with restaurants and cooking.

I had some reservations of going back into the business. I did not want to do the same thing I had done in the past. Neither did I want to do what everyone else did. I wanted something different and I didn't know if that little pizza parlor with chicken wings could provide me enough inspiration to create what I wanted.

First of all, I didn't know exactly what I wanted to do if I got into that business again. Something was holding my hand, putting the car in reverse and driving out of there. I thought of my children: Lisa, 12, Steven, 10 and Joseph, 9, and the responsibilities along the way. So far we were just making ends meet. But the years of schooling and the pains of growing were just ahead of us. I needed to be ready financially and mentally so I could provide both for them.

I checked the money in my pocket and counted $52.50. I had my doubts on going back into the restaurant business with its tortures, work schedules, constant worries and the pressure of performing on a daily basis. Something was keeping me from opening the car door but some other vision kept me thinking of the future. What were my options other than taking my responsibilities more seriously and being more dependable as a parent? I was thinking there was time for me to start building memories. I mechanically opened the door of that old Honda and walked towards the restaurant. As I entered it and walked towards the lady at the front counter. I had a strange feeling it was like I did not want to be there but at the same time I was drawn into it.

The room was small and plain. There were three or four tables scattered around the dining room, covered with red and white checkered plastic tablecloths that matched the curtains covering the windows. A couple of video game machines were standing against the wall. Right in front of me was a square counter to order and pick up the foods. Next to it a plywood wall which separated the kitchen from the dining room and on that wall a couple of Pepsi Cola boards describing the menu. Pizza, subs, and chicken wings were the specialties of the house.

I walked up to the counter. The lady was anxiously waiting for me.

"Can I help you?" she asked, her voice sounding helpful but full of questions.

I glanced back into the tiny kitchen area. A man with a nice smile looked at me and waved. Somehow I felt comfortable and returned the gesture. But with the lady it was different. She talked so much but said nothing. I remember she was bragging about their business and their food.

"You order something?" she said with a heavy accent.

"No, thank you," I answered. As I looked around I saw a puzzled look in her eyes as she looked at the man in the kitchen.

"Are you Italian?" she asked me.

"No, are you?" I asked her back.

"No, no, I am Greek," she said.

"Then why don't you speak Greek so I can communicate with you?" I said.

"You are Greek! Christo, this man is Greek," she exclaimed, turning to the man in the kitchen.

He started to move slowly toward us and offered me his hand and a smile. I liked him immediately. As I shook his hand and looked at his face he inspired me with trust. Then they both came out from behind the counter. They were the same height, about 5´5˝ and on the heavy side, only they were so different in personality. He was quiet, polite and spoke few words. She was loud and spoke constantly. She kept talking about her childhood in Greece and all her accomplishments in this country, subjects which truly bored me. She must have realized that and finally stopped talking!

"I hear this place is for sale," I asked quickly before she could speak again.

She put some fake surprise on her face and said, "God forbid, no, we are doing a great business here. We don't want to sell."

Like I said, she spoke constantly and had nothing to say. I was looking at Christo, waiting for an answer from him. He gestured with his hand asking her to be quiet for a few seconds to give him a chance to speak. "Everything is possible," he said.

"But Christo…" she started to say.

He looked at her with a command to be quiet and she stopped.

"What did you have in mind?" he asked me. We talked for a while about the business. Then I walked with him through the kitchen. There was a double pizza oven, a salad table, a mixer and a two-door stand up refrigerator; mainly set up for pizza making.

"How much do you want for your business?" I asked him.

"Sixty thousand dollars," he said.

I smiled at him and had no doubt he could not read my thoughts. I was short some fifty-nine thousand nine hundred forty six dollars and fifty cents! "I don't know, but I don't think your place is worth that much," I said.

"Make me an offer," he replied.

"Twenty five thousand," I said.

He gave me that humble smile of his and she started talking again. I couldn't understand what she was saying, but I could tell she was offended by my offer. I felt he would negotiate to a logical price and she would take just about anything!

I thanked them for their time and assured them I would return to discuss the business further. As I walked out, I had a feeling that this restaurant on 5024 E. McDowell would be mine and would play a major role in my life.

As I was driving back to Tempe to see my children, I flashed back through my life. At 38 years of age I had experienced so much. I remember my wonderful childhood and how much I learned from it. I was limited in material things but unlimited in love and happiness. I thought of my parents who were mainly responsible. They would forever be my heroes. I would have done anything so my children would have the same feelings when they grew up. It amazed me that my parents had so much energy to give us and I thought of the sacrifices they denied themselves so we could have the necessary upbringing and a carefree childhood. Now I understood their happiness and why they were so content with life. They were doing what they enjoyed best…the happiness that came from simple and noble things like commitment and love and not from riches or material possessions.

Now I knew it was time for me to focus on how my own childrens' minds would be shaped and how well they would look up to me as they grew up. Their mother and I had been separated for nine years, but Claudia and I had remained good friends. We focused on how to take care of our children. We never dwelled at the past or our personal difficulties. We tried our best to focus on our children's future. But for me that was not enough. I could not rest my laurels on traveling the world over and I could not build a future living in the past and a life of uncertainty. Searching for the unknown every day was not going to inspire security in my mind.

I searched my mind for the substance to give me peace and always ended up with three pictures of little faces in my mind. I searched for philosophical teachings and other spiritual guidance to help me with this, but my mind always ended up with simplicity. There are not too many words one can say. It was the commitment we could make, and to be a good example.

I thought about deeds, not words and my mind went back to that little place on McDowell Road. Maybe that was my only opportunity right now to do my deeds. At 38 years old my life had come full circle and I didn't know where the next payment for the rent would come from. How was I going to make that little business blossom? I'd been out of the business a few years and didn't want to go back to it unless I had total control and could practice my own style of cooking. For me food was priority above all. That was what would bring the people back! Yet the place that I wanted it to begin all over again in had all odds against it.

The location was in an area where people would have to drive specifically to it; a strip mall with a couple of bars around it. It was small and out of character. And I was nobody in this town. I had no name and no money. But to me none of these things mattered. I knew once I was in that place I could make things happen. Optimism was a strong part of my personality; to the point it drove the ones who knew me crazy. I always welcomed challenges.

I went back to the restaurant a week later. I was already making plans how to change the restaurant and its menu. I had pulled from boxes hundreds of hand-written recipes which I'd been creating throughout the years. I also saved clippings from newspapers and magazines of restaurants and foods which intrigued me. I know the owners of the restaurant were happy to see me. We talked for a while and I asked them if they had made a decision. They told me they wanted out so they brought the price down to $40,000. That was their final offer.

After further talking we agreed on the price of $35,000. They asked me if I wanted to see sales reports for the restaurant and I told them that wasn't necessary. I asked if I could stay and work with them for a while doing deliveries so I could learn the area and their business. I wanted to buy more time to raise money.

I went to see someone I had borrowed money from before and explained my situation. He agreed to lend me $6,000 with high interest. I went around looking for other friends who I had helped before to round up more money but when it came to money, friends disappeared. All except one who lent me $2,000.

The next day I went to work. On my first delivery I got a 75 cent tip and as I sat down in my car opened my hand and looked at those three quarters. I gritted my teeth so hard I almost broke them. I had never had such an experience in all my years. It was humbling and I felt embarrassed. I closed the three quarters in my fist. I would not go back now. I had made up my mind to go on with this venture. I drove away and as I came to the intersection of 44th Street and McDowell saw a man holding a "will work for food" sign. I looked at him. He looked strong enough to work. Why was he out there on the corner begging for money? I handed him the three quarters and though he smiled at me I felt he was calling me all kinds of cheap names for giving him only 75 cents.

The next day I went to the race track. When I found the man I was looking for I asked him for money he owed me. He said he was broke, but I reminded him that the races had not yet started. After I assured him I would not leave him until he gave me the money he owed me, he gave me $1,000. Now I had raised $9,000.

I went back to work to do more pizza deliveries and for the next few days kept working with Christo. Three weeks later we sat down for another conversation. I told them business was much slower than they had described to me and they had to give me a chance to build up the business. I said I could not invest so much money and after further discussion they understood. We came to an agreement I would give them a $10,000 down payment, two balloon payments of $5,000 every six months and the last $15,000 would be paid in monthly installments through an escrow account.

It was a few days before June of 1984. We set the closing date for June 1, 1984.

The night before the closing, as I had exhausted all efforts of raising the rest of the money, I went to a house where I knew there was a card game. As I sat at the table I focused on the number 3,000. Winning that would leave me a few extra dollars for deposits, supplies, etc. After 16 hours of poker I had what I wanted and at 8:00 a.m. was hoping the game would break up. My appointment with escrow was for 10:00 a.m. I made it there ten minutes late and apologized. After the technicalities of closing the deal I was driving back to 5024 E. McDowell with keys in my hand to open the restaurant. I was excited about life. I was full of energy and ready to go even though I had no sleep the night before.

I locked the door behind me. I wanted to sit there for a few minutes and enjoy the feeling. The restaurant was finally mine and there was no stopping the things I wanted to do. The responsibility to fail or succeed rested\ totally in my hands.

I opened the door for lunch on June 1, 1984 and a big chapter of my life had begun.

THE MOTIVES FOR THE BEGINNING

*I*wanted my restaurant to be different from other restaurants. I remember the places I had worked at in Chicago and Los Angeles. They was nothing exceptional, maybe a different concept than other places, but nothing that would move your taste buds and leave an everlasting memory in your mind. Most people I knew went to restaurants simply because they were hungry. I wanted people to get hungry at the mere thought of coming to *MY* restaurant! I thought of my fathers' taverna and how all the tastes had impressed my mind. It was the freshness and quality of the ingredients that jumped from the plate and captured my imagination. I didn't want a place where I had to reheat food. I wanted it to be freshly made and use the finest ingredients possible. I made the commitment to myself that I would always do that.

I started to experiment with some new dishes. By blending several recipes together the results were surprisingly good. Then I alternated a few traditional recipes and gave them my own flare. I concentrated on four cuisines to take tastes from: Greek, Italian, French and Spanish. At first, people didn't know what to make of it. It was challenging to convince our customers to taste the foods. Some daring ones did, others passed on it and stuck with the pizzas. Some customers tried my lasagne and the compliments started to come in. It was different, freshly made as the customer ordered it. The recipe was a cross between lasagne and Greek pastichio, the cinnamon in the lasagne gave it a mystery taste which intrigued people's palates.

I remember my first day. It went very smooth. A few customers came in to pick up food. At night it was mostly deliveries. When it was finally over and I closed the door, I was tired for not sleeping the night before. But I was also anxious to start moving things around and gathering ideas on how to make this endeavor work. After a few hours I fell asleep in the little store room in the back. A few weeks later the restaurant was already looking different. I added more tables and chairs to the dining room. I changed the red and white curtains and tablecloths. I hung some posters from soccer matches and some scenery of Europe on the walls. I started to play European music. When a customer walked in I wanted them to want to sit down for lunch or dinner!

Waiting for the customers to arrive took a lot of patience. Most business was done by deliveries. I started to stay open until 2:00 a.m., and from time to time attracted some late-night customers who had no other place to go. To my surprise this was a positive move because my late business started to blossom. A few even brought friends.

By now more recipes were developed and I had changed the pizza dough and the sauce. The dough which was developed after much thought and study was crispy, yet soft on the inside. The sauce was simmered for several hours on the back burner to incorporate the flavors. There were six different kinds of cheese used on the pizza and with all fresh and quality ingredients for toppings it captured the imagination of the ones who ate it.

Work was endless: 18 hours a day, seven days a week. In fact, I never left the place for days at a time. I remember the chair my boys had given me. It was blue and opened into a small bed. This was where I would sleep at night, back in that small store room. I had made all 860 square feet of the restaurant my universe. I was determined. The children and their mother helped in the beginning. The boys washed dishes, Lisa waited tables and their mother watched the door and answered the phones.

story continues on page 25

From the early days on McDowell. Delivery boys from Dominos are picking up pizza and other foods. One of them is wearing glasses, as if he didn't want to be identified. Or was he a spy?

Imagination, Respect And Sensitivity

Blending flavors in the kitchen is the art of imagination which allows you to blossom into a picture of things that you have dreamed of creating in your mind. When your mind gives birth and life to those images and as you attempt the near impossible task of developing them to perfection, your feelings get attached with those creations and your love and respect grows.

It is no different with foods. I believe that respect must begin from what the earth has given us and we must be careful not to abuse or waste foods.

Being careless with foods shows disrespect and wasting them shows insensitivity. If you want to be good in the kitchen and bring out the best flavors of the foods you are giving life to, then treat them with sensitivity and respect as if it was your beloved child! The foods which we nurse our bodies with will give pleasure to our palate. Just like a great song lifts our spirits, or like a sincere love brings joy to our hearts. The love and respect will result in bringing great dishes to life. Combinations of foods will spring forth with imagination.

Creating is a great accomplishment, but it is not easy to obtain without the motivation of love to please others as well as to please yourself. Only the love will inspire you with the passion which allows you to imagine and then create hundreds of glorious tastes.

Finally you come to the stage that you can imagine the tastes of the flavors of the cooking ingredients in your mind and picture the final result on the plate. Then you will feel good about yourself because your imagination, your sensitivity and your respect have created a masterpiece from the things that our earth has given us.

The first kitchen on McDowell, sometime in 1987.

Information to assist you
in the kitchen...

THE MYTH OF OLIVE OIL

The olive symbolizes victory, hope and wealth. Today it also heralds unequaled perfection in cooking. Olive oils' pure taste and low cholesterol status has made it the preferred ingredient in kitchens around the world.

Olive oil has long been celebrated in Greek cooking. Legend says the olive sprang forth in 4,000 BC from the magical touch of Athena, the Greek goddess of wisdom. Today, Greece boasts more than 130 million olive trees and includes the olive as a major export industry. It's no wonder since this diminutive fruit is used in cooking, cosmetics, fuel, medicine and Church ceremonies.

For more than its flavor, the Greeks use olive oil as a gift to signify love and friendship. In ancient times massive quantities indicated wealth. In fact, it was an olive branch that the dove offered from Noah's Arc to show peace and prosperity.

In today's markets, olive colors and tastes vary through hundreds of varieties. Green olives are harvested August through November and black olives are culled November through March. A farmers joy, olives can be picked at almost any time with preference for color, texture, and taste. It takes about 1,500 olives to make one quart of oil, hence the product's usually hefty price. The oil is immediately edible, but must undergo extensive quality testing to determine the "status." All olive oils are cloudy and sharp-tasting at first, and settling in cool places determines their labeling.

The traditional method for making olive oil is to crush the olives between two stone wheels until the fruit becomes pulp. Then the pulp is spread on mats and pressed down with weights. Pressure from the weights is low and heat does not build up in the pulp. This method is called "cold pressed." Heat allows more oil to be extracted which results in inferior flavor so "cold-pressed" oils are superior in quality.

The factors that rates olive oil are mainly its level of acidity, color, flavor and aroma. The higher the level of acidity, the less aromatic and refined the oil will be. Extra virgin olive oil has rich depth of flavor and an acid level of less than 1%. Virgin oil has a sharper taste and an acid level of 3%. Acid levels above 3% render an oil "pure," meaning more steam processing was required and the oil was blended for refinement. Pure olive oils are still delectable for connoisseurs. Greeks consume the highest percentage of olive oil per capita. They respect the oil for its life and health benefits. In fact, archeologists have taken special pains to protect Plato's 2,400 year old tree.

Across America, use of olive oils is increasing due to rising income, improved marketing and a trend towards healthier eating habits. All olive oils contain about the same amount of calories which is about 119 per tablespoon. Opened bottles keep for at least two years when kept unrefrigerated but in a cool, dark place.

Extra virgin olive oil enriches hearty soups and sauces such as tomato sauce and mayonnaise. In the Mediterranean countries it is added to some soups just before serving and grilled bread with olive oil is a part of life like Italian "bruschetta" which is grilled, rubbed with garlic and topped with olive oil and sometimes salt. The Spanish top their "pan con tomate" with garlic, olive oil, and tomatoes. In Greece the "Psomi Me Ladi" is toasted on charcoal then sprinkled with olive oil and topped with tomatoes and is eaten with Feta and olives. In France, their beloved "croutons" are fried in olive oil and served with bowls of bouillabaisse.

Olive oil is essential to pasta sauces when combined with garlic. Pure olive oil is preferred in more delicate dishes such as salads and salad dressings. It is also used in delicate seafood dishes and sauces that must not be overpowered by the taste of the oil such as pesto. And if blended with another vegetable oil, olive oil can be used to sauté chicken, fish and other meats, as well as vegetables.

Olive oil also keeps your skin luxurious, protecting it against sunburn and the drying effects of salt water. Included in a diet, it can actually reduce your cholesterol, add a multitude of vitamins, and help guard against ulcers, gastritis, and heart disease.

As you will notice in the following recipes, olive oil is used in almost every one. This allows me to eliminate the use of butter almost completely from my cooking. Also, olive oil, in addition to lemons and wine, gives me enough flavoring to do away with salt. Only when I sauté foods do I blend the olive oil with soybean oil so the flavoring is not overpowered and allows the olive oil to gain more durability under the heat.

"One ought to be acquainted with the power of juices, and what action each of them has upon man and their alliances towards one another. What I say is this. If a sweet juice changes to another kind, not from any admixture but because it has undergone a mutation within itself, what does it first become? Bitter? Salty? Austere? or Acid? I think acid. And hence, an acid juice is the most improper of all things that can be administered in case in which a sweet juice is most proper. Thus if one should succeed in his investigations of external things, he would be the better able always to select the best; for that is best which is farthest removed from that which is unwholesome."

— Hippocrates, 400 B.C.

GARLIC, THE OVER-THE-COUNTER MEDICINE

Garlic is a flavoring in the kitchen we have learned to love. It's a centuries-old drug that is said to cure more ills than any slick potion hyped by a snake oil salesman. It protects us from evil, soothes pain, and is even said to lower blood cholesterol levels. Better yet, it's low cost, legal, almost calorie-free and it tastes great!

Behold the humble garlic bulb. Packed in that parchment-covered head are tender, glisteny cloves rich in flavor and purported benefits for the body. While not listed by doctors as an official drug, it's flavors stimulate the palate for prescription-strength pleasure. Garlic is so popular that many states pay tribute to the herb with their own garlic festivals. Not too long ago, garlic lovers converged in Washington, D.C. for the first world congress on the health significance of garlic and garlic constituents. Health benefits aside, garlic is popular because of its taste.

Garlic is pungent when raw, mellow when cooked, rich when caramelized and robust when roasted whole. Crushing, mincing or finely chopping releases pungent juices and cooking over low heat guards against bitterness. My own way to guard against bitterness is also to marinate chopped garlic in vegetable oil. Simply chop enough garlic to fill a small glass jar, fill the jar with soybean oil (or any other vegetable oil), cover and refrigerate. The oil will take away the harshness of the garlic but will leave its pungent flavor and, most importantly, will not allow the heat to burn it and turn it into a bitter-tasting food.

Garlic can be used with most any meat, in sauces and soups, vegetables, and even some desserts. Garlic is available throughout the year but is most succulent at the end of spring. The head must be firm to the touch to assure freshness. Avoid powder, flakes or any other forms of processed garlic. All its taste and health benefits are lost when it is dried.

The best way to keep garlic is in a cool, dry place and away from light. When stored properly it will keep for several months. The simple way to enjoy the flavor of garlic is on bread. Spread the mixture (see page 116) on French bread and brown under the broiler.

In all my recipes the garlic I use is marinated in oil. I get the best results this way. When the recipe calls for 1 clove of garlic, it is usually the equivalent of ½ tsp of chopped garlic. I am sure that using the garlic in oil will change your opinion about the use of garlic.

OREGANO

This is one of the pride herbs of Greece, even the name derives from the Greek for "joy of the mountains." The Greek mountains are where the herb thrives and it is grown widely. Oregano has a potent flavor despite its soft green leaves.

The herb is native of the Mediterranean and appears in many Italian, French and Greek dishes, especially the ones with tomato-based sauces. The robust flavor of oregano is essential to pizza flavoring.

Oregano is good on salads, poultry, seafood, eggplant, grilled meats, soups, and beans. Dried oregano maintains is flavor well.

BASIL

"Basilikos" is the Greek word for "king." It shows how basil has been regarded throughout the years as one of the most important culinary herbs.

There is hardly a balcony or back yard in Greece that does not include a pot full of basil. The aroma is legendary and it is a gift of friendship and love. Many carry a few leaves of this wonder herb in their hands throughout the day for its aroma.

Basil goes with almost everything but has a special affinity with tomatoes. It is great on salads when fresh, especially when sprinkled with olive oil.

The most famous dish with basil is pesto which turns foods into a feast. But it is also great with fish, soup, chicken, rice, and much more.

The soft green leaves have a strong scent when they are larger. Smaller, young leaves are sweeter. Dried basil loses some of its flavor.

THYME

Thyme is one of the great culinary herbs of European cuisine. It was the most favorite herb in ancient Greece. There are many species of thyme and few dishes cannot be improved by its flavor. Thyme derives from the Greek word "thymari." Its flavor also blends well with many other herbs, especially rosemary. Thyme aids the digestion of foods like lamb, pork, and duck. Also, it tastes great with slowly-cooked dishes such as soups, stews, baked vegetables, roasted or broiled meats, tomato-based sauces, and breads.

Their oval green leaves are aromatic and the fresh leaves are more pungent than dried, but dried leaves retain their flavor very well.

ROSEMARY

This aromatic herb with its needle-like leaves is found in the Mediterranean area and around soil where it thrives in the calcium rich by the sea. The pungent strong flavor of the herb is undeniably pleasant.

It is used best with veal, lamb, poultry and blends well with olive oil, wine, garlic. Rosemary also goes well with tomato-based sauces, fish, pizza and vegetables. Dried rosemary does not lose its flavor, only part of its aroma.

PARSLEY

Parsley originated in southern Europe. There are two types: curly and flat. Both are a rich source of vitamins and minerals. Flat leaf parsley is more flavorful and is best for cooking as it stands up to heat. Look for bright green leaves for the best quality.

A sprinkle of chopped parsley adds color and flavor to many dishes such as potatoes, salads, soups, sauces and goes well with stews, pasta dishes, fish, any dish with Ricotta cheese, rice and eggs.

Dried parsley loses some of its flavor and color.

BLACK PEPPER

Pepper is used and appreciated around the world for its spicy flavor and aroma and gives depth to many dishes. It balances the flavor of meats and picks up the delicate flavor of seafood and eggs. Since the ancient times, pepper was added to bring life to dull, boiled foods and to enhance the flavor of just about any dish – even some sweet dishes.

Black peppercorns are obtained from unripe green berries then are left to dry and then roasted over a smoldering fire. The smoke dries the berries and brings out the aroma of the pepper.

In many dishes peppercorns are used whole. Mediterraneans' most celebrated foods used the whole peppercorns: from Greek Stefado to Italian Salami to French patés.

In this book you will hardly find any recipe without pepper.

LEMON

The cultivation of lemon goes back to ancient Greece where the lemon was used for both its culinary and medicinal contributions.

Both the juice and the skin have endless uses in cooking and garnishing. It brings out the flavor of charcoal-broiled meats, baked seafood and chicken, and just about gives life to any dull food. Used in many desserts and fruit pies or toppings it brings the flavors to life!

The most celebrated soup in Greece is "angolemono." It is made with the juice from lemon and eggs. Its flavor is so much respected that is officially labeled as their Sunday soup.

Using this cookbook you must stock your refrigerator with lemons.

DILL

For the ancient Greeks dill was a symbol of vitality and a cure for the hiccups.

Today dill is used in the Mediterannean region for prized dishes which have unforgettable tastes. Its fresh green leaves with their strong aromatic flavor leaves an overpowering but distinctive taste to any dish used and to culinary imagination.

Dill is a must for stuffed grapeleaves and can be used with seafood, cucumbers, mustard-based sauces, cream-based sauces, veal and soups.

Dill is also known for its digestive use. Dried dill still maintains its color and flavor.

BAY LEAVES

The bay leaf tree goes back to the Mediterranean region as far as history. It's glossy dark green leaves are indispensable in the kitchen. The Greeks' and Romans' respect for the bay tree was such that they used to crown the heads of their victorious athletes and poets with a wreath of bay leaves.

Bay leaves can be used in almost anything from fish dishes to savory meats and is a must for tomato pasta sauces. Bay leaves also blend well with dishes using cloves or cinnamon.

Dried bay leaves lose some of their aroma and flavoring, but they are still powerful enough to bring out almost the same results in taste.

NUTMEG

This evergreen tree, native of the Southeast Asian islands, carries a fruit with a seed that bears two separate flavors. When the fruit is split open the nut inside is covered with a thin-laced skin. That skin is red-colored and is where mace comes from. The inside seed is where nutmeg is produced. In the old days, nutmeg was so precious that it was shipped in special containers of silver.

Mace is used in many desserts, cakes, puddings, and custards, and in some dishes of poultry and fish.

Nutmeg is used in breads, fruits, custards, eggnog, sauces with pasta, vegetables, tomato cream sauce and pasta stuffings. It has a warm perfumed flavor and is friendly to rich foods, not only for its flavoring but also for its digestive properties.

MUSTARD

Mustard has a long tradition in many cuisines. It has been widely used in ancient Greece, Egypt and Rome. Now there are over 100 varieties of mustard. They derive from black, brown or white seeds.

Black mustard seeds have a more distinctive flavor and stronger taste and are used mainly in Indian cuisine.

Brown mustard seeds have mainly replaced the black, because it is easier to harvest.

White mustard seeds are native of the Mediterranean and produce yellowish seeds which produce most of the American prepared mustards.

The preparation of mustard has not changed much. The seeds are left in liquids like grape must, wine, vinegar or water, then are ground to a paste. The use of mustard has a world-wide appeal and its flavors can fit in different occasions.

CINNAMON

This extraordinary spice with its delicate fragrance and semi-sweet taste traces far back in ancient China. It was also used by Romans and Greeks.

Cinnamon comes from a small tree. The spice is peeled away from the outer part of the branches, leaving the inner part to be the cinnamon sticks. Then the outer skin is ground or used whole.

Cinnamon is a must in the kitchen for desserts and a perfect marriage with honey. It is also widely used in cooking, especially in the Greek kitchen where it spices meat stews and poultry.

CLOVES

No kitchen should be without cloves. This nail-like spice gets its name from the Latin clavus (nail) and its history goes back to the islands off of Southeast Asia. It was used in the Chinese kitchen hundreds of years before it was introduced the Europeans.

Cloves are bitter and strong flavored. But as they are cooked they bring out a strong perfume, yet a warm flavor. Now they are widely used throughout Europe in breads, puddings, cakes, cookies, meat stews, soups and marinades. Cloves are essential to foods with festive tastes.

Cloves were also used throughout the centuries to ease the pain of a toothache.

TOMATOES

It is difficult to imagine cooking without tomatoes, yet the tomato was only introduced to European cuisine in the beginning of the 16th century. It started to be widely used in the Mediterranean region in the middle of the 18th century.

Now the tomato is a cooks' best friend. Tomatoes are in their peak of flavor when picked ripe from the vine. They grow best in warm sunny climates. Tomatoes have a great affinity with olive oil.

Tomato products are adequate substitutes in cooking. Sun-dried tomatoes have a smoky flavor and bring out an unforgettable taste when sautéed in olive oil and with dishes which contain garlic. Sun-dried or regular tomatoes can ruin a dish if overused.

LETTUCE

There are many types of lettuce, all are rich in vitamins A and C. Lettuce easily looses its taste. It is best to use as soon as possible while their leaves are firm and not limp. Lettuce provides a wide range of flavors and colors.

Head lettuce is the most popular lettuce with its round shape and soft, tender leaves. They are most popular for salads. The dark leaves on the outside have a stronger flavor and the inside leaves are lighter in color and are more delicate to the taste.

Romaine lettuce is Europe's favorite lettuce. This long-shaped lettuce has a nutty, robust flavor. The dark green, flavorful leaves go well with strong ingredients and cheeses.

ONIONS

Onions can enhance just about any dish. There are hundreds of types of onions mainly distinguished by their color.

Onions are pungent when raw and sweet when cooked. They have been in kitchens since ancient times. The Egyptians and later the American Indians ate them raw. Greeks used them as medicine to cure some illnesses.

The yellow onion is the one most used in this book when we refer to onions (otherwise they are specified as red, pearl or green). Just use your imagination where to use it. It is best in long-cooking recipes.

Red onions give a pleasant sweetness to the flavor.

Pearl onions, tiny onions pickled before growing larger, are ideal for stews or soups.

Green onions (scallions) are immature yellow onion bulbs. They are mild-tasting and sweet in flavor. They are best used in salads and light cooking.

MUSHROOMS

Mushrooms are an all-purpose vegetable. They are used in kitchens all over the world in a wide variety of dishes.

The commercially grown variety of mushrooms are the most versatile and always available. The smaller white mushrooms are harvested at the early stage of development. They are best in salads because they are crispier and their flavor has not matured yet. As the mushrooms mature, it opens its cap and exposes dark gills on the inside. These mushrooms have developed to a full flavor and as the mushroom develops longer in harvest, their caps fan out. It is unattractive because the gills inside are exposed but the mushroom in this stage has come to its best flavor potential.

Wild mushrooms come in many varieties, however many of them are poisonous. Never eat a suspicious type of mushroom picked in the wild unless it is positively identified.

Truffles are regarded as the best of the wild mushrooms. They are usually grown at the bottom of oak trees and are sniffed out by trained dogs. Truffles come in two colors. The black ones are the most common ones. They look like lumps of coal but their flavor is unforgettable. The white variety is found mainly in Italy and all mushroom connoisseurs consider this to be the best flavored mushroom.

Shitake mushrooms are grown mainly in South America. An Oriental variety with a full flavor is used well for long-cooking dishes.

Porcini mushrooms have a rich and pleasant flavor and are also best with long-cooking dishes which brings out more of its flavor.

Chanterelles mushrooms is an extremely flavorful and also beautiful mushroom with a light orange color. You must be gentle when cooking with this mushroom.

Morels mushrooms are spongy-looking mushrooms and are used widely in Europe. Its flavor is compared to that of truffle mushrooms and are full of flavor.

All wild mushrooms take well to drying. In fact, some become more flavorful when dried.

Cleaning mushrooms is a delicate task. If used for salads, simply wipe off with a cloth. The mushroom will become soggy if rinsed alot of with water. If used for cooking, gently rinse with cold water. The mushrooms used in this cookbook are the commercially grown ones. They are avaialble throughout the year.

CAPERS

"Capparion" was used by ancient Greeks as seasoning but it is used as a condiment since about the 12th century.

"Capers" is a bush which grows naturally in the Mediterranean region. Capers are the buds of the flower. They are picked and seasoned in vinegar.

Capers is a natural ingredient for salads and it gives foods a distinctive, slightly salty taste.

ARTICHOKES

The artichoke appears in the 15th century and it was a novelty in France and Italy. The artichoke is a flower bud covered with scales. We can only eat the delicate flesh.

The ancient Greeks ate the leaves and flowers of the artichoke plant which then was known as "Kaktos." Now artichokes inspire some of the most memorable dishes in the southern European region.

The most popular part of the artichoke is the heart. Hidden between the scales the hearts are packed in cans with water and distributed around the world from its main exporter, Spain. At times they are very expensive because of the great demand in Europe, especially in France where they are consume more artichokes than anywhere else in the world. Some artichoke hearts are also marinated and used in salads.

The ones packed in water can be a great addition to salads and are inseparable for my cooking. Use your imagination in such dishes as poultry, vegetables, meats and pasta. If you have never tasted them, you are missing a treat.

THE STAGES OF BUILDING UP

*T*here was a great demand for space in the restaurant as the business was constantly growing. Searching for storage space, the ceiling was converted to storage by hanging shelves. Only a ten foot display case separated the kitchen from the dining room – there were no longer any walls. In the upper part of the case the newly created desserts would be displayed and the bottom part would be used as storage for vegetables. On the top of the case were the jars and cans full of peppers, hearts of palm, artichokes, roasted red peppers, capers and other specialties used for cooking. The case was squeezed against the few pieces of kitchen equipment: a small griddle, a two-burner stove and a pizza oven which made it very difficult to produce all the cooking. Especially as the menu was taking larger shape by each month and continued to grow larger and larger.

The dining room was crowded with tables and chairs, so much so that the server could hardly pass between them. The business had come to this point after we had stopped the food deliveries, deliveries that had really grown into a major business, especially after the restaurant had received the "Best of Phoenix" for the pizza from the *New Times* publication. This award totally surprised me because it was the first time in my life that I had made pizza though I took the time to study the pizza-making concept, especially the dough and the sauce. Our customers loved it to the point that I had six phone lines loaded with calls for deliveries in the evening. To make things easier, we had given our customers numbers so when they called, all they had to say was their number. We would then go to our records and get the rest of the information on where to deliver.

In the middle of 1985, not even a year after I took over the business, I had over 400 numbers of regular calling customers. I remember 8 to 10 years later that some of the "old" customers would walk up to me and say, "Hey, Nick, I'm number 51, remember me?" and from the days I used to do the cooking and deliveries myself, sometimes I would call my friend Dick from the orthodontist shop next door to watch the store while I was taking a delivery.

Now there were three people answering the phones and three to four people doing deliveries, but I was not happy. That was not what I wanted to do. I wanted people to come in and dine in the restaurant so I could see who I was cooking for. I did not want to deliver pizzas for the rest of my life.

I remember it was a Friday afternoon, and as the delivery people came to work, I sent them home, telling them there would be no more deliveries. I told the employees who answered the phones to inform the customers we no longer delivered, and if they wanted the food, they must come in and get it. Everyone thought for sure that the hard work had gotten to me and drove me crazy. But I knew what I wanted from that place, I wanted to see people waiting outside for tables; I wanted to see life and not delivery people running in and out.

Two signs went on the building, one in the front and one on the side. The name was changed to Golden Pizzeria. The little dining room was fixed to be inviting, the lights were dimmer and European music filled the air. Specials on the blackboard started to appear, different every day of the week. The storm of creations filled out the pages of the menu and the guests started to come in and bring their friends. They had to show them the 860 square feet of space where the menu was so large, the food was freshly made and there was always enough for two people. Most could not believe all this was done by one person in that tiny kitchen!

As customers walked in, there was a little hallway. On the right was a wall with awards and write-ups. Directly in front was a display freezer full of gelato and Italian ice, the top of which was used for a counter. In the back of it several coffee flavors were displayed. On the left of the entrance was the dining room and its 40 seats were a hot commodity. If customers had to use the tiny restroom they had to pass directly in front of me and the kitchen. And right before the restroom was the small washing area. The back wall had come down and what used to be the area where I got my sleep was now a work area. The whole place was really hot at times, because of the open kitchen and the bodies of people who crowded the small area. To help cool the place we moved all the motors from the refrigerators onto the roof!

Sometimes while I was sitting out back on the blue chair my boys had given me, I'd think about the long nights I had slept on it as I was trying to build up the business, sleeping in the company of a few crickets. I smile wondering if it was worth it. I never would have dreamed as a young man I would someday work so hard – that was not in my plans. How ironic after traveling the world over, the golden years of my childhood and teenage years, the adventures, the glories and the disappointments, I would end up in Phoenix, AZ of all places of the world working 18 hours a day! The picture of the Greek Islands came to mind, what was wrong with this picture? I had to stay here because after that day which I had decided to stop the deliveries, the customers kept multiplying and it did not seem they were going to stop any time soon.

story continues on page 41

The true lover of knowledge naturally strives for truth, and is not content with common opinion, but soars with undimmed and unwearied passion until he grasps the essential nature of things.
— Plato

Pizza, Bread
and Stuffed Specialties

A complete line of original breads and desserts are available in Nick Ligidakis'
"My Golden Collection of Original Desserts" cookbook.

ABOUT DOUGH

Some of you while living in New York, Chicago, or Florida have made great bread using your favorite recipe. If you moved to Phoenix and tried the same recipes using the same processes you probably found the results were different. You are thinking that you are doing something wrong or have lost your touch of making bread. Relax, you are not doing anything wrong. The poor results are due to elements out of your control that mess up your recipes.

First, it's the weather. That is the main factor which will affect bread making. The more moisture in the air the better. It helps the dough to rise properly. The dry climate in Phoenix is not a good environment for making bread. In my pizza dough recipe I have added a few ingredients which I think helps the dough become softer in the middle, yet crispy on the outside. This dough rises three times to overcome the dryness of the atmosphere and also to break up the chemicals which bring us to the next important element. Water.

If you lived in a town that had clean water before you have moved to Phoenix, where the water is not that great, this will affect the rising of the dough. Chemicals in the water will kill the yeast. In fact, if you wash the bowl you make the dough in with soap and do not rinse it properly, that will also affect your bread making. It is best to wash the bowl with just warm water.

And, of course, flour quality and quantity plays a major roll in the final outcome of the bread. For this recipe I use unbleached flour and your dough must be soft and elastic when it's ready to be pressed into the loaves or rounds for pizza.

Here is the process I use after the dough is ready.

Place dough on a working surface and cover with a towel for about 30-45 minutes or until it has risen to half of its size. Then cut dough to one-pound pieces and form them into balls and place them in an aluminum pan. Cover the pan with a plastic bag and refrigerate overnight. This will give the dough the moisture it needs. When ready to bake, remove dough from refrigerator and knead it with your hands into the shape of a disc. Repeat with all the dough rounds.

Place dough discs on a working surface covered with a lot of flour. Knead the dough with your fingers, pushing it outwards, opening the round more. Then with a rolling pin open the round a little more. Place it in a round tray, sifting flour lightly on the tray. Cover with a plastic bag and let rise for about 1 hour. Now it is easy to open the pizza round to the desired size and you can do so by working from the edges of the round. (You can make bread with this recipe by simply making the dough into the desired shaped loaf after you take it out from your refrigerator. Let it rise until doubled and then bake.)

Pizza, before and after it is baked.

Nick's famous huge calzone.

See Page 28 for additional information about Pizza Dough.

Pizza Dough

4 cups lukewarm water
¾ oz. dry yeast

> *Place in a bowl and mix for 3-4 minutes.*

1 egg
1 cup milk
¾ cup vegetable oil
⅛ cup salt
¼ cup sugar
⅛ lb. margarine, melted

> *Add in and mix well.*

4 lbs. unbleached flour

> *Add in and mix well. Adjust the flour if needed. Dough must not stick to the sides of the bowl. This recipe will make approximately 8 (1 lb.) rounds for pizza. You can use the leftover dough for many other uses: calzones (see page 32), pizza pies (see page 35), pocket pizza (see page 37), stuffed bread (see page 38), garlic strips (see page 39) or simply make a loaf of bread.*

Pizza

To make pizza, simply place the round on a lightly oiled round baking pan and spoon in the middle enough sauce to spread on the round to about 1″ to 1½″ from the edges. Then sprinkle it with shredded Mozzarella cheese and your desired ingredients. On top of those ingredients spread shredded Provolone cheese, white Cheddar cheese, Monterey Jack cheese or any other well-melting cheese you like. Bake in 475° oven for about 25-30 minutes. (Some ovens vary with temperature so you may have to adjust the heat or the timing.)

Here are some recipes for pizzas. You can also make it without cheese or sauce:

Nick's Favorite

Crumbled Feta cheese
Artichoke hearts, sliced
Hearts of palm, sliced
Bacon, cooked
Potatoes, fried

The Greeks found a weed grass growing among bread making cereals. They called that weed "zizania" (tares, in English). These wild oats caused mental troubles and digestive problems when they were mixed with flour.

Red Seafood

(12″ round)

1 Tbsp. olive oil
1 Tbsp. soybean oil
> *Heat in a saucepan.*

2 oz. scallops
4 oz. baby clams
6 oz. bay shrimp
1 clove garlic, chopped
> *Add in and sauté for 3-4 minutes.*

1 Tbsp. white cooking wine
> *Add in and sauté 1-2 minutes.*

8 canned plum tomatoes, chopped
> *Add in and simmer 3-4 minutes*

⅛ tsp. black pepper
⅛ tsp. oregano
⅛ tsp. thyme
⅛ tsp. basil
⅛ tsp. rosemary
1 Tbsp. Romano cheese, grated
1 Tbsp. Parmesan cheese, grated
> *Add in and simmer 3-4 minutes. In this, do not use the pizza sauce. Pour the sauce on after you sprinkle the Mozzarella on the round.*

Grilled Steak Pizza

(12″ round)

1 Tbsp. olive oil
1 Tbsp. vegetable oil
> *Heat in a saucepan.*

6 oz. sirloin steak, cut into thin slices
> *Add in to the saucepan and sauté 2-3 minutes.*

2 cups mushrooms, sliced
2 cups red onions, sliced
2 cups green pepper, sliced
> *Add in and sauté for about 6-7 minutes.*

1 Tbsp. steak sauce
1 tsp. soy sauce
1 tsp. Worcestershire sauce
⅛ tsp. black pepper
> *Add in and simmer 3-4 minutes.*

Texan Pizza
(12″ round)

1 Tbsp. olive oil
1 Tbsp. soybean oil
> *Heat in a saucepan.*

1 onion, sliced
8 oz. ground beef
> *Sauté 4-5 minutes. Discard oil.*

Place the shredded mozzarella on the round.
1 cup B.B.Q. Sauce (see page 202)
> *Pour over mozzarella.*

Place the ground beef and onion on top.
8-10 slices yellow Cheddar cheese
> *Place on top of ground beef.*

Calzones

Lay the 12″ round on a working surface. Place sausage filling in the middle of the round. Wet the edges and fold dough over carefully so you don't spill sauce out. With a fork press the edges to seal and punch a few holes in the top. Bake in a 475° oven approximately 20-25 minutes.

SPANAKI CALZONE:
½ lb. Mozzarella cheese
½ lb. Provolone cheese
1 oz. Ricotta cheese
2 cups Marinara Sauce (see page 115)
¼ lb. Feta cheese
2 cups spinach, cooked and chopped
1 Tbsp. Romano cheese, grated
1 Tbsp. Parmesan cheese, grated
> *Mix well in a bowl.*

GOLDEN:
4 oz. Mozzarella cheese, shredded
2 oz. Provolone cheese, shredded
2 oz. Feta cheese
1 oz. Ricotta cheese
6 strips bacon, cooked and chopped
1 avocado, sliced
1 tomato, chopped
½ cup black olives, sliced
1 Tbsp. Romano cheese, grated
1 Tbsp. Parmesan cheese, grated
> *Mix in a bowl.*

VEGETABLE CALZONE:
Place a 12″ pizza round on a working surface.
1 whole artichoke heart, sliced
1 Tbsp. zucchini, chopped
1 Tbsp. black olives, sliced
1 Tbsp. green olives, sliced
1 Tbsp. green peppers
½ small onion, chopped
4 mushrooms, sliced
1 Tbsp. Ricotta cheese
1 tsp. Romano cheese, grated
1 tsp. Parmesan cheese, grated
2 oz. Mozzarella cheese, shredded
1 oz. Provolone cheese, shredded
½ red onion, chopped
4 Tbsp. Pizza Sauce (see page 117)
Mix in a bowl.

CHEESE CALZONE:
2 oz. Ricotta cheese
4 oz. Mozzarella cheese, shredded
2 oz. Provolone cheese, shredded
2 oz. Monterey Jack cheese, shredded
2 oz. Feta cheese
½ oz. Romano cheese, grated
1½ oz. Parmesan cheese, grated 1 egg
Mix well in a bowl.

SAUSAGE CALZONE:
1 cup Meat Sauce (see page 116)
1 sausage, cooked and sliced
4 oz. Mozzarella cheese, shredded
4 oz. Provolone cheese, shredded
1 oz. Ricotta cheese
1 Tbsp. Parmesan cheese, grated
2 mushrooms, sliced
1 Tbsp. Romano cheese, grated
Mix in a bowl.

SNOW SPAGO:
¼ cup crabmeat
¼ cup bay shrimp
4 oz. Provolone cheese, shredded
4 oz. Mozzarella cheese, shredded
1 oz. Ricotta cheese
1 clove garlic, chopped
⅛ cup Macadamia nuts, chopped
3 asparagus spears, chopped
6 water chestnuts, sliced
½ cup whipping cream
Pinch of rosemary
Pinch of Basil
Pinch of black pepper
1 Tbsp. Romano cheese, grated
1 Tbsp. Parmesan cheese, grated
Mix in a bowl.

SEAFOOD CALZONE:
2 Tbsp. olive oil
Heat in a saucepan.
¼ cup baby clams
1 clove garlic, chopped
½ cup scallops
½ cup bay shrimp
Add in and sauté for 3-4 minutes.
1 Tbsp. white cooking wine
Add in and sauté 1-2 minutes.
5 plum tomatoes, crushed
Pinch of black pepper
Pinch of parsley
Pinch of basil
Pinch of oregano
Pinch of thyme
Pinch of rosemary
Red pepper flakes
Add in and simmer 4-5 minutes.
1 Tbsp. Romano cheese, grated
1 Tbsp. Parmesan cheese, grated
4 oz. Mozzarella cheese, shredded
4 oz. Provolone cheese, shredded
1 oz. Ricotta cheese
Add to other ingredients and mix well.

Pizza Pies

For pizza pies, you will need two 12″ pizza round dough. Place in a lightly buttered baking dish. Place all ingredients in the middle. Lightly water the edges of the round. Cover with the other round and press with a fork to seal the edges. Punch a few holes in the top of the dough with a fork. Bake at 475° for 20-25 minutes.

Here are some fillings for pizza pies:

MEAT PIE:
½ lb. fettuccine noodles, cooked
2 cups Meat Sauce (see page 116)
2 cups Mozzarella cheese, shredded
4 mushrooms, sliced
½ tsp. cinnamon
1 cup Ricotta cheese
½ tsp. black pepper
1 Tbsp. Romano cheese
1 Tbsp. Parmesan cheese
Mix well.

SHRIMP PIE:
2 cups bay shrimp
2 roasted red peppers, chopped
3 artichoke hearts, chopped
2 green onions, chopped
1 cup Marinara Sauce (see page 115)
1 tomato, chopped
2 cups Mozzarella cheese, shredded
¼ cup Ricotta cheese
½ tsp. black pepper
½ tsp. basil
½ tsp. rosemary
Mix well in a bowl.

In the middle of the 2nd century B.C., the technique of grinding grains was developed to make very fine flour. The Greek master bakers began an era of bread making which spread throughout the Roman Empire. Late in the 1st century B.C., there were over 300 bakeries in Rome alone, all run by Greek bakers. There was even a bakery college formed in that era where master bakers developed passwords to protect trade secrets.

VEGETABLE:
1 small zucchini, chopped
2 cups broccoli, chopped
1 small red pepper, chopped
4 mushrooms, sliced
1 clove garlic, chopped
½ cup black olives, sliced
1 cup Tomato (Pizza) Sauce (see page 117)
2 cups Mozzarella cheese
Pinch of black pepper
Pinch of basil
Pinch of rosemary
Pinch of oregano
Pinch of thyme
1 Tbsp. Romano cheese
1 Tbsp. Parmesan cheese
½ cup Ricotta cheese
            Mix well in bowl.

SPINACH PIE:
Use the recipe for Spinach Puffs (see page 69)
1 cup spinach, chopped
¼ lb. Feta cheese
½ cup Ricotta cheese
2 cups Mozzarella cheese, shredded
1 cup Marinara Sauce (see page 115)
            Add to above.

ITALIAN:
1 cup Tomato (Pizza) Sauce (see page 117)
½ cup pepperoni, sliced
2 Italian sausages, cooked and sliced
1 small onion, sliced
5 mushrooms, sliced
½ cup black olives, sliced
1 small green pepper, sliced
2 cups Mozzarella cheese
½ cup Ricotta cheese
1 Tbsp. Romano cheese
1 Tbsp. Parmesan cheese
            Mix well in a bowl.

Pocket Pizza

For this you will need two 6″ pizza round dough. (Split a 1 lb. dough bowl to half, then open to 2 rounds.) Place one round on a lightly buttered pan. Place filling in the middle. Water the edges lightly, cover with the other round and seal edges, pressing with a fork. Punch a few holes on top of the dough with the fork. Bake at 475° for 15-20 minutes. Then cut the rounded pizza in half and you will have two pocket pizzas.

Here are some recipes:

TURKEY:
4 oz. turkey, sliced
½ cup spinach, chopped
¼ cup onions, sliced
2 oz. Feta cheese
2 oz. Ricotta cheese
1 garlic clove, chopped
Pinch of nutmeg
½ cup Marinara Sauce (see page 115)
> *Mix well in a bowl.*

BLUE BROCCOLI:
6 oz. roast beef, sliced
½ cup broccoli, chopped
¼ cup blue cheese, crumbled
½ tsp. horseradish
2 green onions, chopped
4 mushrooms, sliced
> *Mix well in a bowl.*

SAUSAGE:
1 Italian sausage, cooked and sliced
½ cup Meat Sauce (see page 116)
½ green pepper, sliced
3 mushrooms, sliced
1 Tbsp. Ricotta cheese
2 oz. Mozzarella cheese, sliced
1 Tbsp. Romano cheese, grated
> *Mix well in a bowl.*

SHELLFISH:
½ cup bay shrimp
¼ cup crabmeat
½ cup Marinara Sauce (see page 115)
¼ cup baby clams
2 asparagus spears, chopped
¼ small onion, sliced
1 tsp. capers
1 artichoke heart, chopped
1 Tbsp. Parmesan cheese
                    Mix well in a bowl.

PEPPERONI:
¼ cup pepperoni
⅛ cup black olives, sliced
¼ onion, chopped
3 mushrooms, sliced
½ cup Tomato Sauce (see page 117)
2 oz. Mozzarella cheese, shredded
1 Tbsp. Ricotta cheese
1 Tbsp. Romano cheese
1 Tbsp. Parmesan cheese
                    Mix well in a bowl.

Stuffed Bread

Open pizza dough to an oblong shape as if you were making a loaf of bread. Spread filling in the middle, all the way across the dough. Roll in the filling, close the ends and bake at 425° for 25-30 minutes.

GOLDEN BREAD FILLING:
1 avocado, sliced
1 tomato, chopped
1/4 cup Feta cheese
1/4 cup Ricotta cheese
1/8 cup Romano cheese
1/4 cup black olives, sliced
1/4 cup Kasseri cheese
                    Mix well.

Other uses for dough:

GARLIC STICKS:
Place the pizza round in a lightly buttered baking dish and cut it from both sides so you can create small squares about 3´ x 3´. Bake at 475° for about 15 minutes. Dip each square in Garlic Spread (see page 116).

FOR GARLIC BREAD:
Use the above recipe to make garlic bread by simply spreading onto pieces of Italian or French bread and toasting it for a few minutes in the oven.

Whole Wheat Crust for Pizza

1½ cups lukewarm water
2 tsp. dry yeast
> *Mix on low speed of mixer with the bread hook for about 5-6 minutes.*

2 Tbsp. vegetable oil
2 Tbsp. margarine, melted
½ tsp. salt
1 tsp. basil
1 tsp. oregano
¼ cup whole wheat germ
1 tsp. sugar
2 Tbsp. milk
1½ cups unbleached flour
1½ cups whole wheat flour
> *Add to the mixing bowl and mix well. If dough is still sticking to the bowl, add more whole wheat flour. Place dough in a bowl, cover, and let rise to doubled in size. Then follow the instructions for Pizza Dough (see page 35) to make the pizza. This dough can be kept frozen if it is wrapped well, same as regular pizza dough.*

Barley was given to prisoners as punishment by the Greeks and the Romans.

In the middle of the 4th century A.D. St. Patrick, an Irish Monk who travelled in Europe and the Middle East to spread the gospel, learned the process of distillation which already was described by Aristotle to use for the desalination of sea water. St. Patrick brought the technique back to Ireland.

Brioch Bread

2½ oz. milk, lukewarm
10 eggs
> *Mix well.*

½ oz. yeast
> *Add in and mix for 1-2 minutes.*

1 Tbsp. salt
2 Tbsp. sugar
1¼ lbs. unbleached flour
> *Add in and mix for 2-3 minutes.*

½ lb. soft, unsalted butter
> *Add in and mix well for 3-4 minutes. This dough should be a little sticky. Cut to desired size and on a surface with a little flour, shape dough into loaves or rolls. Place in a baking pan, cover with damp towels and let it rise to double. If you have available bread forms, use those, butter the forms and let dough rise in the forms. Bake in 395° oven for about 30-35 minutes.*

The following is a recipe for plain Focaccia bread. You can top it with any topping of your choice before baking. One of my favorites is sliced tomatoes and crumbled feta cheese.

Focaccia

3 cups lukewarm water
¾ oz. yeast
> *Place in a bowl, mix 3-4 minutes.*

1 Tbsp. sugar
1 tsp. salt
2 Tbsp. vegetable oil
> *Add in and mix well.*

2 lbs. unbleached flour
> *Add in and mix well. Add more flour if dough is sticking to the sides of the bowl. Cut to 4 oz. dough balls. Place on a working surface and cover, let rise to double. With a little flour, press the rounds to be flat and open to form a disc, approximately 6-7" round. Let the dough rise until it is soft and elastic. Bake at 375° about 30-35 minutes.*

2 cups olive oil
2 cloves garlic, chopped
> *Mix together. Brush the top of the focaccia while hot.*

1 Tbsp. rosemary
1 Tbsp. basil
1 Tbsp. oregano
1 Tbsp. thyme
1 Tbsp. taragon
1 Tbsp. savory
> *Mix and sprinkle on top of focaccia.*

2 Tbsp. Romano cheese, grated
2 Tbsp. Parmesan cheese, grated
> *Mix and sprinkle on top of focaccia. This bread keeps well in the refrigerator and also freezes well.*

FORMING A PERSONALITY FOR THE FOOD

*I*t is amazing when you think about it that there are so many different styles of cooking and all the glorious tastes that a mind can create! I thought about different styles as different personalities, like in people. I wanted to create my style of cooking, something that I could associate with – a good, likeable personality. I tried to create a personality for food which everyone would be drawn to. It had to be consistent. People like consistency. That was the most important thing. It had to be absolutely sincere. Everyone likes that. It had to be fresh. How can you argue about freshness?

It had to be different, as long as it was not shocking like having green hair or chains hanging from tongues.

It had to have quality and quantity, of course. Quality in personality always draws attention and if it is in abundance then it becomes overwhelming to handle to the point that it is intimidating but yet intriguing to the imagination.

And then it had to be something which would please me to prepare.

So I pick the cuisine that was closest to my imagination and I kept away from things I did not like, such as seasoning that made the food spicy: salt, and later on, butter. Although, I have to make a confession that Chinese is one of my favorite foods and I made a commitment to myself that someday I would create a cuisine which would blend European and Chinese flavors!

Only now my challenge was to create this cuisine with all the above elements in it! In short, I asked myself to create a monster. Since I wanted it so much I worked on this food personality I had imagined in my mind, and like all personalities, it took a while to mature. But when the monster had been created, people took on that personality to the point of addiction. It was sincere and excited. It was consistent and natural. Nothing with stale tastes. No bursting flavors. No lies, no deceiving. It was straight forward.

Consistency was the main secret. Not necessarily the best, but always the same. I do not believe such a thing as "The best" exists. I mean, one can not be the best of all. In order to do that one must be flawless and there is not such a person anywhere. And if we think we are not the best we will always try to reach our limitations. I thought the same about my cooking. It was not the best, but I had room for improvement. Yet it had given it a personality which I really liked, and so did thousands of others.

But as usually happens in any personality, there are people who do not understand you and others who want to change you. Fortunately, there are not that many. In the beginning many complained about the time it took for their food to reach the table. Sometimes in my frustration I'd send them to McDonald's or Dominos. The ones who had the patience to let the personality of the food season were rewarded. Taste, freshness, and wholesomeness does not come out of foods that are premade and reheated. It has to be made as the food was ordered, and that takes a little longer than your average restaurant. Another misunderstanding was the no substitution policy. It was like they were asking me to change the personality I had created. The menu with eight pages of foods was very thoughtfully designed so to cover most people's tastes, and if I went through the trouble to create and offer new recipes, it was distressing to convert the old ones. I felt that I would not have been true to the art. I did not want to complicate the personality of the food. I wanted to deal with consistency and not with Dr. Jekell and Mr. Hyde. At some point I understood that it was impossible to please everyone. It is like any other true art – you do it from the heart and not for the publicity, then you stay true to your beliefs and the ones who will follow will be disciples to spread the word around and stay true to the beliefs of the personality of my cooking. Things started to happen: Best of Phoenix awards, write-ups in newspapers and magazines, television shows, many offers to go wherever people had an interest from San Diego to Florida, from Minnesota to Utah, offers for cooking videos and TV shows, but there was only so much a person can do and still focus on the consistency of the work. That was my priority. I was never going to compromise that because the personality of the food that I had created was my friend for life and for thousands of others.

The diversity of the people who frequent the restaurant was amazing. In the parking lot one would see a Rolls Royce, a Mercedes, a VW bug, or a '64 Chevy. The people who walked into the restaurant would be dressed in suits, dresses, T-shirts or cut-off jeans. From prominent policitians and average workers, well-known athletes and entertainers, to the neighborhood baseball team and little league soccer, everyone felt welcome there. The food had no borders and no discrimination and that suited the personality of the food just fine.

We did not even have beer or wine for the customers but that's okay because they brought their own. I remember we had a special shelf with bottles of wine, labeled with the customers' name, who could not finish their wine but left it there for their next time. I made it my commitment not to let the notoriety of the restaurant consume my personality. I liked my feet planted on the ground. I was very secure there, and kept working to perfect the personality of the food!

I believe that most of the discoveries are accidental; a discovery is something that makes sense to you, and it does not necessarily mean it has to make sense to anyone else. Such a thing is my belief on slow cooking. I sauté my foods over very low heat and I get great results. I do not believe (although there are exceptions) of abusing the foods on high heats, but do not tell that to the scholars of foods. They raise their eyebrows. I had people in my cooking classes that at the time were students of culinary schools. They were, of course, confused at my different techniques, but different ways of cooking does not mean one person is right and another is wrong. It simply supports my belief that there is so much to be explored in the creation of culinary tastes, and in order to do that you must go with your own intuition of what tastes good to you.

Tried this way I think you will be pleasantly surprised. Do not overheat your oil, sauté the meat, chicken, fish or vegetables over low heat. By doing this you give the food a chance to cook slowly and throughout. You will also discover that meats will taste more tender and vegetables more flavorful.

story continues on page 63

Pasta...

PASTA

*I*s it a natural child of Italy or is it adopted? Because of its tremendous popularity around the world, the subject of where pasta was originated is a sensitive subject to the Italians. Was it China, Italy or Greece? Putting the question of origin aside, give the Italians all the credit for, if nothing else, creating wonderful sauces, savory fillings and giving pasta so many different personalities and for making this extraordinary food so popular.

But the question remains. Where, when and how did pasta come to the West? Historians are confused on the subject and even today it is not clear where the birth of this most popular food came about.

To trace pasta, one can go as far back as the 4th century B.C. where Greek writers mentioned this round, thin dough which could be baked or boiled and eaten with olive oil. If one bases the origination of pasta by words, then we have to go back to Greece because the word "macaroni" derives from the Greek word "makarios," which means joy.

And the word "lasagne" comes from the Latin word "laganom" which is also derived form the Greek word "laganon" or "lagana" which is a thin piece of dough baked and eaten with olive oil. But "lagana" resembles focaccia bread more than pasta.

There is nothing written in any history book that Marco Polo brought back any kind of pasta from China. The only thing Marco Polo mentioned was that he ate this paste which was excellent. But the paste was made from the fruit of a tree and not from barley flour.

There are translations from Roman writers of the 13th century mentioning the word "pastilla" as "little pastas." This translation occurred before the time of Marco Polo in the 14th century. Those "small round cakes" were boiled and eaten. The word "macaroni" was also mentioned late in the 13th century by Roman writers as food that was eaten with bread but only by Lords and not from poor people.

But whatever the case may be, we know for sure that the first commercialized production of pasta started in Naples in the early 15th century.

It was not until the 18th century that the process to make dry pasta was discovered. The natural way of drying it involves changes in hot and cold termpatures. Such conditions were found just south of Naples where the climate changed throughout the day.

The great merit of pasta is that it is easily made, takes up hardly any room when stored and above all, tastes great when made fresh. Cooking is also simple. It just takes a pot full of water. Simply bring the water to a boil, drop in the pasta and when the water comes to a boil again, the pasta is ready to eat "al dente" which simply means it will have a resistance to the bite. But this method is used only when cooking *fresh* pasta, which I highly recommend.

There are several good commercialized pastas, but they all vary in their cooking times. To cook any pasta, fresh or dry, you must first make sure that you have enough water so when the pasta swells as it cooks it will have enough room to swim in the water or else will be stuck together. And before you drop the pasta in the water, make sure the water has come to a rolling boil.

If you never made fresh pasta before and you are intimidated by the process, don't be. It is easy and once you have tasted it, you will not want to eat any other type of dry pasta again.

Following are two recipes of the pastas which are used in this book. But use your imagination and try new flavors by starting with the basic recipe of egg pasta and adding tomato, beet, pepper, lemon, jalapeño, whole wheat and so much more.

When making the dough for pasta, use a strong mixer because the dough is dense. You can also mix it by hand by putting the flours on a working surface, opening a hole in the middle, placing all liquid ingredients into that hole and start mixing slowly blending the flours with the rest of the ingredients until it becomes dough.

To cut pasta, you can buy a little hand pasta machine which is very inexpensive and usually makes four cuts of pasta. It makes pasta sheets which can be used for lasagne and is the basis for stuffed pasta and also makes cuts of linguini, fettucini and cappelini. Use linguini in place of spaghetti. When making fresh pasta noodles make sure you sprinkle it with semilina flour so it does not stick together.

Pasta dough can be refrigerated up to two weeks if wrapped well. Then take out as much as you need to make enough pasta for your use. Fresh pasta noodles also keep well in the refrigerator. They can also be frozen but when ready to cook you must drop them in the pot frozen. (This method is not highly recommended.)

Fresh pasta is great and easy to make but cannot be reheated. It will not taste the same as it did when cooked the first time. It is also very difficult to overcook, not like dry pasta which is easily overcooked.

Manicotti Marinara (see page 50)

Egg Pasta

12 eggs
1 lb. durum wheat flour
1½ lbs. semolina
1 oz. vegetable oil
¼ cup water
1 tsp. salt

Mix in your mixer on medium speed for about 12 minutes.

Spinach Pasta

Use the above recipe and add:
1½ cups frozen spinach, drained well and chopped

You may need to add a little more flour.

See pages 44 and 45 for information on how to prepare and cook different pasta cuts.

"The earth gives birth to all creatures and nourishes them, receiving their fertile seed again."
— *Aeschylus (500 B.C.)*

Grain is buried in the ground, then is reborn as a plant which bears grain.

Hard wheat is picked in autumn. Semolina is produced from this wheat. It contains more protein and less starch. It is used mainly for pasta making.

In 300 B.C. Greeks and Italians developed the process of making wheat flour, then durum wheat. Now more than 30,000 varieties of wheat are recorded worldwide and botanists are creating new and better varieties daily.

Wheat first arrived in America late in the 15th century.

Pasta Fillings

BEEF AND CHICKEN:
2 Tbsp. olive oil
1 lb. ground beef
¼ lb. chicken, ground
1 clove garlic, chopped
> *Sauté in a skillet until meats are browned.*

1 egg
1 tsp. lemon peel
½ tsp. nutmeg
2 Tbsp. Romano cheese, grated
2 Tbsp. Parmesan cheese, grated
½ tsp. black pepper
> *Remove from heat and mix the rest of the ingredients together. This filling is good for cappaletti or tortellini.*

SPINACH:
1½ cups spinach (you can use frozen), drained and chopped well
3 oz. cheddar cheese, shreddedddd
1 oz. Parmesan cheese, grated
1 oz. Romano cheese, grated
1 cup ricotta
1 clove garlic, chopped
1/2 tsp. nutmeg
1/2 tsp. black pepper
1 egg
> *Mix all ingredients well. This is great for agnolotti filling.*

CHEESE:
¼ lb. Mozzarella cheese, shredded
⅛ cup Romano cheese, grated
⅛ cup Parmesan cheese, grated
2 tsp. parsley, chopped
2 cups Ricotta cheese
2 eggs
1 tsp. black pepper
> *Mix all ingredients well. This filling is great for spinach pasta ravioli or tortellini.*

CHICKEN – HAM:
2 Tbsp. olive oil
½ lb. chicken, ground
½ lb. ham, ground

>*Sauté in a skillet until meats are browned.*

1 Tbsp. Parmesan cheese, grated
2 Tbsp. Romano cheese, grated
2 eggs
½ tsp. nutmeg
1 tsp. black pepper

>*Remove the skillet from the heat. Mix with the rest of the ingredients. This pasta is good for tortellini filling.*

OTHER FILLINGS:

2 Tbsp. olive oil
4 oz. veal, ground

>*Sauté in a skillet until the veal is browned.*

1 cup spinach (you can use frozen), drained well and chopped
¼ cup Parmesan cheese, grated
¼ cup Romano cheese, grated
1 egg
1 tsp. black pepper
½ tsp. nutmeg

>*Remove skillet from heat and add the rest of the ingredients. Mix well.*

2 Tbsp. olive oil
4 oz. chicken, ground
3 oz. ground beef
3 oz. ground veal

>*Sauté in a skillet until meat is browned. Remove skillet from the heat.*

2 oz. Mortadella cheese, very thinly chopped
1 Tbsp. parsley, chopped
1 Tbsp. Romano cheese, grated
1 Tbsp. Parmesan cheese, grated
1 tsp. nutmeg
1 tsp. black pepper
1 egg

>*Add to the meat and mix well.*

4 oz. Proscuitto, ground
1 cup spinach (you can use frozen), drained well and chopped
2 oz. Romano cheese, grated
2 oz. Parmesan cheese, grated
1 cup Ricotta cheese
1 tsp. black pepper
½ tsp. nutmeg
1 egg

Mix all ingredients well.

2 Tbsp. olive oil
¼ small onion, chopped well
1 clove garlic, chopped
5 mushrooms, chopped well

Sauté in a skillet until onions are lightly browned. Remove from heat.

8 oz. cream cheeese
1 tsp. basil
1 tsp. thyme
1 tsp. black pepper

Mix with the vegetables well.

1 cup Feta Pesto sauce (see page 115)
½ cup Ricotta cheese

Mix well.

½ cup crab meat, finely chopped
½ cup bay shrimp, finely chopped
½ cup Ricotta cheese
2 oz. Mozzarella cheese, shredded
⅛ cup Romano cheese, grated
⅛ cup Parmesan cheese, grated
1 egg
1 tsp. black pepper
1 tsp. parsley, chopped

Mix well.

The French regard cheese as their national specialty. There are more than 375 varieties of cheese in France alone. There are well over 1000 types of cheeses made all over the world.

How To Create Different Tastes

The next two recipes are an example of how much you can create. Here you are simply using the same ingredients but by adding one ingredient to the Stuffed Shells Spinaci (spinach) you have created a completely different taste.

Pay attention to all your recipes. First, what kind of ingredients, herbs and spices go into the dish and then, what kind of tastes those ingredients have created. It is important if you want to create your own style of cooking to develop the tastes in your mind and not on your palate. The imagination is responsible for creating taste. The palate is simply the checking point for your creations. Once you associate the taste with the mixing of your favorite ingredients, there is no stopping how much you can create.

Think of recipes as music. Music is only based on seven notes but you would not know it by the hundreds of sounds of music that we can listen to.

The same is true with your recipes. Stay with the herbs, spices and ingredients you like and you are familiar with. Then you cannot miss. You will create something that you will truly like and if you are pleased with your creations, then the effort of cooking becomes love and passion and will show on the plate and on the faces of your family and friends.

As you are preparing these recipes notice the baking time for all these dishes is less than 30 minutes and the preparation time is just a few minutes. So you see, the making of tasty dishes does not necessarily mean it will be complicated. It's easy! So easy that I bet the biggest skeptic will try these recipes. And once you do and see the reaction of your family and guests, it will encourage you to do more. The whole trick of all this is to organize things. Make sure you have all the ingredients and the necessary preparation done. Then you can make a dinner quicker, and spend your extra time with your family and friends.

Manicotti Marinara

4 pasta strips, approximately 5″ x 10″ (see pages 45-46)
> *Lay strips on a working surface.*

4 oz. Mozzarella cheese, shredded
4 oz. Provolone cheese, shredded
2 oz. Feta cheese
1 cup Ricotta cheese
1 egg
2 Tbsp. Romano cheese, grated
2 Tbsp. Parmesan cheese, grated
> *Mix well. Divide the mixture into 4 parts and place each part on the end of every pasta strip. Spread the mixture across the pasta strip lengthwise. Roll the pasta up. Place the 4 manicottis in a baking dish and cover them with three cups of marinara sauce (see page 115) (about 2½ - 3 cups). Bake in a 425° oven for about 30 minutes.*

Stuffed Shells Spinaci

8 large pasta shells, cooked
> *Place in a baking dish.*

3 oz. Mozzarella cheese
3 oz. Provolone cheese
2 oz. Feta cheese
1 cup chopped spinach
1 egg
1 cup Ricotta cheese
2 Tbsp. Romano cheese
2 Tbsp. Parmesan cheese
> *Mix well and fill the shell with this filling. Cover the stuffed shells with three cups of marinara sauce (see page 115). Bake in a 425° oven for about 30 minutes.*

Lasagne Il Re

5 oz. lasagne pasta, cooked (see pages 45-46)
> *Place in a casserole.*

1 cup meat sauce (see page 116)
> *Add in.*

1 tsp. cinnamon
Pepper to taste
1 Tbsp. Romano cheese
1 Tbsp. Parmesan cheese
1 oz. Ricotta cheese
2 mushrooms, sliced
½ tsp. parsley
> *Place these on top of the meat sauce.*

1 cup meat sauce (see page 116)
> *Pour on top of the spices.*

4 oz. Mozzarella cheese, shredded.
> *Place on top. Bake at 425° for 25 minutes.*

Ravioli Bolognese

12 oz. ravioli, cooked (Preferably spinach pasta filled with cheese)
> *Place in a cooking casserole.*

8 oz. meat sauce (see page 116)
> *Pour half of the sauce and toss with ravioli.*

1 mild Italian sausage, cooked and sliced
> *Place on top of ravioli.*

1 Tbsp. Romano cheese
1 Tbsp. Parmesan cheese
> *Sprinkle on top. Pour remainder of sauce on top. Bake at 425° for about 20 minutes.*

Spaghetti Mozzarella

⅛ lb. spaghetti or linguine, cooked
2 cups meat sauce (see page 116)
1 Tbsp. Romano cheese
1 Tbsp. Parmesan cheese
> *Mix in bowl.*

6 oz. shredded Mozzarella cheese
> *Spread on top.*
> *Bake at 425° for about 20 minutes.*

Ravioli Mozzarella

16 spinach raviolis filled with cheese. (see pages 45-47)
> *Boil in water for about 5-6 minutes. Place raviolis in a mixing bowl.*

6 mushrooms, thinly sliced
3 cups marinara sauce (see page 115)
1 Tbsp. Romano cheese
1 Tbsp. Parmesan cheese
> *Add to the mixing bowl and mix the raviolis with this sauce and place in a baking dish.*

8 oz. Mozzarella cheese, shredded
> *Spread on top of the raviolis. Bake at 425° for about 20 minutes until the cheese on top is lightly browned.*

✯ Spanakofillo

FILLO CRUST:
6 sheets of fillo
> *Lay one fillo in a pie plate approximately 10" wide. Butter it lightly and place the rest of the fillo on top, criss-crossing and buttering them. Fold the ends of the fillo and roll them into the inside of the plate to form the edges of the crust. Bake in 375° oven for 10 minutes.*

1/2 cup Marinara sauce (see page 115)
> *Place in the middle of the crust.*

1 recipe of stuffed shells spinaci (see page 51)
> *Place on top of the sauce.*

2 Tbsp. Marinara sauce (see page 115)
> *Place on top of the filling. Bake in 375° oven for 15-20 minutes.*

Fettuccine Thallasis

2 Tbsp. olive oil
2 Tbsp. vegetable oil
> *Heat in sauce pan.*

½ cup chopped clams
½ cup scallops
1 clove garlic
> *Add in and sauté for 6-7 minutes.*

2 Tbsp. Sauterne cooking wine
2 Tbsp. clam juice
¼ tsp. each of: black pepper, parsley, basil, oregano, thyme, rosemary
> *Add in. Cook 2-3 minutes.*

¹⁄₁₆ tsp. red pepper flakes
¼ cup fettuccine cooked
⅛ cup Romano cheese, grated
⅛ cup Parmesan cheese, grated
> *Add in.*

Fusilli Ladato

3 Tbsp. olive oil
3 Tbsp. soybean oil
½ red pepper, sliced
½ green pepper, sliced
6 mushrooms, sliced
½ zucchini, sliced
1 cup broccoli, chopped in large pieces
1 clove garlic, chopped
> *Sauté until vegetables are soft.*

2 cups fusilli pasta, cooked
> *Add in.*

⅛ cup Mytzithra cheese, grated
> *Add in and stir well.*

Soya has been grown in Asia since 2,000 B.C. Now many farms in Europe produce soya. Soybean oil is extracted from the seeds after they are crushed. Soybean oil is popular because of its neutral flavoring and it is very low in saturated fats.

Green Lasagne

2 Tbsp. olive oil
2 Tbsp. soybean oil
½ green pepper, sliced
½ red pepper, sliced
6 mushrooms, sliced
1 clove garlic, chopped
> *Sauté until soft.*

6 plum tomatoes (canned), crushed
1 tsp. basil
1 tsp. parsley
½ tsp. black pepper
⅟₁₆ cup white cooking wine
1 Tbsp. Romano cheese, grated
1 Tbsp. Parmesan cheese, grated
> *Add in and stir well.*

2 oz. spinach pasta, cooked (see pages 45-46)
> *Pour ½ of the sauce in a baking dish. Place the cooked pasta in and stir gently to mix pasta with little of the sauce.*

2 oz. Ricotta cheese
> *Spread on top of the sauce. Pour remaining sauce on top of Ricotta.*

4 oz. Mozzarella cheese.
> *Spread on top of the sauce. Bake at 425° for 25 minutes.*

Vegetable Ravioli

2 Tbsp. olive oil
2 Tbsp. soybean oil
> *Heat in sauce pan.*

5 mushrooms, sliced
½ red pepper, sliced
¼ onion, slice
1 clove garlic, chopped
½ cup zucchini, sliced
2 artichokes, sliced
⅛ cup sliced black olives
> *Sauté until soft.*

1 Tbsp. white cooking wine
6 oz. ravioli, cooked
> *Add in and mix well.*

½ cup whipping cream.
> *Stir until heated.*

Agnolotti Romana

2 Tbsp. olive oil
2 Tbsp. soybean oil
> *Heat in a sauce pan.*

½ small onion, thinly sliced
> *Add in and sauté 2-3 minutes.*

1 Tbsp. pine nuts
1 tsp. garlic in oil
> *Add in and sauté 2-3 minutes.*

2 whole plump tomatoes (canned)
> *Crush tomatoes well and add to sauce pan along with 1 Tbsp. tomato juice from the can and sauté 6-7 minutes.*

½ cup heavy whipping cream
⅛ tsp. black pepper
⅛ tsp. nutmeg
> *Add in and heat gently for 3-4 minutes.*

2 cups agnolotti pasta
> *Boil for 7-8 minutes. Add pasta to sauce pan.*

2 Tbsp. Romano cheese, grated
2 Tbsp. Parmesan cheese, grated
> *Add to the sauce pan and mix well. Remove from heat. 2 servings.*

Fusilli Primavera

2 Tbsp. olive oil
2 Tbsp. soybean oil
> *Heat in heavy sauce pan.*

½ small onion, thinly sliced
½ small red onion, thinly sliced
½ red pepper, thinly sliced
½ green pepper, thinly sliced
4 mushrooms, thinly sliced
> *Add in and sauté 3-4 minutes.*

1 broccoli flowerette, chopped
½ cup zucchini, chopped
> *Add in and sauté 2-3 minutes.*

2 cloves garlic, chopped
⅛ cup black olives, sliced
⅛ cup green olives, sliced
1 whole artichoke heart, chopped
> *Add in and cook 3-4 minutes.*

½ pint whipping cream
Black pepper to taste
> *Add in and cook on low heat for 4 minutes.*

1 cup white fusilli pasta, cooked
1 cup green fusilli pasta, cooked
> *Add in and stir well.*

½ cup Romano cheese
½ cup Parmesan cheese
> *Add in, stir well and cook 2-3 minutes.*

Fettuccine Formaggi

2 Tbsp. olive oil
2 Tbsp. soybean oil
>*Heat in sauce pan.*

6 mushrooms, thinly sliced
>*Add in.*

1½ cup whipping cream
>*Add in and heat gently.*

Pinch of black pepper
1 Tbsp. Ricotta cheese
½ oz. Mozzarella cheese, shredded
½ oz. Provolone cheese, shredded
>*Add in.*

8 oz. fettuccine, cooked
>*Add in.*

¼ cup Romano cheese, grated
¼ cup Parmesan cheese, grated
>*Add in and stir well.*

Tortellini Romanola

2 Tbsp. olive oil
2 Tbsp. soybean oil
>*Heat in a saucepan.*

1 cup whipping cream
¼ cup walnuts, grated
Pinch of pepper
>*Add in and heat gently.*

8 oz. tortellini, cooked
>*Add in.*

¼ cup Romano cheese
¼ cup Parmesan cheese
>*Add in and stir well.*

MUSHROOM WALNUT TORTELLINI:
>*Sauté 4 mushrooms, thinly sliced, before you add the walnuts and the whipping cream. Then follow the same steps as the preceeding recipe.*

Parmesan cheese was first made in the 12th century in Italy. It needs over 1000 liters of milk to make just one large wheel of Parmesan cheese.

Mostaccioli Primo

2 Tbsp. olive oil
2 Tbsp. soybean oil
> *Heat in a saucepan.*

½ onion, thinly sliced
2 artichoke hearts, crushed (not marinated)
> *Add in and sauté until onions are soft, 3-4 minutes.*

2 Tbsp. white cooking wine
> *Add in.*

1 cup whipping cream
> *Add in.*

1 oz. Ricotta cheese
> *Add in and stir until melted.*

6 oz. mostaccioli, cooked
> *Add in.*

1 oz. Romano cheese
1 oz. Parmesan cheese
Pinch of black pepper
> *Add in and stir well. Place in a small baking pan.*

5 oz. mozzarella cheese, shredded
> *Top over the mixture and bake at 425° for 20-25 minutes.*

Spaghetti Carbonara

2 Tbsp. olive oil
2 Tbsp. soybean oil
> *Heat in a saucepan.*

½ green pepper, thinly sliced
½ red pepper, thinly sliced
4 oz. ham, cooked and thinly sliced
8 slices of bacon, sliced
1 clove garlic
> *Add in and sauté until peppers are soft.*

1½ cup whipping cream
Pinch of black pepper
> *Add in and heat gently.*

12 oz. spaghetti or linguini, cooked
> *Add in.*

¼ cup Romano cheese, grated
¼ cup Parmesan cheese, grated
> *Add in and stir well.*

Lobster Cannelloni

1 spinach pasta sheet approximately 10″ x 5″ (see pages 45-46)
> *Lay on a working surface.*

½ cup shredded Mozzarella cheese
½ cup shredded Provolone cheese
½ cup Ricotta cheese
1 Tbsp. Romano cheese, grated
1 Tbsp. Parmesan cheese, grated
1 egg
¼ cup lobster meat
½ cup crab meat
> *Mix well in a bowl. Place on the end of the pasta sheet and roll filling inside.*

Place cannelloni in a baking dish.
2 cups red clam sauce (see page 210)
> *Pour on top. Bake in a 375° oven for about 25-30 minutes.*

Grilled Spinach Cannelloni

2 pasta sheets, approximately 8″ x 4″ (see pages 45-46)
> *Lay on a working surface.*

2 Tbsp. olive oil
2 Tbsp. soybean oil
> *Heat in a skillet.*

3 mushrooms, sliced
¼ cup chopped spinach
½ small onion, sliced
1 clove garlic, chopped
1 mild Italian sausage, cooked and thinly sliced
½ cup Ricotta cheese
1 Tbsp. Romano cheese
1 Tbsp. Parmesan cheese
¼ cup Mozzarella cheese, shredded
> *Mix in a bowl. Divide filling into two parts. Place each part on the end of each sheet. Roll to close in filling. Grill the cannelloni on flat top griddle with 2 Tbsp. canola oil until both side are golden brown. Place on a serving platter.*

Sauce:

2 Tbsp. olive oil
2 Tbsp. soybean oil
> *Heat in a skillet.*

¼ small onion, sliced
1 clove garlic, chopped
¼ cup chopped spinach
> *Add in, sauté 3-4 minutes.*

⅛ cup white cooking wine
> *Add in.*

4 plum tomatoes, crushed (canned)
1 tsp. nutmeg
1 tsp. pine nuts
1 tsp. black pepper
> *Add in and sauté 4-5 minutes longer.*

¼ cup whipping cream
> *Add in and simmer 2-3 minutes.*

Pour sauce over cannelloni and serve.

Grande Agnolotti de Marre

2 sheets egg pasta, approximately 8″ x 4″ (see pages 45-46)
> *Cut both sheets to resemble half circles and lay on a working surface.*

¼ cup Ricotta cheese
½ cup bay shrimp
¼ cup crab meat
1 egg
1 Tbsp. Romano cheese
1 Tbsp. Parmesan cheese
½ cup Mozzarella cheese, shredded
1 tsp. black pepper
1 tsp. parsley
> *Place in a bowl and mix well. Place mixture in the middle of one of the pasta sheets, wet the edges with a little water and cover with the other sheet. Seal edges with fork. Grill pasta on both sides in 2 Tbsp. canola oil under gentle heat. Place on a serving platter.*

> *Recipe continues on next page...*

Sauce:
2 Tbsp. olive oil
2 Tbsp. canola oil
> *Heat in a skillet.*

4 mushrooms, sliced
4 asparagus spears, cut into pieces
1 clove garlic, chopped
> *Add in and sauté 3-4 minutes.*

1 Tbsp. white cooking wine
> *Add in.*

¼ cup whipping cream
1 tsp. black pepper
2 Tbsp. Romano cheese, chopped
2 Tbsp. Parmesan cheese, chopped
> *Add in and simmer 2-3 minutes. Pour sauce on top of pasta and serve.*

Half Moon Agnolotti

2 sheets of egg pasta, approximately 8″ x 4″ (see pages 45-46)
> *Cut both sheets to resemble half circles and lay on a working surface.*

¼ cup Ricotta cheese
1 Tbsp. Romano cheese
1 Tbsp. Parmesan
¼ cup crab meat
¼ cup lobster meat
1 egg
½ clove garlic, shopped
1 tsp. black pepper
1 tsp. parsley
½ cup shredded Cheddar cheese
> *Mix in a bowl. Lay filling in the middle of 1 pasta sheet, wet pasta on the edges with a little water. Cover with the other pasta sheet and seal edges with a fork. Grill pasta on both sides in 2 Tbsp. canola oil under gentle heat. Place on a serving platter.*

Recipe continues on next page…

Sauce:
2 Tbsp. olive oil
2 Tbsp. soybean oil
> *Heat in a skillet.*
½ cup broccoli, coarsely chopped
1 artichoke heart, sliced
1 clove garlic, chopped
1 Tbsp. almonds, sliced
½ small tomato, chopped
> *Sauté in skillet for 4-5 minutes.*
2 Tbsp. white cooking wine
> *Add in.*
1 tsp. black pepper
1 tsp. parsley
½ tsp. Dijon mustard
¾ cup whipping cream
2 Tbsp. Romano cheese
2 Tbsp. Parmesan cheese
> *Add in and simmer 1-2 minutes. Pour over pasta and serve.*

Fettuccine Marinara

2 cups marinara sauce (see page 115)
> *Warm in a skillet.*
1/4 lb. fettuccine noodles, cooked
> *Add in.*
1 Tbsp. Romano cheese
1 Tbsp. Parmesan cheese
> *Add in and stir well.*

Pinon Ravioli

2 spinach pasta sheets approximately 8″ x 4″ (see pages 45-46)
> *Lay on a working surface.*
1 cup Feta Pesto sauce (see page 115)
½ cup Ricotta cheese
> *Mix well and place filling in the middle of one pasta sheet. Wet the edges with a little water. Cover with the second sheet and seal edges with a fork. Grill over low heat in 2 Tbsp. canola oil until both sides are lightly browned. Place on a serving platter.*

> *Recipe continues on next page...*

Sauce:

2 Tbsp. olive oil
2 Tbsp. soybean oil

Heat in a saucepan.

¼ small onion, sliced
1 clove garlic, chopped
1 cup spinach, chopped
1 artichoke, sliced
1 plum tomato, crushed
1 tsp. pine nuts

Add in and sauté 4-5 minutes.

1 Tbsp. white cooking wine
1 tsp. black pepper
1 tsp. Dijon mustard
½ tsp. nutmeg
½ cup whipping cream
1 Tbsp. Romano cheese
1 Tbsp. Parmesan cheese

Add in and simmer 2-3 minutes. Pour over pasta and serve.

Basil Garlic Fettuccine

2 Tbsp. olive oil
2 Tbsp. soybean oil

Heat in a saucepan.

1 small tomato, chopped

Add in, sauté 2-3 minutes.

1 Tbsp. white cooking wine
1 cup Feta Pesto sauce (see page 115)

Add in and heat for 2-3 minutes.

¼ lb. cooked fettuccine
1 Tbsp. Romano cheese, grated
1 Tbsp. Parmesan cheese, grated
½ tsp. black pepper

Add in and stir to mix well.

GIVING BACK

*T*he popularity of the restaurant happened at a time when I was so much involved with my work. In a way, I did not really watch it grow throughout the months and the years. It was like I closed my eyes for a while and when I opened them, here we were. Thousands of people had invaded my little restaurant, day and night, any time and any day that 860 square feet of space was always full. Our reservation book had tables reserved for weeks and sometimes months at a time. The attention from the critics was unbelievable and the compliments from the customers were endless. I made a promise to myself that I would not let the popularity change me. I had worked hard to arrive at peace with myself and was not going to give it up for a temporary ride to fame. My nature is not to be a materialistic person. I believe happiness and harmony comes from the simple things in life.

As I thought this new-found attention to be a dream world and a temporary high of joy, my way of resisting and keeping my feet on the ground was to keep in touch with the other side of our society, the one you don't talk about in membership clubs or at cocktail parties. There's a side of society most of us want to keep hidden because we're ashamed to say that in the same town we live in, a few miles away from us is another world where children are unhappy and abused, where the elderly live in misery the last few years of their lives; the side of the town we refuse to recognize that's full of people who are sleeping in the streets and digging in the garbage for food. But we must discover that part of town and turn on the lights on so we can see how fortunate we are to have so much, so much that we can give some back.

On Thanksgiving of 1985 I started to look for some of the people that I saw sleeping under the bridges and digging in the garbage cans. The same people that made me feel shameful of our society and puzzled that in the richest country in the world we allow our citizens to go through such misery.

I found some of them sheltered at the Central Arizona Shelter. I asked the executives of the shelter if they would allow me to cook for 250 of their guests. The first Thanksgiving for the Hungry was started from 5024 E. McDowell. That year we prepared a traditional Thanksgiving dinner – turkey with all the trimmings – for them. The Thanksgiving holiday was new to me but its meaning was clear. To sit at a table full of food and know that most is going to be wasted was not acceptable. People filling up their stomachs to the point of misery while others are starving, was unjust and unbalanced. At least on this one day if everyone came together as a community to make sure everybody felt thankful. It could be a start, a ray of hope that is not lost in selfishness and materialism.

In the beginning I never thought that this single act would turn out to be the project that many years later would motivate thousands of people to volunteer with the hope of making our community a better place to live. It all started when a few of the homeless from Central Arizona Shelter returned the pots and pans to the restaurant. It was the day after Thanksgiving. They stood there thanking me. I saw hope in their eyes and joy on their faces and I thought to myself, "My God, is that all that it takes to make someone happy?" From then on it was a commitment.

That event on Thanksgiving made me appreciate the little things that I had. It motivated me to do more and I felt stronger than ever. As the tiny restaurant on 5024 E. McDowell became more and more crowded. It pushed me to every limit humanly possible. I was determined not to stop at anything. The restaurant stayed open long hours and business was never interrupted, even with remodeling and moving equipment in.

I remember one morning we had to bring in a stove, a griddle and a deli case. They arrived at 9:00 am. As we were bringing them in we found out the deli case would not fit through the door. We had to take out the windowto bring it in. Everyone kept saying it was impossible to bring in and connect all that equipment just before opening for lunch. "Nonsense," I thought. All we had to do was believe that it was possible. By 10:30 we were ready as our first customers started to come in. I kept that deli case with me for the next eight years. It came to be known as "the torture case," because in the years to come would be full of desserts that would be loved by everyone.

But besides the desserts the recipes kept coming by the bunches.

story continues on page 84

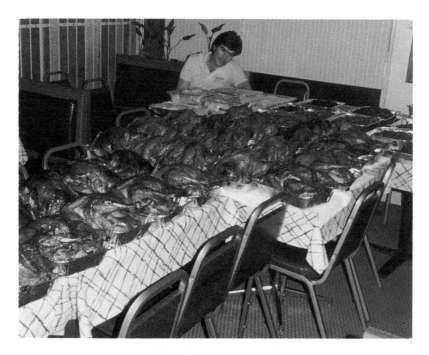

First Thanksgiving on McDowell.

Appetizers...

COOKING WITH VEGETABLES

There are several things you need to know when cooking with vegetables which will affect the results of the final taste. There are groups of vegetables that absorb salt and other groups that absorb herbs, water or oil.

For instance, in the following appetizer section when you bread the vegetables fresh and fry them in clean oil you will see how clean and crisp the taste is. If you are in a restaurant and order fried mushrooms or fried zucchini and it tastes oily and soggy, it is for the following reason. The vegetable was breaded and stored in the freezer where it collects moisture or ice around it. When that vegetable is fried in hot oil, the vegetable absorbs the moisture, especially vegetables which contain water naturally, such as mushrooms or artichokes. That will leave the vegetable soggy tasting.

Other factors are dirty oil and the temperature of the oil. Dirty oil will give you a bitter burned taste. Improper temperature (you must fry between 320° - 350°) will not make the outside crispy fast enough to seal and protect the vegetable from the oil and in this case the oil will be absorbed by the vegetable.

Other groups of vegetables absorb salt. The potato is the prime example. When soup is oversalted, use a potato to soak up the excess salt bringing food to its normal taste. I have not used salt in my cooking for 20 years now (salt added) and not only for health reasons, but I believe salt ruins the cooking. For instance, if you are making a casserole with all vegetables and use salt, your taste will be unbalanced as some of the vegetables will absorb more salt than others. It is best to add salt to accommodate your taste at the table. I love to cook with lemon, black pepper and wine.

You must also be very careful when using bell peppers, especially green bell peppers. When you are having a meat sauce (or any other sauce) that has been simmered for a long time and is getting a sweet peppery taste it is because that sauce contains bell peppers. What the pepper does is act like a sponge and absorb and kills all the herb tastes. It is best to leave it out or add it at the end of the cooking of your sauce.

Oil must also be used carefully. Many vegetables absorb oil. The prime example is the eggplant. If you grill or fry eggplant, make sure you place it on a paper towel before using it to absorb the excess oil.

BREADING MIXTURE

4 cups buttermilk pancake mix
6 cups of water
> *Mix well with a wire whip.*

To bread vegetables and other foods, follow this method:

You will need:
1 bowl of flour
Buttermilk pancake mixture
1 bowl of bread crumbs.

> *Dip vegetable first in the buttermilk mixture, then the flour, then back in the buttermilk mixture. Lastly, place in the bread crumbs. Always start from wet to dry and move from wet to dry.*

With this breading you can do so much. For instance,

MUSHROOMS: *Bread the whole mushroom. Serve with ranch dressing.*

ZUCCHINI: *Cut into about ½" slices. Serve with ranch dressing.*

ARTICHOKE HEARTS: Use the ones packed in water. *Serve with ranch dressing.*

MOZZARELLA STICKS: *Cut into thick strips. Make sure you bread them well. When you fry them, they must be covered completely with oil. Serve with tomato sauce (see page 117).*

Here are some more appetizers that can be breaded with the same method. Always deep fry in 325° - 350° until item is golden brown.

Spanakorizo Balls

4 cups water
> *Heat over medium heat.*

2 cups rice
> *Add in. Boil 6-7 minutes. Cool with cold water.*

½ cup Romano cheese, grated
½ cup Parmesan cheese, grated
1 cup spinach, cooked and chopped
½ cup shredded Mozzarella cheese
> *Mix all ingredients in a bowl. Form small balls the size of golf balls. Make sure the balls are firm. Bread and fry.*

The first cheeses were made from goat's and sheep's milk. Cheeses today are not only made from goat's, sheep's or cow's milk, but also with buffalo's milk which produces Mozzarella.

Grape Rolls

⅔ cup spinach, cooked and chopped
⅔ cup mushrooms, chopped
⅔ cup carrots, chopped
⅓ cup cabbage, chopped
⅓ cup celery, chopped
1 Tbsp. mint leaves
2 garlic cloves, chopped
Pepper to taste

Mix well in a bowl.

32 grapevine leaves

Lay a grapeleaf on a working surface. Place a second one on top of the first. Place a spoonful of filling in the center of the grapeleaf. Roll filling in the leaves. Repeat the process until all grapeleaves are used.
Bread and fry. Serve with tomato sauce (see page 117).

Asparagus Ham Melt

½ lb. cooked ham, chopped
½ lb. of cheddar cheese, chopped
6 asparagus, chopped

Mix well. Make small balls with the mixture. Press the ball with the palms of your hands to flatten them. Use breading mixture (see page 66). Deep fry in 350° oil until golden brown. Serve with ranch dressing (see page 112).

Asparagus Spears

4 pieces of ham, thinly sliced

Lay on a working surface.

4 slices cheddar cheese

Place on top of ham.

8 asparagus spears, blanched in hot water

Place on top of cheese at one end. Roll into tight rolls. Bread and fry. Serve with tomato sauce.

Eggplant Ripieri

8 slices Mortadella cheese
8 slices Provolone cheese
4 slices medium eggplant, ¼ inch thick

Place one slice of Mortadella, top with a slice of Provolone, then a slice of eggplant. Then top with Provolone and Mortadella. Make 4 stacks. Bread and fry until golden brown. Serve with tomato sauce (see page 117).

Spicy Lamb Potatoes

¼ lb. gyros meat, cooked
1 potato, peeled and cooked
1 clove garlic, chopped
½ tsp black pepper

Mix well. Shape mixture into large balls (golfball size) then press down to make it into an oblong shape. bread and fry. Serve with yogurt dressing (see page 113).

Peperoni Tirato

1 mild Italian sausage, cooked, thinly sliced
1 cup Ricotta cheese
1 cup Mozzarella cheese, shredded

Mix well.

2 long roasted red peppers

Fill peppers with mixture. Bread and fry in 325° oil until golden brown. Serve with marinara sauce (see page 115).

Spinach Puffs

2 cups chopped cooked spinach
½ lb. Feta cheese
½ cup pine nuts
½ cup cooked rice
¼ cup onions, chopped
2 green onions, chopped
½ tsp. dill weed
½ tsp. black pepper
1 Tbsp. milk
1 Tbsp. olive oil
2 eggs
1 tsp. cinnamon
½ tsp. mint leaves

Mix well in bowl.

10 pieces of puff pastry dough, 5″ x 5″ size.

Place 2 Tbsp. filling in the middle of the square. Wet the edges and fold the dough into a triangle and press edges gently with a fork. Bake in 395° oven for 15-18 minutes. You can make smaller, bite-size pieces if desired.

Feta Dill Fritters

¼ lb. of gyros meat, cooked (see page 244)
2 cups spinach puffs filling (see page 69)

> *Mix well. Divide into small balls, press balls with the palms of your hands to flatten into small hamburgers. Bread and fry.*

Broccoli Melt

½ lb. yellow Cheddar cheese, shredded
½ lb. broccoli flowerets, finely chopped

> *Mix well. Make balls the size of golf balls. Bread and fry. Serve with ranch dressing (see page 112).*

Fried Rice Balls

2 cups cooked rice
¼ cup Mozzarella cheese, shredded
2 Tbsp. Romano cheese
2 Tbsp. Parmesan cheese

> *Mix well, form into balls. Bread and fry. Serve with tomato sauce (see page 117).*

Vine Pesto Chili

Grapeleaf Pesto:
4 Tbsp. butter
8 grapeleaves, chopped
¼ cup Parmesan cheese, grated
½ tsp. pepper
3 cloves garlic
¼ cup olive oil
¼ cup pine nuts
¼ cup walnuts, chopped

> *Place all ingredients into a mixing bowl and mix on medium speed for about 6-8 minutes until thick and creamy.*

6 green chilies

> *Open cut from one side, lay them on a working surface. Place about 1 Tbsp. in the middle of each of the chilis and roll. Bread according to the method on page 66. Deep fry in 350° oil until golden brown.*

Tiropitakia

¾ lb. Feta cheese
¼ lb. Ricotta cheese
1 tsp. nutmeg
3 eggs, beaten
2 Tbsp. parsley, chopped
1 cup Romano cheese
1 cup Parmesan cheese
> *Mix well.*

Melted butter
> *Cut fillo sheets into 3" or 4" strips. Place 2 strips together. Place 1 Tbsp. on the end of the strips. Fold into triangles. Bake in 375° oven or deep fry in 325° oil. For easier use, you can use puff pastry dough, cut into desired size.*

CHEESE PUFFS:
> *Use the same filling. Place 2 Tbsp. filling on 5" x 5" pastry dough. Brush the edges with water and fold over. Press the edges with a fork. Bake in 425° oven for about 15-20 minutes.*

Seafood on Pastry

2 puff pastry squares (approximately 5" x 5")
> *Place in a small oiled pan.*

2 Tbsp. olive oil
> *Heat gently in a saucepan.*

2 green onions, chopped
½ cup of bay shrimp (small)
> *Add in. Sauté for 2-3 minutes.*

1 clove garlic, chopped
1 Tbsp. white cooking wine
> *Add in.*

4 plum tomatoes (canned)
Pinch of black pepper
Pinch of oregano
Pinch of basil
Pinch of thyme
Pinch of rosemary
Pinch of parsley
> *Add in. Simmer for 3-4 minutes.*

1 Tbsp. Romano cheese
> *Add in. Stir, remove from heat. Pour filling on top of puff pastry. Divide into equal parts. Bake at 425° for about 15-18 minutes.*

Puff Pastry dough is available in specialty markets.

Clamcakes

2 puff pastry sheets (approximately 5˝ x 5˝)

Place in a small, oiled baking ban.

2 Tbsp. of olive oil

Heat gently in a saucepan.

½ cup clams, chopped
2 green onions, chopped
1 clove of garlic, chopped
¼ cup of zucchini, chopped

Add in. Sauté for 3-4 minutes.

1 Tbsp. white cooking wine
½ tsp. black pepper
½ tsp. basil
½ tsp. rosemary

Add in. Simmer 2-3 minutes. Place filling on top of the two puff pastry squares, dividing evenly.

4 Tbsp. Mytzithra cheese, grated

Place on top of the filling. Bake in a 425° oven for about 15-18 minutes.

Romeiko

2 puff pastry squares (approximately 5˝ x 5˝)

Place in a small oiled baking pan. Bake in a 425° oven for about 5 minutes. Remove from oven.

6 sun-dried tomatoes, finely chopped
4 oz. of Feta cheese

Mix well, and divide into two parts.

2 Tbsp. of tomato sauce (see page 117)

Place 1 tsp. on each pastry dough. Put on top of this the tomato-Feta mixture.

2 oz. of Mozzarella cheese

Place on top of mixture. Sprinkle a little rosemary on top. Bake for 8-9 minutes longer.

Ham Puffs

½ lb. cooked ham, chopped
¼ lb. of Swiss cheese, chopped
½ cup of Ricotta cheese
½ tsp. black pepper
1 egg

Mix well. Place 1 Tbsp. filling in the middle of a puff pastry dough, 5˝ x 5˝. Brush the edges of the dough with water, and fold it over. Press the edges with a fork to seal. Bake at 425° for 15-20 minutes.

Asparagus Puffs

2 Tbsp. olive oil
1 lb. asparagus, chopped
1 Tbsp. garlic

> *Melt butter, sauté asparagus with garlic, about 2-3 minutes.*

¼ cup. sliced almonds

> *Add, heat 2-3 minutes longer. Transfer filling into a large bowl. Mix well with the following ingredients.*

½ cup shredded Swiss cheese
2 eggs
¼ lb. Ricotta cheese
Pepper to taste
1 Tbsp. Romano cheese
1 Tbsp. Parmesan cheese

> *Place 1 Tbsp. of filling on each pastry square. Form triangles. Bake at 450° 15-20 minutes.*

Asparagus Logs

Use asparagus puff filling (see page 73)

> *Place 2 Tbsp. of filling on a puff pastry dough square, fold the filling in by rolling the dough, seal the seam and the edges. Repeat to make desired logs. (Remaining filling can be refrigerated). Deep fry in 350° oil until pastry dough is lightly brown. Serve with Ranch dressing.*

Another way of breading is to substitute the bread crumbs with a mixture of:

2 cups corn meal
1 cup flour
2 cups matzo meal
1 cup Semolina

> *Mix well.*

And the following items are the best to bread this mixture with:

ONION RINGS:
> *Cut into thick rings. Use the outside, larger, rings. Bread just like the preceding recipes except you are using the corn meal mixture instead of the bread crumbs. Serve with Ranch dressing.*

FRIED CLAMS:
> Use the whole baby clams.
> *Serve with pineapple cocktail sauce (see page 78).*

FRIED OYSTERS:
> *Serve with tartar sauce (see page 114).*

FRIED SCALLOPS:
> *Serve with tartar sauce (see page 114).*

ONION HEARTS:
> Best to use the hearts of red onions.
> *Serve with Ranch dressing (see page 112).*

Another easy way to use breading is:
Dip the food into the buttermilk pancake mix, then into the flour. Here are some things you can do this way:

BAY SHRIMP: Use the small shrimp.
Serve with pineapple cocktail sauce.

POPCORN CALAMARI:

10 small Calamari tubes
Cut into small pieces. Serve with tomato sauce.

Dolmades

48 grapevine leaves (approximately)
3 Tbsp. of olive oil
Heat gently in a saucepan.
6 green onions, chopped
1 Tbsp. fresh parsley, chopped
1 cup of raisins
2 cups rice
1 cup pine nuts
1 Tbsp. fresh dill, chopped
1 tsp. black pepper
Add in. Simmer for about 5-6 minutes.
½ cup white cooking wine
Add in. Simmer 2-3 minutes. Stir well. Place one grapeleaf on a working surface, then put another grapeleaf on top of the first one, overlapping almost half way. Place 1 Tbsp. filling on top, fold the leaf from the bottom to cover the filling. Tuck in the edges, then roll.
½ cup olive oil
Place in the bottom of a small cooking pot. Place rolled grapeleaves in the pot. Repeat the process until the filling is used. Arrange grapeleaves on the bottom of the pot fitting them tightly together. Then start a second layer on top of the first one.
Juice of 1 lemon
Squeeze on top of the grapeleaves.
1 tsp. black pepper
Sprinkle on top.
Cover the grapeleaves with two plates (or any other heavy item just to keep them on the bottom of the pot). Fill the pot with water approximately 4-5" over the grapeleaves. Boil on medium heat for about 60 minutes. Add more water if needed. Let cool completely before removing. Serve with yogurt sauce (see page 113).

Artichoke Vinaigrette

⅛ cup olive oil
2 cups artichoke hearts
> *Heat in saucepan.*
½ cup mustard vinaigrette (see page 113)
> *Add in.*

Feta Leaves

1 cup Feta cheese
½ cup sun-dried tomatoes, finely chopped
> *Mix well. Place 1 Tbsp. of the mixture in the middle of a grapevine leaf and roll, continuing the process until all the filling is used. Grill with olive oil.*

Potato Skins

> *Cut 2 potatoes in half, lengthwise. Scoop out the pulp so you can have the shells left. Deep fry the potato shells for a few minutes until golden brown. Lay the shells in a baking dish with the cavities up. Place in the filling and bake 10-15 minutes in a 375° oven. Serve the skins with yogurt dressing.*

Assorted Fillings:

BACON
> *Fry approximately 16 strips bacon. Place them in the skins and cover them with 8 slices of Cheddar cheese.*

TURKEY
1 cup mushrooms, thinly sliced
1 Tbsp. olive oil
6 oz. cooked turkey, sliced
> *Sauté for a few minutes until mushrooms are soft. Spoon into the skins. Top with 5 oz. shredded Mozzarella cheese.*

WESTERN
1 Tbsp. olive oil
1 cup green peppers, thinly sliced
1 small onion, thinly sliced
4 oz. sliced ham
> *Sauté for a few minutes until vegetables are soft. Place filling into skins.*
12 slices of Cheddar cheese.
> *Place on top of filling.*

SPINACH
2 cups of the spinach puff filling (see page 69)
Spoon into the skins.
1 cup Ricotta cheese
¼ cup spinach, cooked and chopped
Mix and place on top of skins.

PURE GREEK
6 oz. gyros meat (see page 244)
8 artichoke hearts
Grill together until meat is brown on top. Place on top of potato skins.
½ cup Feta cheese
Crumble on top.
1 cup of Kefalograviera cheese
Cover the feta with it.

MEAT SKINS
1½ cup meat sauce (see page 116)
Place in skins.
4 mushrooms, thinly sliced
Place on top.
4 mild Italian sausages, cooked, thinly sliced
Place on top.
5 oz. Mozzarella cheese, shredded
Sprinkle on top.

VEGETARIAN SKINS
¼ cup onions, thinly sliced
¼ cup red onions, thinly sliced
¼ cup mushrooms, thinly sliced
¼ cup green peppers, thinly sliced
¼ cup zucchini, thinly sliced
¼ cup artichoke hearts, thinly sliced
¼ cup green olives, thinly sliced
1 heart of palm, sliced
Grill with 2 Tbsp. oil. Place in a bowl. Mix with ¼ cup Italian dressing. Place in skins.
4 oz. Provolone cheese, shredded
Spread on top.

Chicken Wings

Place 12 chicken wings in a fry pan with 2 cups frying Canola oil. Fry for about 8-10 minutes until wings are brown.

Flavor Variations

N.Y. Style
1 cup Bar-B-Que sauce (see page 202)
>*Pour into a bowl.*

1 clove garlic, chopped
>*Add.*

½ tsp. black pepper
½ tsp. parsley
½ tsp. oregano
½ tsp. thyme
½ tsp. rosemary
6-7 hot red pepper flakes
>*Add. Put the wings in the bowl and mix well. Place the above mixture on a baking sheet and bake 375° for 10-15 minutes.*

Follow the same procedure for the following flavors:

Grecian
2 Tbsp. olive oil
1 clove garlic
juice of ½ lemon
½ tsp. rosemary
½ tsp. thyme
½ tsp. oregano
½ tsp. parsley
½ tsp. black pepper

Blue
½ cup blue cheese dressing
½ cup blue cheese crumbles

Honey Dipped
½ cup honey
¼ cup water
Pinch of cinnamon
>*For* HONEY MUSTARD, *add 1 Tbsp. Dijon mustard to this honey mixture.*

Coconut Fried Bananas

4 bananas, peeled, sliced horizontally into 1″ slices
2 cups buttermilk pancake mix
3 cups water
>*Mix well.*

Flour
2 cups shredded coconut
Oil for deep frying, heated to 350°
>*Dip bananas into the buttermilk mix, then into the flour and back into the buttermilk mix. Roll them into coconut. Fry until golden. Makes 4 servings.*

Pineapple Cocktail Sauce

1 cup chili sauce
1 Tbsp. horseradish
Pinch black pepper
2 Tbsp. onions, finely chopped
½ tsp. hot sauce
1 tsp. celery, finely chopped
Juice of ½ lime
Juice of ½ lemon
¼ cup pineapple juice
>   *Mix all ingredients well.*

Baby Shrimp Cocktail

1 lb. baby bay shrimp, cooked
1/2 cup pineapple cocktail sauce (see recipe above)
>   *Mix. Chill before serving. Makes 4 servings.*

Brochettes of Snails

24 large snails (escargots)
>   *Use 4 wooden skewers and thread 6 snails on each. Roll skewer in bread crumbs.*

2 Tbsp. olive oil
2 Tbsp. soybean oil
>   *Heat in a saucepan and brown snails to golden on both sides.*

½ cup butter
2 green onions
1 clove garlic, chopped
>   *Heat in a saucepan and sauté onions and garlic for about 3 minutes.*

½ cup white cooking wine
1 cup whipping cream
1 tsp. black pepper
>   *Add in. Simmer gently until cream thickens, about 5-6 minutes. Serve snails with sauce.*

Taste is a physical sensation which causes the arousal of most of our senses. Presentation and color of food is an enticement to the sight. Flavor brings pleasantness to the lips, tongue and palate. The aroma of herbs and spices inspires excitement to the smell.

Each one of those senses acts together to motivate the sense of taste to its fullest and to bring a physical desire before and after the meal.

Taste, therefore, is an intellectual act because it involves the majority of our senses with analysis to taste. As we become more educated about the subject of taste, we will be able to detect bitterness, sweetness, salinity and acidity of foods so we can pick the partner of preference among herbs and spices to fulfill our needs to the best possible taste.

Baked Stuffed Mushrooms

2 Tbsp. olive oil
2 Tbsp. soybean oil
> *Heat in a skillet.*

12 large mushroom caps
> *Add to the skillet. Sauté until lightly brown, about 5 minutes.*

2 Tbsp. white wine
> *Add to the skillet. Remove caps from skillet and place on a baking sheet.*

¼ lb. Feta cheese
2 Tbsp. capers, chopped
4 large artichoke hearts (not marinated), chopped
> *Mix well. Fill mushroom caps. Bake in 375° oven for about 15 minutes. Makes 2 servings.*

Here are more fillings for stuffed mushrooms:

BLUE CRAB STUFFED MUSHROOMS
Follow the same way of preparing the mushroom caps as above.

½ cup crabmeat
> *Place in mushroom caps.*

½ cup chopped blue cheese, crumbled
> *Place on top of crabmeat. Bake in 375° oven about 15 minutes.*

PESTO STUFFED MUSHROOMS
Follow the same way to prepare mushroom caps as above.

½ tomato, sliced
> *Place on top of mushroom caps.*

2 Tbsp. Feta cheese, crumbled
> *Sprinkle on top of tomatoes.*

½ cup pesto sauce (see page 115)
> *Place on top. Bake in 375° oven for 10-12 minutes.*

Just before the 3rd century B.C., the great explorer Pythias believed in Pythotherapy. The only treatment he suggested was juice from fruit and a diet from plants.

Garlic Press

½ cup chopped eggplant
2 cloves garlic, chopped
½ red roasted pepper, chopped
1 tomato, chopped
1 tsp. dill
1 tsp. black pepper
1 egg
3 Tbsp. bread crumbs
1 tsp. parsley
2 Tbsp. flour

Place all ingredients in a bowl and mix well. Make flat round patties from the mixture about 1/2 cup each.

3 Tbsp. olive oil
3 Tbsp. soybean oil

Heat well in a skillet. Fry the patties until brown on both sides. If a flat top griddle is available, it's best to use that.

Stuffed Calamari

12 large calamari tubes
1 cup (approximately) of Feta Pesto sauce (see page 115)

Stuff the calamari with the pesto using about 1 Tbsp. for each tube.

4 Tbsp. olive oil
4 Tbsp. soybean oil

Heat well in a skillet.

1 cup buttermilk pancake mix
2 cups water

Mix well. Dip calamari in.

Flour

Roll them in flour. Fry until browned, about 7-8 minutes.

Garlic Walnut Fritters

2 potatoes, boiled, skinned

Mash in a bowl.

2 cloves garlic
1 Tbsp. red wine vinegar
2 Tbsp. walnuts, grated
1 tsp. black pepper

Add in to the bowl, mix well.

2 Tbsp. olive oil
2 Tbsp. soybean oil

Place in a skillet (or on a flat top griddle). Divide filling to approximately ¼ cup each part, flatten and dip in flour before placing on the skillet. Brown well on both sides.

Kaltsounakia

1 lb. of pizza dough (see pages 28-30)

> *Divide to about 1 oz. pieces. Form small rounds and flatten the rounds to very thin.*

½ cup Ricotta cheese
¼ cup Feta cheese
¼ cup Myzithra cheese, grated
1 tsp. pepper
1 egg
1 Tbsp. dill

> *Mix well Place 1 Tbsp. (approximately) of filling in the middle of each round. Wet the edges with a little water. Fold over one end of the dough to enclose the filling and form a half-moon shape. Press with the fork on the edges to close the filling in well. Deep fry, preferably in Canola oil until golden brown.*

Zucchini Fritters

1 small zucchini, chopped
⅛ cup Feta cheese, crumbled
⅛ cup Kefalotyri or Kaseri cheese, shredded
1 potato, peeled, chopped
1 tsp. dill
1 egg
1 tsp. pepper
1 tsp. parsley
1 tsp. oregano
3 tsp. bread crumbs
2 tsp. flour

> *Mix well in bowl. Spoon out mixture to ¼ cup (approximately). Form flat round patties. Roll them in flour.*

3 Tbsp. olive oil
3 Tbsp. soybean oil

> *Heat in a skillet (or on a flat top griddle). Fry until brown on both sides.*

Basil Keftedes

1 lb. white gyros (see page 224)
½ cup Feta Pesto sauce (see page 115)

> *Mix well in bowl. Form small flat round patties. Dip in flour.*

Flour
3 Tbsp. olive oil
3 Tbsp. soybean oil

> *Place in a skilled (or on a flat top griddle). Fry until brown. Serve with yogurt sauce (see page 113).*

Skordalia

5 cloves garlic, chopped
½ cup old bread, soaked in a little water
1 cup walnuts, grated
1 cup olive oil
Juice of ½ lemon
2 Tbsp. red wine vinegar
1 potato, boiled and peeled

> *Place in a mixer and mix until all ingredients are smooth.*

Use this spread with fish, especially fried fish, or just spread on bread. It has a strong garlic taste.

Taramosalata

½ lb. Tarama (carp fish roe)
½ small onion, chopped fine
½ cup dry bread, soaked in a little water
1 small potato, boiled, peeled

> *Place in a bowl and mix well.*

1 cup olive oil
Juice of 2 lemons

> *Add the oil and lemon, slowly, a little at a time. Mix for about 10-12 minutes until the mixture is smooth.*

This spread can be used as a side dish with just about anything but it is so addictive that you'll want to eat it with a spoon before it reaches the table.

Taramokeftedes

4 green onions, chopped
½ cup tarama (carp fish roe)
1 potato, boiled, peeled
1 tsp. dill
1 tsp. parsley
2 Tbsp. bread crumbs
1 tsp. black pepper
Flour

> *Mix well in a bowl. Form small round flat patties. Dip in flour.*

3 Tbsp. olive oil
3 Tbsp. soybean oil

> *Heat in a skillet or on a flat griddle. Fry until golden brown on both sides.*

Spinach Puffs (see page 69)

Feta Leaves (see page 75)

GOOD ENERGY IS THE SECRET

*T*he hours of hard work had now become an everyday routine. The days went by quickly as if clocks and windows did not exist. The clock was definitely running faster than me, and I was running after it trying to catch it. It seemed impossible to slow down that clock. I remember in one stretch it was 24 months straight without a single day off, 18 hours a day of work, cooking, baking, creating and for the next three years very little changed. Now I wonder where all that strength came from?

I remember so many times my legs felt weak, the mornings were my biggest challenge, how to get from the bed to the shower. Now I know that was all in the power of the mind, the mind that so many of my heroes have inspired. It was that power that kept my legs from giving up. It was that power that got me out of bed. The heroes in my life who gave me the strength to go on, were many. Those who had sacrificed their lives for their beliefs and have contributed to mankind to visualize a better life. Those who have planted beliefs into our minds and inspired love into our hearts. Respect and love are valuable virtues to my inspiration. The respect and the love for my two biggest heroes in life, a man and a woman, had entered into my thoughts so deep that now they are a part of my everyday life. They are also my inspiration for the love for the three people I have loved most in my life: a girl and two boys who have inspired me with responsibility and motivate to never give up, even after my so-called failures. My parents are my inspiration. My children are my love. They all give me the energy to go on, energy that is all good. Energy that is not motivated by money and material things or selfish reasons to be better than the next person.

All that good energy I use to my advantage the supplies of which are endless. I have learned now not to have people around me that draw that good energy away. We only have so much energy to give. We must have heroes that will inspire us with motives of personal achievements of self control and balance and not cause disturbance in our minds and hearts; people who are useful to our peace of mind and do not require constant attention and waste our energy. Positive people bring positive results. Negative people cause disturbance and make us weary.

It was that energy that kept me going for endless hours, every day. I remember when orders have overflowed into the kitchen and single-handedly I prepared them, one motion for hours. Now I am amazed at how I did it. The stamina to go through so many years of endless hours can only come from inspiration and not physical strength. Everything that has built up or accomplished was started with an idea. If you have this idea, do not give it up, even if it seems impossible to accomplish at that time.

Plato's republic was an idea in his head. Acropolis was a vision and many thought it impossible to complete. Beethoven could not hear his music, it was all in his mind. Picasso could not see Jaconta's smile. He imagined it.

One must have the inspiration to accomplish and that inspiration will come from your heroes. That inspiration will become good energy to create and accomplish positive things in life. If you think you are running out of energy, all you have to do is reach up and get more supplies of it. Your heroes will inspire endless energy for you. These heroes can be anyone: your parents, your friends, your children, your teachers, a statesman who truly believes in democracy, students fighting for freedom. Anyone can touch your life in a positive way. You just have to let it happen.

Some of the people I have looked up to had strong influences over my everyday life. The energy that I can get from them is overflowing in my mind and keeps my legs from bending, my eyes from closing, and my mind alert. Energy is the secret and it is available, and free, and that energy will create the opportunity to think for the positive and never for the negative. Even my children gave me energy and I know that later in their lives that energy was returned to them in the same positive way. It works. And not only to the people that are close to you, but to many others whom we come in contact with.

The customers of my restaurant, for example, whom I have seen throughout the years walking into the restaurant with smiles and telling me wonderful stories. I wish I could remember them all. A family which every Friday night would come into the restaurant on McDowell and because they could not find an open table, always brought their trailer and order their food to go, then park the trailer in front of the restaurant and eat their dinner watching TV. I remember an older lady that for years, twice a week, drove to the restaurant in a taxi cab to pick up her food. A couple who were traveling from New York to Los Angeles and on purpose changed planes in Phoenix with five hours delay so they could eat in my restaurant. Someone who called from Florida and asked me to send him meals and desserts for a special dinner party. I remember businessmen from Dallas who used to fly into Phoenix on their private plane once a month just to eat in my restaurant. A lady who pre-ordered food to go from Chicago and picked it up on her way home from the Phoenix airport.

Sometimes when I checked the reservation list there were many out of state phone numbers. A 92-year-old lady once told me the reason she lived to be old was so she could enjoy my cooking. I remember a family who planned their reunion (from Detroit, Utah, and Denver) in Phoenix so they could eat in the restaurant. More recently, I saw them in "Nick's on Central," with a newborn baby. The father of the baby told me the baby was "Nick's Next Generation" and that part of his parenthood job was to make sure the child would enjoy "Nicks' " food. A young man stopped me recently and told me his father brought him to the restaurant when he was 12 years old. That was 11 years ago. Now that he was expecting a child of his own, he would do the same for his child.

Recently I went to court for a ticket and was sitting in the courtroom among 30-35 others when the Judge walked in, took a look at the crowd, then looked quickly through his cases. He picked one out from the middle of the stack, then said, "Nick, come over here." As I walked to his bench he talked to me for about ten minutes about the restaurant and how much he enjoyed the food through the years.

Not too long ago a young girl called me to her table and with sparks in her eyes said, "You were in that little place on McDowell, right?" And when I said, "Yes," she told me the story that her father took her to McDowell when she was eight years old. Then they moved to Texas. Twelve years later she came to Phoenix and her friends took her to the restaurant for lunch. She had no idea that this was the same restaurant from the

McDowell days, but as she took the first bite of her food, she remembered the taste from when she was younger and associated this restaurant on Central with the one on McDowell. The good energy works and will generate endless supplies if we keep the healthy thoughts on our minds.

I remember the days on McDowell when every customer who walked into the restaurant was a celebrity and that has not changed at all. But some celebrities were more well known than others. One day I met Rita Davenport from the TV show "Cooking with Rita," and she invited me to her show on which I appeared twice. Both times the response was tremendous and my already busy restaurant became busier. Reservations were days and weeks in advance. Also around that time, I met Brad Steiger, a famous author of many books. We became good friends. He became a big fan of my cooking. He encouraged me to preserve my recipes into a cookbook, and so with his help my first cookbook was published. The most difficult thing about that book was to measure every ingredient for the recipes because when I cook, I never measure anything. That book and that energy motivated me to create even more recipes.

story continues on page 88

I had the wonderful opportunity of working with Nick for over six years and learned so much about cooking, as well as life's philosophies. I have always found Nick's cooking fascinating, and his culinary abilities artistic. Nick cooks and creates everything with care and love.

When I saw this book I knew this was *the* cookbook to own. Each recipe is a work of art and has a little part of Nick in all of them. The book has everything from soups, salads and appetizers to main dishes. Everything on his menu and more can be found in this book.

But not only is this a fabulous cookbook, it is full of interesting information about the food and also a story that won't let you put the book down until you have finished it.

I wish Nick nothing but the best with this incredible cookbook and all the endeavors he embarks in.

Best wishes,

Kathy Karros-Clarke

Benefit dinners were donated by Nick's for the special olympics to put a little smile on the special athlete's faces. The restaurant closed for the evenings hosting the special guests.

IT IS AN ART, NOT WORK

*F*requently I was asked the question why I was working so hard and how I can accomplish so much in such a short time. The answer is simple. What I do is not work. It is an art. It is part of my life like nursing or breathing. I have understood throughout the years to take care of my body with healthy, nutritious foods and have learned that only natural thinking can give me peace of mind free of the pollution of drugs and alcohol. So among the other important elements of my life, creating dishes became another necessity. I wanted it to improve that to the best of my ability, as I tried to improve my soul and my mind. The urge was powerful for spiritual growth without the motivation of notoriety and greed. The need to expand and express the thought I had pictured in my mind, it was my mission. It was important to me to create new ideas and new tastes for others to experience. It was that attitude which pushed me to open the "Pita Stop," a unique take-out place in the food court of Tri-City Mall. All sandwiches were made on Pita bread with unique fillings.

The little take-out place sat in the upstairs of the Mall among a pizza parlor, a 50's diner, a Chinese place, a yogurt shop and a movie theater. But come lunch time the line at the "Pita Stop" was much longer than any other.

To introduce the "Pita Stop" to our regular customers, I decided to close the restaurant on McDowell for two months. Our customers would then have to drive to Mesa for a taste of our food and our desserts from the display case that in the storefront of the "Pita Stop."

Hundreds of customers went out of their way to visit the "Pita Stop." The success of the new place was beyond my expectations and two months after the opening, I thought it was time to reopen the restaurant on McDowell. About one week before we opened the restaurant, I informed a few of our customers about the reopening, hoping to have a few customers for the first days. I went back the following Monday to prepare for the opening and as I walked in, felt I was coming home even though the place looked empty and deserted. It felt warm. For the next two days I prepared the desserts, dressings, sauces and all I needed to open the restaurant. The smells of melting chocolate and the odors of the fresh-cooked foods gave that small area back its character. By Wednesday morning I was ready to open the doors. I figured that a couple of days before the weekend would be enough to prepare me for the weekend crowd, but what happened those two days before the weekend was beyond belief. From the time the doors opened, people flooded in all day long and went into the late night, until midnight. I had to lock the door to keep people from coming in. I was pleasantly surprised with the overwhelming reception of the reopening. But I could not understand how all the people knew? There was no advertisement or any formal announcement.

For the first time it made me realize how powerful the network of people was. From mouth to mouth, hundreds of people knew about it. The next day was more of the same, hundreds of people visiting the restaurant and many more that went into the weekend and from then on it was reservations only. If anyone wanted to get into that small space, resevations were needed two weeks in advance.

The return to McDowell was a triumph. The business was reaching new heights, and my mind was creating new recipes. As if I wanted to reward my customers with new tastes, recipes were coming with so much ease, it was almost no effort to create something new. I remember writing my first cookbook. I was adding recipes to it without even trying them. I knew in my mind the taste. Ingredients were dancing in my head instead of in my mouth and putting them together was an easy task.

story continues on page 104

Our customers celebrating the re-opening on McDowell.

Pitas and other Sandwiches...

Gyros (see page 92)

Artichoke Chicken Pita (see page 95)

Pita Sandwiches

Fold the filling in a warm pita bread. Simply warm the pita in 2 tsp. canola oil in a skillet (or on a griddle) over very low heat. Grill the filling with canola oil (use a skillet if griddle is unavailable).

GYROS:

6 strips gyros meat, grilled (see page 244)

Serve with lettuce, tomatoes, onions and Yogurt Sauce (see page 113).

FETA GYROS PITA:

6 strips gyros (see page 244)
2 artichoke hearts

Grill together. Place in a bowl.

½ cup Feta Dressing (see page 112)

Mix with above.

TURKEY YOGURT:

6 oz. turkey, cooked and sliced
4 mushrooms, thinly sliced

Grill together. Place in a bowl.

½ cup Yogurt Dressing (see page 113)

Add to above and place in pita.

3 slices Swiss cheese

Place on filling and melt under gentle heat.

B.B.Q. BEEF:

6 oz. roast beef, cooked and sliced
½ small onion, sliced

Grill together. Place in a bowl.

½ cup B.B.Q. Sauce (see page 202)

Place filling on top of pita and melt 3 slices Cheddar cheese by covering pita with filling.

PASTRAMI CREAM:

6 oz. pastrami, sliced
½ avocado, sliced

Grill together.

1 Tbsp. Thousand Island Dressing (see page 114)

Place on top of pita

2 Tbsp. cream cheese

Place on top. Place grilled pastrami and avocado on top.

PEPPER STEAK:
4 oz. rib eye steak
>*Grill.*

¼ green bell pepper, sliced
¼ small onion, sliced
3 mushrooms, sliced
¼ small red onion, sliced
1 Tbsp. black olives, sliced
>*Sauté in a skilled. Add a few drops of steak sauce, soy sauce and Worcestershire sauce. Place on top of steak while still on the grill. Melt 3 slices of Swiss cheese on top.*

PITA BLUE:
4 oz. turkey, cooked and sliced
4 slices ham, cooked and cut into pieces
>*Grill and place in a bowl.*

2 Tbsp. blue cheese, crumbled
1 Tbsp. Ranch Dressing (see page 112)
>*Add to above and return to griddle. Top with 2 slices of Swiss cheese until cheese is melted.*

BEEF AND CHEDDAR:
6 oz. roast beef, cooked and sliced
>*Grill.*

3 slices Cheddar cheese
>*Place on top of roast beef and melt cheese.*

AVOCADO FETA:
6 strips white gyros (see page 244)
½ avocado, sliced
>*Grill and place in a bowl.*

½ cup Feta Dressing (see page 112)
>*Add to above and mix well.*

HAM AND SWISS:
4 slices ham, cooked
>*Grill.*

3 slices Swiss cheese
>*Place cheese on top of ham and melt cheese.*

ANTIGYROS:
6 strips white gyros (see page 260)
>*Grill. Serve with Yogurt Sauce (see page 113), lettuce, tomatoes and onions.*

B.B.Q. WHITE GYROS:
6 strips white gyros (see page 260)
½ small onion, sliced
> *Grill and place in a bowl.*

½ cup B.B.Q. Sauce (see page 202)
> *Add to above and mix well.*

PITA OF HEARTS:
6 strips white gyros (see page 260)
2 artichoke hearts, sliced
1 heart of palm, sliced
> *Grill and place in a bowl.*

¼ cup Mustard Vinegarette Dressing (see page 113)
> *Add to above and mix well.*

SPARTAN:
¼ onion, sliced
¼ red onion, sliced
¼ green bell pepper, sliced
4 mushrooms, sliced
1 Tbsp. green olives, sliced
1 artichoke heart, sliced
½ small zucchini, sliced
1 heart of palm, sliced
> *Grill and add 1/4 cup Italian Dressing (see page 112) while still on the grill.*

3 slices Swiss cheese
> *Place on top of above and melt cheese.*

MONTE CRISTO:
4 oz. turkey, cooked and sliced
4 slices ham, cut into pieces
1 egg
1 Tbsp. heavy cream
> *Place in a bowl and mix well. Grill. When almost done, place 3 slices Swiss cheese on top to melt.*

SAN FRANCISCO PITA:
6 oz. pastrami, sliced
½ avocado, sliced
4 slices bacon, cooked
> *Grill together. Add 1 Tbsp. Thousand Island Dressing (see page 114) while still in the griddle. Melt 3 slices of Swiss cheese on top.*

ARTICHOKE CHICKEN:
4 oz. chicken breast, cut into strips
2 artichoke hearts, sliced
½ small onion, sliced
> *Grill and place in a bowl.*

½ cup Yogurt Dressing (see page 113)
> *Add to above and mix well.*

ASPARAGUS CHICKEN:
4 oz. chicken breast
> *Grill and when almost done, place on top:*

2 slices ham, cooked
3 asparagus spears, cooked
3 slices Provolone cheese
> *And when the cheese melts top it with 1 Tbsp. Mustard Vinaigrette Dressing (see page 113).*

BLT, T:
Lettuce, tomatoes, sliced turkey, cooked bacon

TURKEY:
Lettuce, tomatoes, sliced turkey, Provolone cheese

TUNA:
Provolone cheese, tomato, tuna salad

NICK-A-BOB:
6 oz. gyros meat (see page 244) made into a long patty
> *Grill and when almost done top with 2 slices Kefalograviera cheese. Serve with Yogurt Sauce (see page 113).*

HAWAIIAN TUNA:
4 oz. Ahi tuna
> *Grill and top with:*

Cream cheese
3 tomatoes, grilled
¼ red onion, sliced and grilled

MANGO CHICKEN:
4 oz. chicken breast
> *Grill and when almost done top with:*

¼ small red onion, sliced and grilled
2 slices mango
1 Tbsp. blue cheese, crumbled
2 slices turkey, cooked and sliced
3 slices Swiss cheese
> *Serve with Yogurt Dressing (see page 113)*

CELERY GYROS PITA
4 oz. white gyros, sliced (see page 260)
½ small red onion, sliced
½ celery heart, chopped (available in specialty shops)
½ tomato, sliced
1 Tbsp. canola oil
> *Grill or sauté in oil. for about 4-5 minutes.*

½ cup yogurt dressing (see page 113)
> *Mix in a bowl with the grilled ingredients. Place in the middle of warm pita bread and fold.*

FRANCHEEZE PITA
1 large hot dog, cut lengthwise to form a pocket
2 slices Cheddar cheese
> *Stuff into the hot dog pocket.*

5 slices bacon
> *Wrap around the hot dog, secure with toothpick. Deep fry until bacon is done. Remove toothpicks. In warm pita bread fold the hot dog in with lettuce, tomatoes and onions, if desired.*

LAMB TURKEY PITA
4 oz. sliced lamb
4 oz. cooked turkey breast, sliced
> *Grill separately in canola oil.*

1 Tbsp. blue cheese, crumbled
> *When lamb is cooked, place blue cheese on top of meat to melt slightly.*

2 slices Swiss cheese
> *When turkey is warm, place Swiss on top to melt.*

1 warm pita bread
2 Tbsp. yogurt dressing (see page 113)
> *Place yogurt in the middle of pita. Place chopped lettuce and sliced tomatoes on top of yogurt. Place lamb and then the turkey on top of the lamb. Fold pita.*

Focaccia Sandwiches
> *Use a 6" focaccia bread (see page 40)*
> *Heat in oven.*

The following are fillings for the Focaccia sandwiches. Simply spoon on top of this open face sandwich. Use 1 Tbsp. olive and 1 Tbsp. soybean oil to sauté the fillings.

GRECIAN PEPPER BEEF:
6 oz. roast beef, sliced
⅛ cup roasted red pepper, sliced
⅛ cup green bell pepper, chopped
> *Grill in oil. Place in a bowl.*

2 Tbsp. mustard vinegarette dressing (see page 113)
> *Add to the bowl and mix well. Spoon onto focaccia bread.*

PEPPERY CHICKEN:

1 6-oz chicken breast, cut into strips
⅛ cup roasted red pepper, sliced
⅛ cup green bell pepper, sliced
4 mushrooms, sliced
⅛ cup onions, sliced
½ garlic clove, chopped
Grill in oil. Add a few drops of steak sauce, soy sauce, Worcestershire sauce.
3 slices Swiss cheese
Melt on top.

WHITE SAUSAGE:

8 oz. white gyros (see page 260)
Make into a long patty. Fry in oil. Place on top of Focaccia bread.
⅛ cup green bell pepper, sliced
⅛ cup red bell pepper, sliced
⅛ cup onion, sliced
Sauté until vegetables are soft.
1 Tbsp. white cooking wine
½ cup marinara sauce (see page 115)
Add to vegetables. Spoon on top of meat.

COUNTRY GYROS:

6 strips gyros meat, grilled (see page 244)
Place on top of Focaccia bread.
2 eggs
Beat the eggs.
3 slices tomato, chopped
1 oz. Feta cheese
Add to eggs and mix. Place in a bowl.
2 Tbsp. Feta Dressing (see page 112)
Add to egg mixture and mix well. Place on top of gyros.

ATHENIAN LAMB:

6 oz. lamb, cooked, sliced and heated
Place on top of Focaccia bread.
⅛ cup onions, sliced
⅛ cup red onions, sliced
½ tomato, chopped
1 artichoke heart, chopped
½ clove garlic, chopped
Sauté in the oil.
1 tsp. red cooking wine
Pinch of black pepper
Pinch of oregano
Pinch of mint
2 oz. Feta cheese
Add. Spoon on top of the lamb.

HAM AND CHICKEN BLUE:
4 oz. chicken breast, cut into strips
1 Tbsp. onions, sliced
3 slices ham, cut into strips
½ clove garlic, chopped
> *Sauté in the oil until chicken is done.*

1 tsp. white cooking wine
> *Add to skillet.*

Pinch of black pepper
1 Tbsp. heavy cream
2 Tbsp. blue cheese, crumbled
> *Add and heat until cheese is melted.*

STEAK:
1 6-oz. rib eye steak
> *Fry to your likeness.*

⅛ cup red bell pepper, sliced and grilled
4 mushrooms, sliced and grilled
> *Place on top of steak.*

3 slices Provolone cheese
> *When melted, place on top of vegetables. Place all on top of steak on the Focaccia bread.*

Croissants

Here are different toppings for croissants. Cut the croissant in half lengthwise and place the filling in the bottom part of it.

AVOCADO CRAB:
4 oz. crabmeat
> *Place bottom croissant on a baking dish. Pub crabmeat on top of it.*

½ avocado, thinly sliced
> *Place on top of crabmeat.*

3 slices Swiss cheese
> *Place on top of avocado. Bake in 375° oven about 5-6 minutes.*

GOLDEN CLUB:
> *Place on top of the croissant bottom:*

½ cup lettuce, shredded
3 slices tomatoes
4 oz. turkey, sliced
4 strips bacon, cooked
3 slices Provolone cheese

Feta Crab Croissant

3 oz. crabmeat

Place the bottom of the croissant on a baking dish. Put crabmeat on top.

4 oz. Feta cheese, crumbled
3 artichoke hearts, chopped

Place on top of crabmeat.

3 slices Swiss cheese

Place on top. Bake in 375° oven about 5-6 minutes.

Steak and Eggplant

6 oz. rib eye steak

Grill to your likeness.

4 slices eggplant

Grill until done. Place on top of steak.

3 slices Provolone cheese

Place on top of eggplant. Grill until melted.

Turkey Melt:

6 oz. sliced turkey
2 artichoke hearts

Grill together for a few minutes.

3 slices Swiss cheese

Place on top, grill until melted.

Zucchini Chicken:

6 oz. chicken breast

Grill until meat is cooked.

4 slices zucchini

Grill until done and place on top of chicken.

3 slices Provolone cheese

Place on top of zucchini until melted.

Sandwiches

Use a 9 grain roll.

Mushroom Steak:

6 oz. rib eye steak

Grill to your likeness.

4 slices mushrooms, grilled
Swiss cheese

Place on top of steak, and grill until cheese is melted.

GOLDEN STEAK:
6 oz. rib eye steak
> *Grill to your likeness.*

Green bell peppers
Onions
> *Grill and place on top of steak.*

Provolone cheese
> *Place on top of vegetables and rill until cheese is melted.*

Lamburgers

To make a lamburger, mix 6 oz. gyros meat (see page 244) with the filling, grill and serve on 9 grain roll with Yogurt Sauce (see page 113).

OLIVE CHILI:
2 chopped green chilis
1 Tbsp. sliced black olives

MEDITERRANEAN:
3 chopped sun-dried tomatoes
2 Tbsp. Feta cheese
1 Tbsp. capers

ARTICHOKES:
2 artichoke hearts, chopped
3 slices Swiss cheese, chopped

CORN PEPPER:
3 baby corns, chopped
1 small roasted red pepper, chopped
1 Tbsp. blue cheese, crumbled

Pocket Subs

> *Use a 8″ sub roll cut on the side ends to create a pocket. Place filling into the pocket. Bake in 375° oven approximately 8-10 minutes.*

GRECIAN BEEF:
1 oz. roast beef, sliced
Red peppers
Green peppers
Onions
> *Place in a skillet and grill.*

2 Tbsp. Mustard Vinaigrette Dressing (see page 113)
> *Mix in a bowl with the above ingredients.*

REUBEN:
6 oz. pastrami, sliced
3 oz. sauerkraut
> *Grill.*

¼ cup Thousand Island Dressing (see page 114)
> *Mix in a bowl with pastrami and sauerkraut. Place in sub pocket. Top with 3 slices of Swiss cheese.*

SAUSAGE:
> *Place in the sub pocket:*

1 cup Meat Sauce (see page 116)
1 Italian sausage, cooked and sliced
3 slices Mozzarella cheese

TUNA MELT:
> *Place in the sub pocket:*

1 cup tuna salad (see page 127)
2 slices tomatoes
3 slices Swiss cheese

RED CABBAGE PASTRAMI:
6 oz. pastrami, sliced
3 oz. red cabbage
> *Grill and mix in a bowl.*

¼ cup Thousand Island Dressing (see page 114)
> *Add to bowl, mix and place in the sub pocket. Top with 3 slices of Swiss cheese.*

BBQ CHICKEN:
6 oz. chicken breast, cut into strips
½ red bell pepper, sliced
½ small onion, sliced
> *Grill and mix in a bowl.*

½ cup B.B.Q. Sauce (see page 202)
> *Add to bowl and mix. Place in the sub pocket and top with 3 slices of Cheddar cheese.*

BLUE ROAST:
6 oz. roast beef, sliced
½ small onion, sliced
> *Grill and mix in a bowl.*

2 Tbsp. blue cheese, crumbled
2 Tbsp. Ranch Dressing (see page 112)
> *Add to bowl and mix. Place in the sub pocket and top with 3 slices of Swiss cheese.*

CHICAGO BEEF:
6 oz. roast beef, sliced
½ small onion, sliced
> *Grill and mix in a bowl.*

½ cup B.B.Q. Sauce (see page 202)
> *Add to above ingredients then place in the sub pocket. Top with 3 slices of Cheddar cheese.*

VEGETARIAN:
½ small onion, sliced
½ small red onion, sliced
½ small green pepper, sliced
4 mushrooms, sliced
½ small zucchini, sliced
1 artichoke heart, sliced
1 heart of palm, sliced
> *1 Tbsp. green olives, sliced*
> *Grill and mix in a bowl.*

2 Tbsp. Italian Dressing (see page 112)
> *Mix together with above and place in the sub pocket. Top with 3 slices of Provolone cheese.*

Burger Subs

8 oz. ground beef, molded into shape of a sub roll, white or whole wheat. Here are some of the toppings. Place toppings on top of the hamburger after you turn it to cook on the other side.

BACON BURGER:
3 slices Cheddar cheese
4 strips bacon, cooked

WESTERN:
3 slices Canadian bacon
3 slices ham
3 slices Cheddar cheese
> *Top with B.B.Q. sauce (see page 202).*

HAWAIIAN:
3 slices Canadian bacon
Pineapple tidbits
3 slices Swiss cheese
> *Top with Thousand Island Dressing (see page 114).*

ATHENIAN:
Feta cheese
Black olives, sliced
Peperoncinis
> *Top with Yogurt Dressing (see page 113).*

CALIFORNIAN:
3 slices Cheddar cheese
1/2 avocado, sliced
4 strips bacon, cooked

ACAPULCO:
Jalapeños
2 slices roast beef, cooked
3 slices Cheddar cheese
> *Top with Thousand Island Dressing (see page 114).*

ITALIAN:
Tomato Sauce (see page 117)
6 slices pepperoni
3 slices Provolone cheese

CRAB ASPARAGUS:
> *Crabmeat*
> *Cream cheese*
> *3 asparagus spears, cooked*

Vegetable Burgers

½ **small onion, finely chopped**
1 clove garlic, chopped
½ **zucchini, finely chopped**
½ **red pepper, finely chopped**
½ **cup eggplant, finely chopped**
1 tsp. black pepper
1 tsp. dill
1 tsp. thyme
1 Tbsp. Romano cheese
1 Tbsp. Parmesan cheese
1 egg
2 Tbsp. bread crumbs
> *Mix all ingredients in a bowl. Form patties of desired size and grill in canola oil.*

FOR VEGETABLE FRITTERS:
> *Use the above recipe, make small patties, dip in flour and grill on flat top griddle or fry in a skillet until done. This makes an excellent appetizer.*

THE WRONG MOVE

*F*ive years after the opening of Golden Pizza on McDowell and at a time everything was going well in my life, business was at its best. Two to three week reservations were needed to get into the restaurant. All the necessities of life were available. One month of every summer the restaurant closed so I could take some time off. Mondays we would close to recuperate and prepare for the week, and Sundays would be Special Dinner reservations only. But there was something missing. I envisioned in my head creating endless tastes of foods and cases full of delicious desserts. I knew that was not going to happen here. This place was way too small. I started to look for options and pay more attention to people who were offering me opportunities to relocate. In the past five years countless offers were dismissed, but now I was open to suggestions. The kitchen here was too small for my dreams. There was no room for anyone to be in the kitchen to help me.

My body needed a break from the grueling daily abuse. The electric power was so overloaded that breakers always went off in the middle of the customer rush. When it rained, most of the time the kitchen flooded with water. I remember water up to my ankles as I was working, and several times on stormy days the power of the whole block would go off. More than once I remember cooking under candlelights and customers being amused by dining in the darkness by candlelight. Outside the back door I had built a small room to store the paper products and next to it, under a small roof top, was the big mixer because it could no longer fit it into the restaurant.

Searching for more room, the whole ceiling of the restaurant had become a storage room. Everything was full to capacity. Tables and chairs squeezed one next to another in the dining room. Equipment crowded into the kitchen. My cooking area was so small my body was a few inches away from any equipment. Within a couple of steps I covered the whole line of the kitchen.

The air conditioning was also at its capacity. All motors for refrigeration were moved up onto the roof to create less heat in the dining area. Electricity was loaded to maximum. Storage was limited. It was a daily guessing game to have enough products for the day to produce the foods of the large menu and all the new recipes. I was planning to add more recipes and more desserts. Most people shook their heads with disbelief.

I started to explore the possibility of expanding next door. There was a barber shop there and I made them an offer to move into the vacant space next to them. But they refused. That would have been an ideal set up for my operation, expanding the kitchen a little, making room for a few more tables and I would have been happy there. Sometimes I think about how some small events change the destiny of our lives and how it would have been if we had followed other directions. But the bottom line is we make our own destiny and if we choose to go one way rather than another that is our decision and it becomes our responsibility. If we are true to our responsibilities there is no one to blame for the direction or misdirection of our ways of life but ourselves.

In 1989 an opportunity came. It had the face of a doctor, a lawyer, a businessman, and a hustler. The team was formed with the purpose of making "Nick's," a household name. First, we were going to franchise the "Pita Stop." The next project was to market the salad dressings, publish my cookbooks and build up a commissary to provide for the "Pita Stop" stores.

It all started when I met the hustler. After he had dinner in the restaurant, he approached me smoking a cigar and talking fast about the things he was able to accomplish with me and my talent. I listened to him, smiling. I'd heard this before, so many times, in fact, that I left it at, "We'll see." But he was serious and determined to make his talk work. He brought me this lawyer who headed a large law firm. After several meetings in the attorney's office we decided to look for investors to make the move to a bigger place that would enable us to accomplish all our goals.

The first investor was a friend of the lawyer. A businessman, he made a commitment of investing $90,000. The other investor was a frequent customer of my restaurant, a doctor, who was going to invest $250,000. More meetings followed to finalize the deal and layout the plans for the future. When all was done we went to work to make our plans become a reality.

At that time I felt I had to be cautioned of crossing the street because four insurance policies were taken out in my name to protect their investment. The search for a new location started, and finally we found a place on 40th Street and Thomas. It was an existing restaurant commissary for a failing chain of restaurants. It was a good opportunity and the restaurant was bought. But it needed a general remodeling to serve our needs and bring it up to date. New equipment was needed to replace the old, plumbing and electrical work was necessary and we started to remodel. At the same time we started to search for future investors for the "Pita Stop" franchise and the other ventures that we had planned.

The new restaurant was about 9,000 square feet. Some of the investment money came in to start the project and as soon as the remodeling started I had to close the restaurant on McDowell so I could organize the opening on 3903 East Thomas which was planned about 30 days after the closing of the McDowell location.

It was a day with mixed emotions moving out of McDowell. I felt I was leaving behind a life I never knew before – experiences of hard work, unbelievable memories and an army of regular customers which some people compared to a cult following.

Later I compared this experience of the last five years to another experience in my life that helped shape my mind. It was in the Greek Army where, as a young man, you were called to a mandatory service to your country. Of course, as a young man, it is difficult to give up those so-called beautiful years of your life just to be in the service. But when this is done and years later I was thankful I did it because I came out with so much more knowledge of life and responsibility. Most of all it raised a tremendous sense of pride that I was able to give something of myself to the country and the culture I love so much.

Those five years on McDowell did the same to me and my profession. I went in uncertain about what style of cooking I was going to follow, and I never had dreamt the dimension it was going to take. When I came out I was a seasoned chef with tremendous confidence of my work and the ability to create dishes or desserts without special effort. Most of all it had given me a direction in life with a lifestyle my children would someday look up to. Maybe they'll find an example that it is only through hard work and commitment you're able to look back and feel good about the things that were accomplished.

Yes, when I left McDowell, the feelings were mixed, but mostly good. I never regretted the move. I looked at 5024 E. McDowell as a place that was used for my schooling to learn about my business and, most importantly, about my life. I never regretted the move out of there even when a few days after closing that little place the whole deal fell apart.

An emergency meeting was called by the investors. The doctor revealed that his wife of 22 years just filed for a divorce and all his assets were frozen until the settlement. He promised he would find other ways to honor his investment, but I knew deep inside that was never going to happen.

As the businessman was certain that no other investment was coming in, he too pulled back feeling his money was not enough to finish the project. Suddenly all meetings stopped and all future plans were put on a permanent hold. Everyone washed their hands and walked away leaving me with an unfinished restaurant of 9,000 square feet. Friends told me to walk away and go back to McDowell, but for me there was no looking back. I had to move forward and there went my only hope to do it.

Probably the normal thing to do was to look for another option, something that would have made more sense and would have been more practical to start and operate. For a moment I thought of going back to McDowell but that was a fleeting thought. I told myself I would only look back in life for lessons to be learned and not for comfort of a thought on how life would have been. There was no money to move any place else and there was pressure from my customers to open the restaurant.

After that meeting I went back to the restaurant. It was getting dark outside. All the workers had gone home. The huge place was dark and cold. Piles of dirt were on the floor from the plumbers who were trying to replace damaged pipes and drains. Piles of wood were all over the place from walls being rebuilt. The kitchen was bare from most of the equipment that was going to be replaced. I thought of the equipment coming in and the price tag on them. Now I had to find a way to pay for them. Then there was the neon sign, the electrical work, the utility deposits, plates, glasses, all types of foods to order to be able to serve my large menu, liquor to fill the bar. And there I was all alone with very little money to do it! But I was determined. In life everything is possible. At least I would give it the best try I could.

That night I stayed up most of the time thinking of ways to finish the project. There had to be a way that it could be done. I had to keep on building memories. But there were more challenges ahead to accomplish that goal...challenges of tremendous dimension. Dimensions I never knew existed.

THE WAY UP TO THE MOUNTAIN

*T*he day after I learned about the investors backing out I had a meeting with the general contractor. I explained the situation and asked him if he could finish the job and I would pay him after the business opened. He agreed. Then I found a leasing company to lease the equipment that was coming in. I discovered an insurance company which would put up utility bonds for the deposits. After spending everything I had saved from McDowell, borrowing money from a few friends and using my credit cards to their limit, the restaurant was opened on time as planned.

In the meantime, since I was putting all my effort into opening the "Golden Cuisine of Southern Europe," I was neglecting the "Pita Stop." Business there was dropping off and the little profits from the "Pita Stop" were used to support the opening of the new restaurant. The restaurant was a success, customers welcomed the new place with open arms. For me, the operation now was much bigger and a bit more complicated since I had no staff trained for the kitchen. My plan was to train some of the help who had worked for me at McDowell. At first, I only opened a small section of the restaurant's main dining room. Later on when some of my assistants were trained, they helped me in the kitchen. I would open the food service in the bar area. Much later, and as more people were trained, the back dining room would also open. But for several months, I would be the only one in the huge kitchen which opened from 7:00 am till midnight every day. I was back doing 18 hours a day, but was determined to overcome this mountain. The more obstacles that appeared on my way, the more determined I became to reach the top.

The restaurant was old and as we went into the summer months, problems began to appear. Refrigerator compressors started to break down and air conditioners did the same. Replacing those things was expensive. Plumbing was also a problem, drains started to back up frequently. But I was not going to let this discourage me. I was on a mission and was determined to overcome it.

The months were moving too fast. At times I wish I had the power to slow down time. The first of the month seemed like it was there every other week and I had to struggle to pay the rent. The payroll seemed like it was there every other day and by now I employed about 50 people. In order to do all the projects I had started, I began making use of the space and creating other avenues to help with expenses.

All utilities were paid on the dates of the disconnect notice, especially the extremely high electric bill. It was a trying time, but I was optimistic that all things must pass. I was looking forward to the next step of my life. I had a responsibility to try my best not to fail. Despite all the financial troubles of keeping up with expenses and at the same time trying to pay back all the loans and debts, the business was doing extremely well. So well, in fact, one day the so-called investors/partners came back. I am sure it was the work of the hustler who was still looking for a way to make an easy dollar by easing his way into someone else's hard work and ideas.

I remember the day we met in the restaurant. Along with him there was the lawyer and the businessman. Once they saw how good my business was doing they started demanding part in the corporation as it was written in the original agreement, despite the fact none of them had fulfilled their original obligation and had abandoned me in my time of need.

I thought to myself about this society that has become so greedy and how some people have ill thoughts of pretending to be the most powerful animals of this jungle because they have a title or money. After a short conversation with them, I took out the restaurant key from my keychain and smiled. I laid the keys on the table and said, "As of now, my name, my menu, and all that has to do with me personally are finished here. You can operate this place the way you want, and you can also take over all the debts to satisfy the creditors. But you have to do it without me."

I got up from my chair, ready to leave. The lawyer, being the good lawyer he was, asked me to please sit down. "We know nothing about restaurants, and there is no way we can be here running this place," he admitted. He looked at the other two, trying to get a reaction from them. But no one had an answer. "You can have all the corporations except for the restaurant and the Pita Stop," I said. They agreed to take them. I guess it was better than nothing. As they were walking away I thought of them as vultures who came to retain whatever possible. They left holding a few worthless documents, which I'm sure are now sitting on some shelf collecting dust or got thrown away in the garbage.

The "Pita Stop" by now was suffering because I could no longer pay attention to it. All my energy was going into saving the "Golden Cuisine." The results were to close the doors of the "Pita Stop." Soon I made an effort to trim down the 50 employee payroll. I discontinued the distribution of my dressings, stopped the dinner theater, and quit the food basket runs to offices. Despite this uphill battle I remained optimistic that the business would overcome the difficulties and someday I would be able to say I had made it. People close to me shook their heads with disbelief and some of them urged me to give up my Thanksgiving project as a part of trimming down the expenses. But that was not going to change. This project was a part of my life and a commitment that I had made to myself.

As the difficult times were mounting up, I tried to block my mind from the world of destruction. The only thing that mattered was saving of the restaurant. I once again reached up to my heroes for inspiration and energy. I thought of some of them that I had learned to admire and the difficult times they went through: the wars to save their land. The prosecution to spread their beliefs. Losing their lives to preach the truth. Denial to themselves for their families. Thinking about the ones that I've admired throughout my life, their wisdom and their determination for the things that they believed, it made me realize what I was going through was just a minor inconvenience. On the contrary, I felt very fortunate I had so much more than some of them. I was not threatened by wars or hunger.

I shook my head and smiled thinking how we've become so spoiled from the structure of our society and the circumstances in our life. The simple things which fill our lives with joy are no longer present. Now we have taken most of them for granted. I looked around me and realized I had more than others. I thought of my children and insured my thoughts that this possession alone was a precious one and that I had a responsibility because of them. Their minds had to spring forward with healthy thoughts. I believe that somehow these troubled times will be an inspiration to bring those healthy thoughts into their minds, away from drugs, alcohol, abuse, and insecurity. They were part of my inspiration of survival and I did not want them to see me fail. And how could I fail in life with my parents energy for strength and my children's love for perseverance?

I have learned from my parents that courage is an act of virtue. One is not courageous if he jumps from a tall building to the ground to prove his courage. That's stupidity. My parents had courage to ignore the distractions of the time: war, poverty and danger so they could infuse to their children love and security. I found myself acting the same way. I tried my best to keep the trouble in the backstage of my life and always keep an optimistic view. I did not want my children to worry and grow insecure. Even though, through the struggle to survive the restaurant I had lost the "Pita Stop" and its franchise dreams, I had my home and cars repossessed, and my credit cards revoked. I was down to limited options. Survival was from day to day. But I was there fighting for survival and very seldom would I show stress. I kept upbeat and strong for I had faith that all was going to work out.

The business was doing good except for the later evening business. By now crime in the plaza the restaurant was located in was on the rise. Cars were stolen on a regular basis. Night clubs around me brought drug traffic in the parking lot, and fights and shootings frequently appeared near the restaurant. The bad reputation of Tower Plaza Mall spread and our customers were skeptical of coming after dark. Despite the plea from all of the tenants to beef up security, management of the Plaza showed very little interest in doing so. They were fighting their own war of survival as they were entering into a bankruptcy protection program.

But despite all that, I did not neglect my work. I was more determined than ever to go through with this. I had focused on making the restaurant survive. I still had the love for my art left in me. Everything else had disappeared from my life: marriage, material things and simple pleasures. Yet I kept my mind and sanity on creating more recipes.

story continues on page 132

The human good turns out to be activity of soul in conformity with excellence, and if there is more than one excellence, in conformity with the best and most complete.

But we must add in a complete life. For one swallow does not make a summer, nor does one day; and so too one day, or a short time, does not make a man blessed and happy.

— Aristotle

From the grand opening on Thomas Road.

Dressings and Sauces...

Feta Dressing

2½ cups Feta cheese, crumbled
¾ cup red wine vinegar
2 tsp. oregano
3 Tbsp. olive oil
½ tsp. black pepper
3 cups mayonnaise
2 garlic cloves
1 tsp. thyme
1 tsp. basil

Mix well. Makes about 6 cups.

Ranch Dressing

2 cups mayonnaise
2 cloves garlic
1 tsp. Worcestershire sauce
Dash of tabasco
1 cup sour cream
1 cup buttermilk
2 tsp. black pepper
1 tsp. Dijon mustard

Mix well.

Italian Dressing

2 cups vegetable oil
2 cups olive oil
Juice of 1 lemon
1 clove garlic
1 tsp. basil
1 Tbsp. Romano cheese
1 Tbsp. Parmesan cheese
½ tsp. black pepper
½ tsp. dill weed
1 cup red wine vinegar
1 tsp. oregano
1 tsp. thyme
1 tsp. parsley
1 Tbsp. minced onion
½ tsp. rosemary
½ cup pickle juice (if available)

Mix well.

Horseradish Sauce

1 cup sour cream
½ tsp. black pepper
1 clove garlic, chopped
⅛ tsp. horseradish
Mix well.

Yogurt Dressing

1½ cup mayonnaise
½ cup chopped cucumbers
1 Tbsp. Romano cheese
1 Tbsp. Parmesan cheese
1 cup sour cream
1 cup plain yogurt
2 green onions, chopped
Juice of 1 lemon
1 tsp. Dijon mustard
½ tsp. black pepper
Mix well. Makes about 6 cups.

Grapeleaf Dressing

4 Tbsp. butter
8 grapeleaves, chopped well
¼ cup Parmesan cheese, grated
3 cloves garlic, chopped
¼ cup olive oil
¼ cup pine nuts
¼ cup grated walnuts
1 tsp. black pepper
In a mixer, mix well, about 6-7 minutes.
2 cups Italian dressing
Add in and mix well.

Mustard Vinaigrette

2 eggs, well beaten
⅛ cup Dijon mustard
Mix well.
2 cups Italian dressing (see page 112)
Add and mix well.

Blue Cheese Dressing

2 cups mayonnaise
1 clove garlic, finely chopped
1 cup blue cheese, crumbled
1 tsp. Worcestershire sauce
1 cup sour cream
1 cup buttermilk
1 tsp. black pepper
1 tsp. Dijon mustard
Mix well.

Thousand Island Dressing

1 quart mayonnaise
½ cup diced onion
3 hard boiled eggs, chopped
1 tsp. Worcestershire sauce
¼ cup diced pimentos
8 oz. dill relish
12 oz. chili sauce
½ tsp. black pepper
1 clove garlic, minced
½ tsp. Tabasco sauce
1 tsp. capers
Mix well.

Cheddar Bacon Dressing

1 cup shredded Cheddar cheese
1 tsp. red wine vinegar
1 tsp. Worcestershire sauce
6 strips bacon, cooked and chopped
2 cups mayonnaise
1 cup buttermilk
½ tsp. black pepper
Mix well.

Tartar Sauce

1 cup mayonnaise
2 Tbsp. green onions, chopped
¼ cup green olives, chopped
1 Tbsp. red pimientos, chopped
Juice of 1 lemon
2 Tbsp. dill relish
¼ tsp. dill weed
¼ tsp. black pepper
Mix well.

Marinara Sauce

2 Tbsp. olive oil
2 Tbsp. soybean oil
> *Heat in saucepan.*

1 small onion, chopped
2 cloves garlic, chopped
> *Sauté until onions are soft.*

1 can tomatoes in juice (1 lb. 12 oz.)
> *Crush tomatoes and discard juice.*

1 tsp. basil
1 tsp. oregano
1 tsp. thyme
1 tsp. parsley
½ tsp. black pepper
> *Add, simmer about 7-8 minutes.*

1 Tbsp. Romano cheese
1 Tbsp. Parmesan cheese
> *Add. Makes about 5 cups.*

This marinara sauce is so simple and it can be prepared in a just a few minutes. This also supports the theory that simplicity can bring great satisfaction in life. The following are some of the dishes you can prepare with this sauce:

STUFFED SHELLS SPINACI, see page 51
MANICOTTI MARINARA, see page 50
EGGPLANT PARMIGIANA, see page 45
RAVIOLI MOZZARELLA, see page 52
FETTUCCINE MARINARA, see page 61
SHRIMP MARINARA, see page 237
SPANAKI CALZONE, see page 32

Feta Pesto

4 Tbsp. butter, unsalted
¾ cup fresh basil, chopped
3 cloves garlic, chopped
> *Mis well in a mixer for about 2 minutes.*

¼ cup olive oil
⅛ cup Parmesan cheese, grated
⅛ cup Romano cheese, grated
¼ cup pine nuts
¼ cup walnuts, chopped
½ tsp. black pepper
> *Add in and mix until thick and creamy, about 7-8 minutes.*

FOR GRAPELEAF PESTO: *Substitute the basil with 1 cup chopped grapevine leaves.*

Meat Sauce

1 cup margarine
> *Melt gently in a large pot.*

3 lbs. ground beef
> *Add and simmer until lightly browned.*

2 small onions, chopped
4 cloves garlic, shopped
12 mushrooms, sliced
1 celery stalk, chopped
1 small carrot, chopped
> *Add in and simmer until vegetables are soft.*

1 #10 can tomato puree (6 lbs. 1 oz.)
1 #10 can plum tomatoes in juice (6 lbs. 6 oz.)
> *Add in puree and wash can with 1/4 can water. Crush plum tomatoes and add to pot with juice.*

6 bay leaves
2 Tbsp. basil
2 Tbsp. thyme
2 Tbsp. black pepper
1 Tbsp. parsley
1 Tbsp. oregano
1 Tbsp. rosemary
⅛ cup Romano cheese
⅛ cup Parmesan cheese
> *Add in and simmer for about 3 hours.*

This meat sauce can be used in many recipes. The reason for this large recipe is so some can be refrigerated for up to 3 weeks. It also can be frozen. Keep it on hand and you will be able to prepare meals within 30 minutes. The following dishes are some of the examples that you can do with this sauce.
LASAGNE IL RE, see page 51
RAVIOLI BOLOGNESE, see page 51
SPAGHETTI MOZZARELLA, see page 52
EGGPLANT MOZZARELLA, see page 52
SAUSAGE CALZONE, see page 33
or simply serve over pasta.

Garlic Spread

1 cup margarine
2 Tbsp. grated Parmesan Cheese
2 Tbsp. grated Romano cheese
½ cup mayonnaise
4 cloves garlic, chopped
3 Tbsp. parsley flakes
> *Mix well. Spread on top of sliced French bread. Toast bread in oven for a few minutes.*

Sautéed Vegetables

¼ cup olive oil
1 red pepper
1 zucchini
10 mushrooms
1 clove garlic
> *Heat until soft.*

⅛ cup white wine
Pinch black pepper
Pinch parsley
Pinch oregano
Pinch basil
Pinch thyme
Pinch rosemary
> *Add. Makes a great side dish.*

Pizza Sauce (Tomato Sauce)

1 cup margarine
> *Melt in large pot.*

4 cloves garlic
2 onions, chopped
> *Add, cook over low heat until soft.*

1 #10 can tomato puree (6 lbs. 1 oz.)
Fill can ¼ full of water
> *Add.*

1 #10 can whole tomatoes in juice (6 lbs. 6 oz.)
> *Crush and add.*

1 cup oregano
½ cup basil
¼ cup dill
¼ cup thyme
½ cup black pepper
⅛ cup grated Romano cheese
> *Add, stir until mixed well.*

This sauce can also be used as a tomato sauce dip and can be refrigerated up to four weeks. It also freezes well.

Pesto Butter

½ lb. unsalted butter
> *Mix well until smooth.*

½ cup feta pesto (see page 115)
> *Add in and mix well.*

Mushroom Rice Pilaf

¼ lb. margarine

Heat in a pot.

1 onion, chopped
12 mushrooms, sliced
2 cloves garlic, chopped

Add and sauté for about 6-7 minutes until onions are soft.

½ cup white cooking wine
1 tsp. black pepper
1 tsp. parsley
1 tsp. oregano
1 tsp. basil
1 tsp. thyme
1 tsp. rosemary
3 cups rice
6 cups water

Add in and stir well. Cover the pot and simmer for about 15 minutes or until rice is done.

Seafood Sauce

1 cup mayonnaise
2 Tbsp. green onions, chopped
¼ cup green olives, chopped
1 Tbsp. pimentos, chopped
Juice of 1 lemon
2 Tbsp. dill relish
½ tsp. dill
½ tsp. black pepper

Mix well.

Garlic Walnut Spread

2 potatoes, peeled and boiled
3 cloves garlic
1 cup walnuts, grated
1 tsp. black pepper

Mix until potatoes are pureed.

1½ cups olive oil
½ cup red wine vinegar

Add in and mix slowly until mixture is creamy. This spread goes well with seafood, especially fried seafood.

Artichoke Spread

8 artichoke hearts
1 cup mayonnaise
⅛ cup Parmesan cheese, grated
⅛ cup Romano cheese, grated
1 tsp. black pepper
Juice of ½ lemon
1 Tbsp. chives

Mix well. Place in a small baking dish, bake in 350° oven for about 9-10 minutes. Makes a nice side dish.

Sun-Dried Tomato Spread

8 sun-dried tomatoes, chopped
1 cup of Feta cheese
1 Tbsp. capers
1 tsp. oregano
1 Tbsp. olive oil

Mix well until smooth.

Egg-Lemon Sauce

½ cup water
1 Tbsp. cornstarch

Place in a saucepan and mix well over gentle heat.

3 eggs

Beat well in a bowl.

Juice of 3 lemons

Add to the eggs, beat well.

8 cups broth, heated (use vegetables, chicken or beef, see page 134)

Add to the bowl with the eggs very slowly, beating constantly. Add to the cornstarch, beating constantly.

Coconut Fried Bananas (see page 77) with Pineapple Cocktail Sauce (see page 78)

Salads...

Grilled Steak and Eggplant Salad

1 Tbsp. olive oil
1 4-oz. rib eye steak
½ eggplant sliced
> *Grill until steak is cooked and eggplant is soft, cut steak and eggplant into strips.*

¼ red cabbage, chopped
> *Place on a serving platter.*

1 tomato, cubed
1 small red pepper, sliced
6 green onions, chopped
> *Place in a bowl and add the steak and eggplant.*

½ tsp. mint
1½ Tbsp. olive oil
½ Tbsp. red wine vinegar
> *Add in bowl, toss and place on top of red cabbage.*

Deep Fried Ravioli Salad

½ lb. cheese-filled ravioli
> *Fry until crispy.*

¼ cup Romano cheese, grated
¼ cup Parmesan cheese, grated
> *Place in a bowl. Place ravioli in, toss together.*

1 Heart of palm, cut into small pieces
1 Tbsp. sweet peas
2 Slices of salami, cut into small pieces
¼ of a red pepper, cut into small pieces
¼ of a green pepper, cut into small pieces
¼ cup sliced black olives
½ of green (unripened) tomato, chopped
½ of a small red onion, chopped
> *Place in bowl.*

½ cup mustard vinaigrette dressing (see page 113)
> *Add in and toss.*

Ravioli was usually deep-fried and eaten like fritters in the 14th century.

Pasta Salad

1 cup white fusilli pasta, cooked
½ cup green fusilli pasta, cooked
½ cup gardiniera (mixed marinated vegetables)
2 pepperoncinis
2 artichoke hearts, sliced
2 cherry peppers
2 slices of zucchini, chopped
6 pitted black olives, sliced
6 pitted green olives, sliced
¼ cucumber, peeled and cubed
⅛ cup green pepper, sliced
⅛ cup sliced mushrooms
⅛ cup sliced red onions
⅛ cup sliced onions
⅛ cup sliced red peppers
1 Tbsp. chopped red pimentos
¼ tomato, cubed
1 cup Italian dressing (see page 112)

Mix all ingredients in a large bowl. Add 1 cup Italian dressing to the tossed salad before serving.

Greek Peasant Salad

2 tomatoes, cut into wedges
Place on a serving platter.
1 cucumber, peeled and cubed
Add on to the tomatoes.
1 small red onion, sliced
1 small yellow onion, sliced
1 small green pepper, sliced
Place on top of cucumbers.
8 oz. Feta cheese, crumbled. Place on top.
10 kalamata olives
Place on the edges of the platter.
6 pepperoncinis
Place them between the olives.
¼ cup olive oil
Pour on top.
1 Tbsp. red wine vinegar
Sprinkle on top.
Pinch oregano
Pinch thyme
Pinch basil
Sprinkle on top.

Shrimp Pasta Salad

1 romaine lettuce, chopped
> *Arrange on a platter.*

1 cup salad shrimp, cooked
> *Place on top of lettuce.*

½ small green pepper, sliced
4 green onions, sliced
¼ red onion, sliced
4 mushrooms, sliced
1 small tomato, diced
½ small cucumber, diced
⅛ cup sliced black olives
⅛ cup sliced green olives
Place on top of shrimp.
½ cup white fusilli pasta, cooked
½ cup green fusilli pasta, cooked
> *Place on top of vegetables. Serve with choice of dressing.*

Golden Salad

1/2 head of iceberg lettuce
> *Cut into salad-size pieces and place on a platter.*

½ red onion, sliced
4 mushrooms, sliced
3 green onions, chopped
½ cup sliced black olives
½ tomato, cubed
> *Place on top.*

2 slices of ham, cut in strips
2 slices of turkey, cut in strips
2 slices of Swiss cheese, cut in strips
2 slices of Provolone cheese, cut in strips
6 slices of cooked bacon
> *Place on top of vegetables. Serve with choice of dressing.*

Red wine vinegar is produced from red wine. The quality of the vinegar depends on the wine. The best wine vinegars are the ones where the wine is allowed to ferment slowly in oak barrels at 75°. But this method is costly and most manufacturers raise the temperature to speed up the process. Then the vinegar costs less, but the taste is much inferior.

Sliced Lamb Salad

¼ small red cabbage, sliced
> *Place on a platter.*

4 green onions, chopped
1 tomato, cubed
> *Place on top of red cabbage.*

2 Tbsp. olive oil
1 small red pepper
6 slices of eggplant
½ lb. leg of lamb, sliced
> *Grill all above ingredients until vegetables are soft and lamb is cooked.*

1 cup of mustard vinegarette dressing (see page 113)
1 Tbsp. Dijon mustard
> *Place in a bowl and mix well. Place lamb, red peppers and eggplant into the bowl. Mix well and place on the top of the vegetables. Pour rest of dressing on top.*

Antipasto Salad

2 roasted red peppers
> *Place on a platter.*

½ romaine lettuce
> *Cut into pieces and place on the platter.*

½ small onion, sliced
½ small red onion, sliced
½ small red pepper, sliced
½ small green pepper, sliced
4 mushrooms, sliced
⅛ cup sliced black olives
⅛ cup sliced green olives
> *Place on top of lettuce.*

1 cup of gardiniera (mixed pickled vegetables)
Place on top.
2 slices of salami, cut into strips
2 slices of ham, cut into strips
2 slices of Mortadella, cut into strips
2 slices of Provolone cheese, cut into strips
2 slices of Swiss cheese, cut into strips
4 slices of pepperoni
> *Place on top.*

¼ cup cooked fusilli pasta
> *Place on top.*

2 pepperoncinis
2 cherry peppers
2 artichoke hearts
> *Arrange around the platter. Serve with Italian dressing (see page 112)*

Crab Avocado Salad

½ romaine lettuce
> *Cut into pieces. Arrange on a platter.*

½ cup cooked crabmeat
> *Place on top.*

½ avocado, sliced
> *Place on top.*

⅛ cup sliced black olives
1 small tomato, cubed
½ small cucumber, cut into pieces
4 mushrooms, sliced
½ red pepper, sliced
> *Place on top.*

¼ cup shredded Mozzarella cheese
> *Sprinkle on top.*

2 artichoke hearts
> *Arrange on platter. Serve with choice of dressing.*

Seafood Salad

1 Tbsp. olive oil
> *Heat gently in a saucepan.*

8 scallops
⅛ cup lobster meat
½ cup small bay shrimp
1/8 cup crab meat
> *Add in and sauté for 2-3 minutes.*

½ red pepper, sliced
6 green onions, chopped
1 Tbsp. capers
1 Tbsp. sliced black olives
> *Add in and sauté for 4-5 minutes longer.*

½ romaine lettuce, chopped
½ avocado, sliced
½ tomato, sliced
> *Arrange on a platter.*

3 Tbsp. olive oil
Juice of ½ lemon
1 Tsp. chopped parsley
> *Place in bowl and beat together with a fork, about 1-2 minutes. Add warm salad into the bowl with the dressing. Mix gently and arrange on top of lettuce.*

Pasta and Bean Salad

1½ cups white fusilli pasta, cooked
1½ cups green fusilli pasta, cooked
¼ onion, sliced
½ green pepper, sliced
1 cup gardiniera (mixed pickled vegetables)
½ cup sliced black olives
½ cup sliced green olives
2 hearts of palm, sliced
½ tomato, sliced
1 tsp. capers
¼ cup black beans
¼ cup butter beans (or use any other beans that you like)
½ cup Italian dressing (see page 112)

Mix all ingredients together and place on a platter.

Nick's Chicken Salad

1 8-oz. boneless chicken breast

Grill and cut into strips.

½ romaine lettuce, chopped
½ red pepper, sliced
1 heart of palm, sliced
1 Tbsp. capers
2 artichoke hearts, quartered
4 mushrooms, sliced
½ tomato, sliced
½ cucumber, sliced
¼ cup Feta cheese, crumbled
2 Tbsp. red wine vinegar
2 Tbsp. olive oil

Place all in a bowl.

Dill weed
Oregano
Basil
Thyme
Rosemary

Add a pinch of each to above ingredients. Mix together and arrange on a platter. Place chicken on top and serve.

Seafood Steak Salad

1 Tbsp. olive oil

Heat in a saucepan or a flat top grill.

1 4-oz. rib eye steak
¼ cup lobster meat
8 scallops
½ red pepper, sliced

Grill in the oil. When steak is done, cut it into strips.

½ romaine lettuce
1 tomato, sliced
1 tsp. capers
4 green onions, chopped
6 Chinese pea pods
2 Tbsp. olive oil
2 Tbsp. red wine vinegar
Pinch of basil
Pinch of rosemary

Place in a bowl and mix well. Arrange on a platter, then place grilled items on top.

Athenian Potato Salad

5 potatoes, boiled, peeled and cubed
4 oz. bacon, grilled and cut into pieces
1 small red onion, chopped
½ stalk celery, chopped
6 cornicorns, chopped
½ tomato (unripened, if possible), chopped
1 Tbsp. Dijon mustard
1 Tbsp. sliced black olives
1 Tbsp. sliced green olives
1 Tbsp. chives
Pinch black pepper
½ tsp. prepared horseradish
3 cups Feta dressing (see page 112)
1 Tbsp. olive oil
1 Tbsp. red wine vinegar

Mix well together.

Tuna Salad

2 lbs. tuna (canned)
1 tsp. Dijon mustard
1 cup dill relish
1 cup green olives, chopped
1 small onion, chopped
1 cup mayonnaise
½ tsp. black pepper

Mix well.

Broiled Chicken Salad

1 8-oz. chicken breast, grilled and sliced
½ romaine lettuce, chopped
½ avocado, sliced
½ tomato, sliced
> *Arrange vegetables on a platter, set chicken aside.*

1 roasted red pepper, sliced
4 green onions, chopped
3 artichokes, quartered
1 Tbsp. black olives, sliced
1 Tbsp. pecans
¼ cup mustard vinegarette dressing (see page 113)
Juice of ¼ lemon
> *Place in a bowl and toss well. Place on top of lettuce and arrange chicken on top.*

Ahi Tuna Salad

1 8-oz. Ahi tuna, grilled, sliced
¼ red cabbage, chopped
1 roasted red pepper
4 cornicorns
4 sun-dried tomatoes, cut in pieces
1 tsp. sliced black olives
¼ red onion, sliced
½ tomato, sliced
1 tsp. pistachio nuts
½ cup grapeleaf dressing (see page 113)
> *Toss above ingredients except tuna in a bowl. Top with tuna.*

Fruit Salmon Salad

1 8-oz. fillet of salmon
1 Tbsp. olive oil
> *Grill.*

¼ romaine lettuce, chopped
> *Place on a platter.*

Melon
Grapes
Strawberries
Apples
Oranges
Kiwi
Mangos
> *Cut fruit in pieces and arrange on top of the lettuce. Slice salmon and place on top of fruit. Serve with yogurt dressing (see page 113) and mix with 1 tsp. honey.*

Grilled Seafood Spinach Salad

2 Tbsp. olive oil
8 scallops
4 oz. sea bass, cut into strips
4 oz. Ahi tuna, cut into strips
6 medium-sized shrimp
½ red pepper

> *Grill.*

6 oz. spinach leaves
6 Chinese pea pods
4 green onions, chopped
1 tsp. grated Romano cheese
1 tsp. grated Parmesan cheese
1 tomato, sliced
1 tsp. dill weed

> *Place in a bowl and mix well. Put on a platter and place grilled items on top in the bowl.*

¼ cup mustard vinegarette dressing (see page 113)

> *Add dressing and toss well. Place on top of spinach mixture.*

Calamari Salad

½ cup buttermilk pancake mix
1 cup water

> *Mix well.*

10 small calamari
Flour

> *Dip the calamari into the buttermilk pancake mixture then roll into flour. Deep fry the calamari until golden brown.*

¼ romaine lettuce, chopped
3 cups red cabbage, chopped
¼ red onion, chopped
1 tomato, sliced
1 Tbsp. sliced black olives
1 tsp. capers
2 Tbsp. Balsamic vinegar
1 Tbsp. olive oil

> *Place in a large bowl and mix well. Place on a platter and top with fried calamari.*

Korinthian Salad

1 small head romaine lettuce
6 mushrooms, sliced
1 tomato, cubed
1 avocado, sliced
1 clove garlic, chopped
8 kalamata olives
½ onion, thinly sliced
1 red pepper, thinly sliced
3 artichoke hearts, quartered
Pinch black pepper
Pinch basil
Pinch oregano
Pinch thyme
Pinch rosemary
½ cup olive oil
⅛ cup red wine vinegar

Place in a bowl and mix well.

Black Bean Tortellini

½ cup red peppers, sliced
¼ cup red onions, sliced
4 slices ham, sliced
4 slices turkey, sliced
2 hearts of palm, sliced
2 green chilies, sliced

Place all of the above ingredients in a bowl.

1 cup cooked black beans
¼ lb. cooked tortellini

Add.

½ cup mustard vinegarette dressing (see page 113)
⅛ tsp. cumin

Add and toss well.

Balsamic vinegars are made in Movena in northern Italy. This unique vinegar is aged in wooden casks and can be aged from 10 to 30 years. The name comes from the Italian "balm" which means smooth, mellow. Commercialized versions are available in markets.

Tortellini Salad

4 oz. meat-filled spinach tortellini
4 oz. meat-filled white tortellini

Cook for 7-8 minutes in boiling water. Cool and place in a bowl.

2 oz. ham, diced
½ onion, thinly sliced
½ red onion, thinly sliced
1 small red pepper, thinly sliced
1 small green pepper, thinly sliced
½ cup sliced black olives
½ cup sliced green olives
6 mushrooms, thinly sliced

Place all ingredients in bowl with pasta and mix well.

¼ cup mustard vinaigrette dressing (see page 113)

Pour over ingredients and toss well. Place on a large platter and garnish with artichoke hearts, pepperoncinis, banana peppers and cherry peppers. Serves 3-4.

Seafood Pasta Salad

2 oz. white fusilli pasta
2 oz. green fusilli pasta

Cook for about 6-7 minutes in boiling water. Cool.

1 small head iceberg lettuce

Break into small pieces and place on a large platter.

1 small green pepper, sliced
½ small onion, sliced
½ small red onion, sliced
4 mushrooms, sliced

Place on top of lettuce.

4 oz. bay shrimp, cooked

Place on top of vegetables.

6 bay scallops

Sauté 3-4 minutes and place on top of shrimp. Place pasta on top.

2 oz. sliced black olives
2 oz. sliced green olives

Put on top of pasta.

1 whole artichoke heart, diced

Place on sides of platter. Garnish with pepperoncinis, banana peppers and cherry peppers. Serve with dressing of your choice. Serves 3-4.

In the Balkans, a large number of people live to be over 100 years old. They owe this longevity to a simple diet consisting mainly of yogurt.

STEPPING IN THE MUDDY WATERS
OF OUR SOCIETY

*F*or the past few months my attorney was trying to convince me of filing for bankruptcy protection, but I rejected the idea because that would be a sign of failure. I told him I could do it; I could pay everyone and bring the business out of this mess. It had been almost two years since the Golden Cuisine had opened, and it was still difficult to keep up with the demand of the overhead and the decline of late evening business. I kept being optimistic, still working over 100 hours a week. My mission was to preserve what I had created.

The pace remained as frenzied as it had begun two years ago. Work continued from dawn till past midnight. It was a torturous schedule physically and an endless puzzle mentally. I felt I was in a neverending chess game, every day a new move to defend and protect the restaurant from being killed. If it was not the loans, it was the rent. If it was not the suppliers, it was the electric company or the payroll. Every day I took a deep breath to withstand the pressures the day would bring.

Days kept coming and going without relief in sight. My attorney was still pressuring me to file for bankruptcy protection. "It's your only chance," he kept saying. The word "bankruptcy" was giving me a nauseated stomach, and I kept telling him it was not right. "But everyone is doing it," he insisted. "It is not bad; on the contrary, it will give you time to reorganize."

The chess game was growing intense. Every morning as I opened the restaurant my mind was preoccupied with how I would face the ones that would show up to collect. Each time someone asked for me or anytime the phone would ring I had to make tremendous efforts to protect the space I felt was mine. All of this was distracting to the work that has given me so much pleasure throughout the years.

Finally after the continued pleas from my attorney, I filed for bankruptcy protection. For a while things got better, but then business started to decline mainly because of the crime in Tower Plaza. During this time I started thinking of moving the restaurant. I looked for options. The Thomas restaurant was a showplace. The kitchen was totally open, practically in front of the dining room. People stood in lines to watch the cooking, which most of the time involved 20-25 sauté pans along with the other food preparation around it. It could not come to an end. Too many people enjoyed the food and the concept.

I had lost a bit of interest in the restaurant. Tremendous pressure was starting to take its toll on me. I had to move on before I lost complete interest in my work. Once those thoughts started to enter my mind it was easy to be convinced of moving on. Failure to make it was completely mine. We can always find excuses for our mistakes, but we must take full responsibility if we want to learn from those mistakes. Sometimes we have to look at the whole picture. Me, I was blinded with the effort to make it work and let things get out of control.

It was time for another new beginning. Somewhere I could preserve the passion of creating my work which, amazingly enough, became my escape to create more recipes.

story continues on page 145

With my long-time friends, Christina and Mario Monacelli, just before leaving McDowell to move to Thomas Road.

Broths and Soups...

Vegetable Broth

2 onions, sliced
8 mushrooms, sliced
2 ribs celery, chopped
3 carrots, sliced
5 cabbage leaves, chopped
1 head lettuce, chopped
2 leeks, sliced
1 tsp. thyme
1 Tbsp. parsley, chopped
4 bay leaves
1 tsp. black pepper
2 quarts water

Simmer in a soup pot for about 1 hour.

Chicken Broth

1 lb. chicken parts (wings, legs)
1 bulb garlic
4 cloves
1 onion, chopped
2 carrots, sliced
6 mushrooms, sliced
1 tsp. pepper
1 rib celery, chopped
5 quarts water

Simmer for about 2 hours.

Beef Broth

2 lbs. beef shanks
2 lbs. beef short ribs
2 lbs. chicken parts
1 tsp. black pepper
5 carrots, sliced
1 onion, chopped
1 bulb garlic
5 quarts water

Simmer for about 4 hours.

Fish Broth

2 lbs. fish with bones
1 onion, sliced
1 carrot, sliced
1 leek, sliced
1 rib celery, chopped
2 quarts water

Simmer for about 1 hour.

Potato Parmesan Soup

10 potatoes, peeled and cut into large pieces
4 cups chicken broth
¼ lb. butter

Put in soup pot and add water to cover the potatoes by a few inches. Boil about 10 minutes.

2 cloves garlic, chopped
1 lb. chopped spinach
1 tsp. nutmeg
1 tsp. black pepper
½ tsp. Tabasco sauce

Add in and boil gently until potatoes are cooked (approximately 15-20 minutes). Add water if needed.

2 cups heavy cream

Add in and boil another 5 minutes.

½ cup Romano cheese, grated
½ cup Parmesan cheese, grated

Add in and stir. Remove from heat.

Even late in the 17th century, the potato was still a mystery. The Germans fed potatoes to pigs and believed that potato eating would cause leprosy. The French proved that was not the case by eating them. The potato diet reached its peak during the French Revolution. People were so hungry and turned to potatoes for a filling meal. Despite the difficulty of reaching the vegetable markets, the potato now is the most widespread and versatile of all vegetables. It is used in cooking by millions of families. Thousands of restaurants use industrially-prepared potatoes. Potatoes are bought by millions of consumers from supermarkets as chips or in dehydrated form.

Provolone Soup

½ lb. butter
> *Melt in a pot.*

2 cups flour
> *Remove pot from heat, add flour in, stirring constantly until smooth.*

¼ cup Dijon mustard
> *Add in, stirring constantly.*

6 cups whipping cream
> *Add in, stir well. Place on low heat.*

6 cups chicken broth
> *Add in, stir well.*

2 onions, finely chopped
2 carrots, finely chopped
1½ lbs. spinach, chopped
> *Add in.*

1 tsp. nutmeg
1 tsp. black pepper
> *Add in. Simmer for about 1 hour. Pour soup into bowls and before serving, sprinkle top with shredded Provolone cheese.*

FOR BAKED SOUP: Pour soup into individual serving cups, cover with sliced Provolone cheese and bake until cheese is melted, about 10-12 minutes.

Soup has been a tradition in the European diet since the dark ages. Soup was poured in a bowl with a piece of bread in it, a method still popular in many European countries with some types of soup, especially in France. Soup derives from the Latin word "suppa" which means to soak.

Mediterranean Fish Soup

2 cups olive oil
Heat in soup pan.
1 red pepper, chopped
1 potato, cut in pieces
1 small onion, chopped
2 cups leeks, chopped
2 cloves garlic, chopped
2 ribs celery, chopped
4 asparagus, chopped
About 3 lbs. assorted fish such as:
    Sea bass
    Tuna
    Halibut
    Swordfish
    Snapper
        Add in and sauté about 4-5 minutes.
1 cup mussels
1 cup scallops
1 cup small shrimp
1 cup chopped clams
1 tsp. fennel
1 tsp. parsley
⅙ tsp. red pepper flakes
1 tsp. saffron
2 bay leaves
1 tsp. thyme
1 tsp. rosemary
        Add in, and cook for about 4-5 minutes.
¼ cup white cooking wine
2 cups clam juice
        Add in.
1 small can plump tomatoes in juice (1 lb. 12 oz.)
8 cups water
        Break tomatoes and add with the juice. Simmer 1½-2 hours.

Black Bean Soup

1 lb. black beans

> *Place beans in a soup pot and cover with water. Soak for a few hours. Boil for about 15 minutes and add water if needed.*

1 onion, chopped
1 rib celery, chopped
½ red onion, chopped
2 carrots, sliced
½ cup ham, diced
2 bay leaves
1 Tbsp. parsley
½ tsp. coriander
¼ cup red wine vinegar
1 tsp. cumin
3 cloves garlic, chopped
1 tsp. chili powder
1 tsp. paprika
1 tsp. cayenne pepper
4 cups chicken broth

> *Add and simmer for about 10 minutes. Add water if needed to keep all ingredients well under it.*

1 small can plum tomatoes, crushed (1 lb. 12 oz.)
2 green chilies, chopped
3 drops of Tabasco sauce
1 tsp. black pepper
1 tsp. rosemary
1 tsp. thyme

> *Add in and simmer for 50-60 minutes or until beans are cooked.*

FOR BAKED BLACK BEAN SOUP: Place in individual bowls. Cover with a thin layer of cream cheese. Sprinkle with a little chili powder and bake in 350° oven for 10 minutes.

Beans and lentils were the foods of the poor for the Greeks and the Romans and since there were a lot of poor people they ate alot of beans and lentils. In fact, still today, "fasolada" (bean soup) symbolizes the national soup of the poor in Greece. Lentils and beans are rich in phosphorus and iron. The main supplier for lentils were the Egyptians.

Peas were very common in the Mediterranean but split peas did not become popular until the 19th century when we had the idea of removing the skin which is indigestible. Today it is the most widely eaten pea.

Beans grow mainly in Central America and Mexico where the tropical weather favors these kind of vegetables. They are rich in protein. Beans, along with corn, is very important to the Latin-American diet.

Peanut Lentil Soup

1 lb. lentils

> *Place lentils in soup pot and cover with water. Soak for a few hours.*

1 onion, chopped
2 carrots, sliced
1 rib celery, chopped
3 bay leaves
2 cups chicken broth
¼ cup olive oil
¼ cup red wine vinegar
1 tsp. black pepper

> *Add water to cover, simmer for about 1 hour or until lentils are cooked. Keep adding water as needed.*

1 cup creamy peanut butter

> *Add in and stir well. Remove from heat.*

Smoked Cabbage

2 white cabbages, chopped
4 cups chicken broth
¼ lb. butter

> *Put in a soup pot and cover with water. Boil for about 5 minutes.*

1 cup ham, diced
½ lb. bacon, cooked and chopped
1 tsp. black pepper
1 tsp. nutmeg

> *Add in and simmer for about 30-40 minutes. Add water as needed.*

FOR BAKED CABBAGE SOUP: Place in individual soup bowls and cover with slices of Fontina cheese. Sprinkle with a little nutmeg and bake in a 350° oven for about 10 minutes.

Cabbage is said to be the oldest of vegetables. Now there are almost 450 varieties of cabbage. The Greeks and the Romans ate cabbage to prevent drunkenness. In fact, today farmers of the Mediterranean will not grow cabbage near vineyards.

The famous Greek philosopher Diogenes ate cabbage and drank water, mainly for economic and idealistic reasons. Aristippus, another philosopher, opposed the idea saying that cabbage would cut your life short and would dull the mind. Diogenes lived to be 90 years old. Aristippus died in his 40's. On one of Captain Cook's expeditions in the 17th century, members of his crew were injured in a great storm. The doctor saved the victims from gangrene with compresses of cabbage leaves.

Dijon Chicken and Bacon Soup

1 cup butter
> *Melt in a soup pot.*

8 slices bacon, cooked and diced
1 rib celery, diced
1 carrot, sliced
1 small onion, chopped
8 oz. chicken, diced
6 mushrooms, sliced
> *Add in and sauté until chicken is lightly browned, about 10-12 minutes.*

2 Tbsp. Dijon mustard
> *Add in and stir well.*

4 cups chicken broth
> *Add in with water to cover all ingredients well. Simmer for about 30-35 minutes.*

FOR BAKED SOUP: Place in individual bowls and cover soup with Swiss cheese. Bake in 350° oven for about 10 minutes.

Eggplant Okra Soup

1 cup olive oil
1 large eggplant, diced
2 red bell peppers, diced
> *Place in a soup pot and sauté well until eggplant is soft, about 10-12 minutes.*

1 small can garbanzo beans
1/2 lb. okra (you can use frozen)
2 cloves garlic, chopped
1 small can baby onions
4 sun-dried tomatoes, chopped
1 small can plum tomatoes with juice (approximately 2 cups)
1 tsp. rosemary
1 tsp. thyme
1 tsp. cumin
> *Add in with water to cover. Simmer for about 60 minutes.*

FOR BAKED EGGPLANT SOUP: Place in individual bowls and cover with sliced Mozzarella cheese. Bake in 350° oven for about 10 minutes.

Asparagus grows in light soil because its roots and buds grow underground and in the spring the buds will grow upwards and pierce the surface of the earth. They become the asparagus spears.

Country Bean Soup

1 lb. white beans

> *Put in a pot and cover with water. Soak for a few hours. Boil for about 15 minutes.*

1 onion, chopped
8 mushrooms, sliced
2 cloves garlic, chopped
2 Italian sausages, cooked and sliced
½ cup ham, diced
1 4-oz. rib eye steak, diced
2 carrots, sliced
1 rib celery, chopped
1 tsp. thyme
1 tsp. black pepper
8 whole cloves
1 tsp. rosemary
1 Tbsp. steak sauce
1 Tbsp. Worcestershire sauce
4 cups chicken broth
6 oz. chicken, diced

> *Add in and cook until beans are soft, about 60-70 minutes. Add water if necessary.*

FOR BAKED BEAN SOUP: Place in individual bowls and over with sliced white Cheddar cheese. Bake in 350° oven for about 10 minutes.

In the kitchen on Thomas Road, working on several dinners at a time.

Pasta and Bean Soup

1 lb. red beans

> *Put in a pot and cover with water. Soak for a few hours. Boil for about 10 minutes.*

8 oz. chicken, diced
1 onion, chopped
2 cloves garlic, chopped
1 carrot, diced
1 small green bell pepper, chopped
2 cups chicken stock
2 bay leaves
¼ cup okra, diced (you can use frozen)
1 tsp. rosemary
1 tsp. parsley
1 small zucchini, diced
1 cup spinach, chopped
1/4 cup olive oil
1 tsp. basil
5 plum tomatoes, crushed (from a can)

> *Add in, cover with water and simmer for about 60 minutes or until beans are cooked.*

½ lb. orzo pasta
¼ cup Parmesan cheese, grated

> *Add in and cook for about 10 more minutes or until orzo is cooked.*

Blue Cauliflower Soup

1 small cauliflower (use flowerettes only)
1 small head cabbage, chopped
½ lb. butter
2 cups chicken broth
6 green onions, chopped

> *Put into a soup pot, cover with water and boil for about 10 minutes.*

2 cloves garlic, chopped
1 tsp. white pepper
2 drops Tabasco sauce

> *Add in and simmer for about 30 minutes.*

1 cup heavy cream
6 oz. blue cheese

> *Add in and simmer for 10 more minutes.*

Avgolemono Soup

1 lb. rice
2 quarts chicken broth
1 tsp. black pepper
> *Boil for about 15-18 minutes until rice is done.*

8 eggs, separated
Juice of 3 lemons
> *Beat the egg whites until frothy in a separate bowl. Beat the egg yolks and add the yolks to the whites, beating, then add the lemon juice. Take out a small bowl of the hot broth from the soup pot and add it to the egg/lemon mixture slowly and beating constantly. Add the mixture to the soup pot, stirring slowly. Remove from heat.*

OPTIONAL: 1 lb. of cooked, diced chicken may be added.

Teaching cooking classes on Indian School Road.
Baked Provolone Soup (see page 137)

FIGHT FOR SURVIVAL

*I*t was time for a change, and once I made up my mind, my focus turned to finding another location where the overhead was not too big. I looked at several locations and once I found the space at 3717 E. Indian School Road which was only a few miles away from the restaurant on Thomas, my mind was made up. This was going to be my next restaurant. But how was I going to open it? There was no money available for a project like this!

The space on Indian School was half the size of Thomas, and was just four walls. Everything had to be built up. But somehow I knew this was where the new restaurant was going to be. At the same time I had to operate a troublesome business, I was also trying to open a new restaurant without funds.

The days of worries
> were many

The nights without sleep
> were endless

It was not the inconvenience or the danger of losing everything at any given time, it was the threat of being without a place to express my passion.

The so-called inconveniences of life were a small price to pay in order to keep what I believed in alive. One of my teachers kept telling me, "You can't live a life of pleasure which is without pain." I was prepared for the worst, and those were the days that very few believed I could withstand. To many it did not make sense what I was putting myself through. "Give it up, it is not worth it. You can work anywhere and make a lot of money," they kept telling me. But the easy answers were not for me. That was not how I wanted to live my life and I was not about to give up.

Many images went through my mind: my children, my parents, the loyal customers, the faithful employees, and the art that I had created. It was a possession I could not give away. I thought about the Thanksgiving project and how we had touched thousands of citizens. There were too many feelings to give up without a fight. My wish to keep the restaurant going was a cause and not a fear, yet I finally realized pain was part of life and suffering was unnecessary. I had come to the point that this one restaurant was causing me to suffer. When I found the space at 3717 E. Indian School Road and the landlord was willing to lease me the space and do some improvement, the money was just enough for some of the remodeling. There was so much more to do to build a full-scale restaurant out of four plain walls.

The new space was much smaller than the restaurant on Thomas. Somehow the restaurant was built. Plumbers, electrician's, carpenters and equipment. People I had hired to work were people I knew and also were willing to do the work and receive payments after the new restaurant was opened. Some personal loans helped me to take care of the opening expenses.

It had also been some time since I had created new recipes. While I was waiting for the place to be finished, it gave me time to create more dishes and design a new menu which would contain old and new recipes alike.

"Nick's Cuisine of Southern Europe" was supposed to open its doors on May 10, 1992, the day we celebrate the existence of our mothers and show our appreciation to the ones that gave us birth, taught us how to walk, and tried to get that precious first word out of our mouths. I thought of my mother who came to visit me while I was on McDowell. It was not long ago, but it seemed that so many things have occurred since them.

A few days before the opening date there was still alot of work to be done. The restaurant had to pass inspections, the menu was not back from the printer, foods had to be ordered and prepared. The inspectors kept finding more things to do, and up until the Friday before Mother's Day we were still correcting things. Everyone wanted to go home for the weekend. Finally after several calls and hard work to correct minor problems we got the green light and the gas company arrived to turn on the gas. Thank God for that because our reservation book was almost full.

That was in my mind all day Friday, thinking I had to open the doors on Sunday. I couldn't imagine all these people coming to celebrate Mother's Day and finding the doors closed. It came very close to that point because by 4:00 pm Friday afternoon we were still waiting for the last inspector to come for the plumbing and the gas. The electrical inspector gave us a lecture, but finally gave us the green light. By 4:30 a group of people were hanging on the plumbing inspectors words which would authorize the gas company to turn on the gas. Workers from the gas company were waiting by the meter, looking at their watches, saying that in a few minutes they had to go home. The final issue was the big bakery oven. There was nothing wrong with it, but the inspector could not find the type and model number in his book. He said he had to wait until Monday before he could authorize the use of it. After I assured him we were not going to use the oven over the weekend, he gave us a temporary tag to open.

I felt the sound of the gas moving through the empty pipes and kept hoping the pressure tests would turn out okay because that was the only test left.

After all the commotion of the day I realized the menus had not yet arrived; the printer assured me by Saturday afternoon they would be ready, and Saturday we had scheduled all the deliveries for the food items to arrive, and then we had to be prepared so we could be ready to open the restaurant doors on Sunday.

In everything there is a portion of everything, except mind.

— Anexagoras

A city or the state is not a mere aggregate of persons, but a union of them sufficient for the purpose of life.

— Aristotle

A New Beginning

On Sunday, Mother's Day of 1992, we opened the doors of Nick's Cuisine of Southern Europe. The 4,000 square foot facility was half the size of the restaurant on Thomas. The dining room sat about 110 people. It was surrounded by eight cases full of desserts. Behind the desserts was the open kitchen and the work station of the servers. As you came in the front door you would go past the shelves of the specialty shop, neatly stocked with specialty items and on the wall along the other side were write-ups, awards and letters displayed the length of the restaurant. In the back there was a small bakery and preparation area. The whole setup was comfortable and convenient for guests and employees.

The Sunday after we opened the doors, it was standing room only and never let down since. Only in the beginning was it difficult. Summer came too soon, business slowed down a bit, but the biggest difficulty was moving as it took customers quite some time to find our new location. I remember three years later I still had people coming in, glad they had finally found us! I heard too many stories from people trying to find the new location, from the telephone operators to the calls to the newspapers. A family told me once as they walked into the restaurant that as they drove to the place on Thomas and saw it had closed, drove up and down Thomas and then Indian School to find the new restaurant. "We knew you were around here somewhere," the father said.

Another couple saw our delivery van with the name on the side and followed it to the restaurant. A couple from Prescott talked to a friend who told them their favorite restaurant in Phoenix had closed its doors and when they mentioned the name, their friends responded that "He is not out of business, he's on Indian School Road now." They drove to Phoenix the same day to have dinner.

One of my favorite stories is that a lady went to the bank on the other side of the plaza and she told me somehow she sensed the smells of the food and knew I was around there. She asked the bank teller and found out she was right. I'd seen them through the year coming in, glad they had found the restaurant. For me it was gratifying to see so much loyalty and I was glad to see my "lost children," as I call my lost customers, coming home.

I had seen most of them grow with me and the restaurant. I've seen them single and now married, some of them had their first date in the restaurant. Others had met at the restaurant and many of those couples had babies. I had seen a generation grow up as I had seen my children become adults.

My children were bringing their friends to eat in the restaurant and show them the creations with pride. Most of their friends worked in the restaurant when they needed a job. Along with all of them I had grown also. I was settled in my thoughts and comfortable with myself. Despite the difficulties and the hard work I was peaceful with my life and content to be who I was. Difficulties were going to be overcome. There were so many important things in my life: my parents, brothers, sister, my children, my culture, my work that left little room for anything else. I lived alone, but was never lonely. I couldn't understand the meaning of the word. My feelings were rich and that stopped me looking for happiness in material things. This restaurant was a new beginning in many ways. And most of all, it was the beginning of a maturity that I took to a different level.

With the students of the Scottsdale Culinary School.

Talking with guests on Thomas Road.

Nothing Should Break The Peace

I heard it all the time; capitalize on my fame of the restaurant and that of the Thanksgiving project to gain wealth and live the "good life." I always wanted to know what the definition of "good life" was. How do you define the word "good?" To many it means material wealth, to others it means parties, drugs and distraction. To some it means prestige in society and yet to others it means having a great family and a good job.

Where do we draw the line of where we are satisfied with the "good life" or is it even possible? I think some can draw the line by discarding things they do not want. But it is only a few who have the strength to resist the temptations of the society, the belief and the idealism of making the place which we call home a better place to be for us and generations to come. Failures are easy to understand. Envy of those more fortunate is nonexistent. If we understand that we cannot live in a society the way it is but in the one it could be. I wish more people's definition of "good life" had a noble explanation. Then, things would be less complicated. Less people are going to sleep on the streets. Less people are going to be hungry. More children are going to be in school and more elderly are going to smile. And we, who are going to understand that definition, are going to be in peace and harmony and nothing is going to break that peace. Nothing could!

The struggle to survive continued. Debts which occurred at the previous restaurant haunted me. In the second year of business things got harder. The initial loans to open this restaurant were slowly paying off, the restaurant was busy but could only generate so much revenue to pay the loans off. Plus the debts of the previous business' operation expenses started to fall behind. It was a daily battle to operate, but slowly we were making progress.

And in the third year even though things were very difficult, I was seeing the light. At that time I decided to publish my dessert cookbook. Later that proved to be a bad business decision because it cost so much more than I had anticipated. But the signing of the book that was held at the restaurant brought unbelievable success. People lined up most of the night to get a signature copy. Approximately 500 people came through the restaurant that night. It was a bad financial decision that felt good.

The unexamined life is not worth living.

— Socrates

It would perhaps be thought to be better, indeed to be our duty, for the sake of maintaining the truth even to destroy what touches us closely for while both are dear, piety requires us to honour truth above friends.

— Aristotle

NEVER GIVE UP
THE THINGS THAT YOU LOVE

*I*t was the business decision I made on Thanksgiving of 1995 that broke my back. It all started like every other year. A few months before Thanksgiving we start to organize our project. We set a goal to feed about 22,000 needy citizens. As the day of Thanksgiving approached, everything seemed under control.

The last few years before Thanksgiving came we tried to find people who were forgotten from our community; the elderly living alone and unable to provide or cook a Thanksgiving meal for themselves, the disabled and the sick, poor families where children went hungry, abused women and children living alone. And along with the many shelters and organizations who we provided meals for, we suggested reaching people who would otherwise go uncared for. In search of finding those people we asked the help of school districts, churches and the City of Phoenix to give us lists of people in need. This year of 1995 the Human Resource Department of the City of Phoenix asked us if we could feed 5,000 people. That number brought our total to 22,000 people.

I closed the restaurant the Sunday before Thanksgiving. I knew I needed time to be ready for all those meals and what usually happens every year, the people start to come and bring us their donations; turkeys, canned goods, stuffing, potatoes and other foods started to pile up. On the Monday before Thanksgiving the City asked if we could handle another 5,000 people and without hesitation I said, "Yes, we could do it." I figured there was enough time to collect and prepare enough donated food to feed all those people. On Tuesday they asked if they could add another 3,000, and I said "Why not?" I mean, how could I deny food to hungry people? But I said that was it. We would not be able to handle any more.

They brought us piles of forms which they had collected and more came through the fax. On Wednesday, more names came through the fax machine. We asked the City of Phoenix to stop sending names. Later on in the evening we started the deliveries. This year we deliveried uncooked foods the day before Thanksgiving so people who were able to cook for themselves would be able to feel the spirit better by preparing their own meal and at the same time would ease up our deliveries for the next day.

As volunteer drivers were coming back, some complained the people who they took the food to did not seem like they needed it. Some lived in nice homes and others seemed unthankful of the gifts. Soon we found out what had happened. The City of Phoenix had opened the project to its agencies around the city. The form they passed out for the donations read that if you wanted a turkey dinner for Thanksgiving, simply sign this form. There was no screening of the people to see if they were in need or not.

Almost everyone started to sign up, including case workers and other employees, and the disarray of the bureaucratic system was on display at its best. Names had piled up to well over 30,000 people. In a last minute effort to discard people who didn't need the meals so we could provide to the ones who were really in need, we started calling the families who signed up. Fifty percent of them said they had a meal and this would be extra that they could save for another time!

For endless hours our volunteers made hundreds of calls. We were running out of time. The first 18,000 people which we had in our computer and who we fed throughout the years went smoothly. Then the problems started. It was Thanksgiving morning and we still were receiving names through the fax. We finally turned the machine off. Besides our worry to feed over 30,000 people now we had to waste our energies on finding out who really needed the food.

Early in the morning volunteers lined up to take deliveries. The line went on for almost two blocks. By early afternoon more were lining up because the deliveries were endless. Our volunteers frantically tried to discard names who did not need the food and desperately tried to fill up the forms which the drivers would use to bring the deliveries to the right place. The cooking continued most of Thanksgiving day. Everything was under control except there were too many names. I never saw such a gallant effort from hundreds of people to bring this project to completion. We worked till 10:00 o'clock at night and finally had to stop. We had run out of time and run out of volunteers. The phones were still ringing and I felt guilty because we had missed people who really needed to be fed. Unfortunately we had provided to others who kept the meal for another day.

I didn't sleep that night. I couldn't understand how some people could be so greedy as to deny others meals. Was it their fault or was it bureaucracy which messed up again?

I should have been happy. We were able to provide food for 32,000 people. We went through well over 4,000 volunteers, not counting hundreds who brought us food and donations. The spirit of giving was displayed this year by people so much more than in years past. But I was bothered thinking of the ones I had disappointed. I tried to picture their faces and the sadness I brought them. It tortured me all night. Feeding 32,000 people was not a consolation to me. I could only make it a lesson for years to come not to trust other agencies to screen people in need. It made me more determined than ever to look forward to more Thanksgivings. I was not about to give up the things I loved. That night, reading some of the newsletters of years past, I was comforted thinking that through the years we had done more good than damage.

Besides the anguish that went through me that year it cost me much more than that. In a last minute effort to provide food for the extra people who we did not plan for, and our supplies were running low, we had to go out and spend the restaurant fund. Emergency deliveries were called to our suppliers and volunteers ran constantly to stores to get supplies as we needed them. The bill to complete the project cost almost $26,000 which came from the restaurant. And if one can figure the revenue lost for five days of closing the restaurant doors and the utilities and the rent wasted on those five days then the price becomes extremely high for a project that was going to be spoiled by a few greedy people.

None of this mattered. The money or the hard work of five days straight did not even matter. I made one more bad business decision that down the road would come back and haunt me. In my mind I had no second thoughts. I did what was right for me and not what would be convenient for the future. Sometimes things that bring us pleasure are costly. At least along with my pleasure we brought a smile to 32,000 people and if I had to do it again I would do so without a second thought.

Like I said, never give up the things that you love.

story continues on page 173

My children and their friends during one of the children's birthdays on Indian School Road.

Poultry...

Chicken Palm

3 Tbsp. olive oil
3 Tbsp. soybean oil
> *Heat in a saucepan.*

1 8-oz. breast of chicken
Flour
1 egg, beaten
> *Roll in flour, dip in egg then back in flour. Place in saucepan. Sauté until lightly brown on one side, approximately 5-6 minutes on a medium-low heat, turn chicken over.*

¼ cup white cooking wine
> *Add in.*

2 artichoke hearts, chopped
> *Add in.*

1 heart of palm, chopped
> *Sauté 3-4 more minutes.*

2 oz. pecan pieces
¼ pint whipping cream
> *Add in.*

Pinch of pepper
> *Add.*

I Tbsp. Dijon mustard
> *Add in.*

2 oz. Swiss cheese, shredded
> *Simmer 2-3 minutes longer. Place chicken on a serving platter. Stir sauce until cheese is melted, pour sauce over chicken.*

Chicken Plaka

3 Tbsp. olive oil
3 Tbsp. soybean oil
> *Heat in a saucepan.*

1 8-oz. chicken breast
Flour
1 egg, beaten
> *Dip in flour, then in egg and back in flour. Place chicken in the saucepan. Sauté 4-5 minutes on one side until lightly brown. Turn chicken over.*

Juice of ½ lemon
> *Squeeze in.*

½ small onion, thinly sliced
6 mushrooms, sliced
2 artichoke hearts, sliced
> *Add in; sauté until onions are soft; 4-5 minutes.*

⅛ cup white cooking wine
Pepper to taste
> *Add in; simmer 3-4 minutes longer.*

⅛ cup whipping cream
> *Heat 2-3 minutes. Place chicken on serving platter; pour sauce over it.*

Feta Pesto Chicken

1 8-oz. boneless chicken breast
> *Pound gently to make it thinner.*

2 Tbsp. Feta Pesto sauce (see page 115)
1 Tbsp. Feta cheese, crumbled
1 Tbsp. of Ricotta cheese
> *Mix in a bowl. Place in middle of chicken and close it in.*

Flour
> *Cover the chicken breast with flour.*

1 egg, beaten
> *Roll breast in, coat with flour again.*

3 Tbsp. olive oil
3 Tbsp. soybean oil
> *Sauté chicken until brown on both sides, about 4-5 minutes for each side.*

½ onion, chopped
1 clove garlic
> *Add in, sauté 3-4 minutes.*

8 oz. plum tomatoes in juice, crushed
1 Tbsp. pine nuts
½ tsp. black pepper
½ tsp. oregano
½ tsp. thyme
½ tsp. basil
½ tsp. parsley
> *Add in, sauté 6-8 minutes.*

1 tsp. Romano cheese
1 tsp. Parmesan cheese
> *Add in leave it on the heat for 1-2 minutes longer.*

Chicken Palm (see page 154)

Salonika Chicken

3 Tbsp. olive oil
3 Tbsp. soybean oil
> *Heat in a skillet.*

1 8-oz. breast of chicken
Flour
> *Cover the chicken breast with flour.*

1 egg, beaten
> *Roll breast in, coat with flour again. Place in skillet, brown lightly on one, side about 5-6 minutes. Turn chicken over.*

⅛ cup white cooking wine
> *Add in.*

1 mild Italian sausage cooked and sliced
> *Add in.*

4 mushrooms, sliced
4 pepperoncinis
1 Tbsp. capers
1 Tbsp. pine nuts
> *Add in.*

Black pepper to taste
½ tsp. oregano
> *Add in. Sauté 5-6 minutes longer.*

1 Tbsp. Grand Marnier
> *Add in and simmer 2 minutes.*

Asparagus Chicken

1 8-oz. breast of chicken
> *Place breast of chicken on working surface.*

4 slices ham
4 slices provolone cheese
> *Place 2 slices of ham and 2 slices of provolone in this order, on each side of the chicken.*

3 asparagus
> *Place on top of cheese.*

1 Tbsp. Romano cheese, grated
1 Tbsp. Parmesan cheese, grated
> *Place grated cheese on top of asparagus. Fold chicken to enclose fillings.*

Flour
Egg
Bread crumbs
> *Dip the folded chicken in these items in this order.*

3 Tbsp. olive oil
3 Tbsp. soybean oil
> *Sauté the chicken until both sides are browned well. Place in baking dish. Bake for 30 minutes in 425°. Place on serving plate.*

Sauce:
2 Tbsp. olive oil
2 Tbsp. soybean oil
> *Heat in a saucepan.*

4 mushrooms, sliced thinly
> *Sauté 3-4 minutes.*

1 Tbsp. sliced almonds
> *Add in.*

¼ cup whipping cream
1 Tbsp. Romano cheese
1 Tbsp. Parmesan cheese
½ tsp. black pepper
> *Add in and heat gently for 2-3 minutes. Stir well. Pour sauce over chicken.*

Romaine Chicken

3 Tbsp. olive oil
3 Tbsp. soybean oil
> *Heat in a saucepan.*

1 8-oz. chicken breast
Flour
1 egg, beaten
> *Dip chicken breast in egg and then in flour. Place chicken in the saucepan. Sauté until lightly brown on one side, 6-7 minutes. Turn chicken breast over.*

⅛ cup white cooking wine
> *Add in.*

½ small Romaine lettuce, cut in small pieces
4 green onions, chopped
4 artichoke hearts, crumbled
Juice of ½ lemon
1 tsp. dill week
1 tsp. parsley
½ tsp. black pepper
> *Add in and simmer until lettuce is soft, 8-9 minutes.*

½ cup whipping cream
> *Add in and simmer 2-3 minutes. Place chicken breast on a serving platter.*

Yolk of 1 egg
> *Add in to the sauce and stir well. Place sauce on top of chicken.*

All of the domestic fowl we eat today was found in Roman kitchens. Romans ate more poultry (except turkey) than we do today. The chicken reached Greece around the 5th century B.C. In the 19th century chicken became a regular food for their diet. Today, people eat chicken almost every day of the week. The quality of chicken has declined and it is not like it used to be. The demand for chicken has pushed farmers to adopt methods of fast growing, but this leaves the chicken flat tasting.

Caper Chicken

3 Tbsp. olive oil
3 Tbsp. soybean oil
> *Heat in a saucepan.*

1 8-oz. chicken breast
Flour
1 egg, beaten
> *Dip in egg and then in flour. Place chicken in the saucepan. Sauté on one side until lightly brown. Turn chicken over.*

1 small tomato, chopped
1 tsp. of capers
5 sun-dried tomatoes, cut in large pieces
1 clove of garlic, chopped
> *Add in.*

⅛ cup white cooking wine
> *Add in.*

1 tsp. black pepper
1 tsp. basil
1 tsp. parsley
1 tsp. oregano
1 tsp. thyme
1 tsp. rosemary
> *Add in and sauté for 8-10 minutes.*

Chicken Kapama

3 Tbsp. olive oil
3 Tbsp. soybean oil
> *Heat in a saucepan.*

1 8-oz. chicken breast
Flour
1 egg, beaten
> *Dip in egg and then in flour. Place chicken in the saucepan. Sauté on one side until lightly brown. Turn chicken over.*

½ small onion, sliced
1 clove of garlic, chopped
⅛ cup white cooking wine
> *Add in and sauté for about 5-6 minutes*

6-7 Italian plum tomatoes (canned)
> *Crush them into a bowl and add to the saucepan.*

1 cinnamon stick
2 bay leaves
Pinch of cinnamon
Pinch of nutmeg
½ tsp. of black pepper
6 whole cloves
> *Add in and simmer for 8-10 minutes.*

Chicken Piccata

3 Tbsp. olive oil
3 Tbsp. soybean oil
> *Heat in a saucepan.*

1 8-oz. chicken breast
Flour
1 egg, beaten
> *Dip in egg and then in flour. Place chicken in the saucepan. Sauté on one side until lightly brown. Turn chicken over.*

Juice of ½ lemon
> *Squeeze on top of breast.*

1 small zucchini, sliced
6 mushrooms, sliced
½ tsp. black pepper
> *Add in and sauté 2-3 minutes*

⅛ cup white cooking wine
> *Add in and sauté 5-6 minutes*

Turkey Tostada

3 Tbsp. olive oil
3 Tbsp. soybean oil
Slice of cooked turkey, approximately 1″ thick
Flour
> *Dip turkey in flour, then sauté on both sides until lightly browned. Place turkey in a small baking dish.*

4 slices ham
6 slices Provolone cheese
> *Layer ham on top of turkey and then layer provolone on top of ham.*

4 mushrooms, sliced thin
6 slices of zucchini
> *Place in the saucepan.*

1 tsp. black pepper
⅛ cup of white wine
> *Add in and sauté until mushrooms are soft. Top the ingredients in the baking dish with mushrooms and arrange zucchini on top. Bake in 375° oven for about 15 minutes.*

A young chicken which is not too big or too fat is ideal for roasting. You can detect a young chicken by the skin. It should be smooth. Older chickens are best to boil or to use in casseroles. Their skin is thick and pitted and shows a lot of fat. There is an old saying in Greece telling that "the old chicken makes the best broth," which is used by women who are teased for their older age.

Chicken Blue

3 Tbsp. olive oil
3 Tbsp. soybean oil
> *Heat in a saucepan.*

1 8-oz. chicken breast
Flour
1 egg, beaten
> *Dip in egg and then in flour. Place chicken in the saucepan. Sauté on one side until lightly brown. Turn chicken over.*

½ small onion, sliced
3 slices of ham, chopped thickly
1 clove of garlic, chopped
> *Add in and sauté 3-4 minutes.*

1 tsp. black pepper
⅛ cup white cooking wine
> *Add in and sauté 3-4 minutes longer.*

¼ cup blue cheese, crumbled
2 Tbsp. whipping cream
> *Add in, stir cheese to melt.*

Mustard Grain Chicken

1 whole chicken
Black pepper and rosemary
> *Sprinkle pepper and rosemary on chicken and place in an oiled baking pan. Bake for about 15 minutes in a 350° oven. Remove, cool, cut in half.*

3 eggs beaten
> *Roll chicken half in the egg*

1 cup of 9 grain cereal
½ cup Dijon mustard
> *Mix in a bowl. Roll the chicken in this mix. Deep fry until golden brown.*

Citrus Chicken

1 whole chicken
Black pepper
Rosemary
> *Sprinkle the chicken with a little black pepper and rosemary. Place in an oiled baking pan and bake at 375° for about 15 minutes. Remove, cool, cut in half.*

2 Tbsp. olive oil
2 Tbsp. red cooking wine
Pinch of each: black pepper, oregano, thyme
> *Mix in a bowl for marinade. Place chicken halves on a charbroil and grill, basting with this marinade.*

Juice of ½ lemon
Juice of ½ orange
> *Mix in a bowl and start brushing the chicken when about half done.*

Cornish Hen Spinaci

2 cornish hens
Juice of ½ lemon
Juice of ½ lime

Wash and sprinkle the cavities of the hens with the lemon-lime juice.

½ tsp. brandy
2 tsp. olive oil
½ tsp. thyme
½ tsp. oregano

Mix in a bowl and rub the hens inside and outside including the cavities.

1 Tbsp. soybean oil
¼ cup of chopped onions
⅛ cup of the hens livers

Sauté in a saucepan until onions are soft. Place in a bowl and mix with:

½ cup chopped spinach
2 strips of bacon, cooked and chopped
⅛ cup Ricotta cheese
⅛ cup Feta cheese
½ tsp. oregano
¼ tsp. nutmeg
½ tsp. black pepper

Stuff the hens with the stuffing and place them in a baking pan with a little water and 1 cup of chicken broth. Bake in a 350° oven for about 25-30 minutes, basting frequently with the juice in the baking pan.

Cornish Hens Spinaci

Apricot Cornish Hen

2 cornish hens
1 cup of mayonnaise

> *Rub hens with the mayonnaise, inside and outside including the cavities.*

1 cup breadcrumbs
½ tsp. ginger
1 Tbsp. sherry
⅛ cup chopped liver giblets of the hens
4 green onions, chopped
1 Tbsp. apricot jam
1 tsp. soy sauce

> *Mix in a bowl and stuff the hens. Place in a baking dish with about a cup of water. Bake the hens in a 375° oven for about 25-30 minutes.*

½ cup sherry cooking wine
½ tsp. tabasco sauce
1 cup apricot jam
1 Tbsp. soy sauce
1 tsp. ginger

> *Place in a saucepan and heat. Stir until well heated. Baste hens frequently with this mixture while they are baking. Place hens in a serving platter.*

1 cup chicken broth
⅛ cup sherry cooking wine

> *Add to baking dish and boil and then pour over the hens.*

Gorgonzola Chicken Fettuccine

3 Tbsp. olive oil
3 Tbsp. soybean oil

> *Heat in a skillet.*

1 8-oz. chicken breast, cut into strips

> *Add in and sauté 5-6 minutes.*

⅛ cup white cooking wine

> *Add in.*

½ small red roasted pepper
1 clove garlic, chopped
1 tsp. black pepper

> *Add in and sauté 3-4 minutes.*

½ cup whipping cream

> *Add in and heat for 1-2 minutes.*

¼ cup Gorgonzola cheese, crumbled

> *Add in and heat for 1-2 minutes.*

¼ lb. fettuccine noodles, cooked
2 Tbsp. Romano cheese, grated
2 Tbsp. Parmesan cheese, grated

> *Add in and stir to mix well.*

Celery Chicken

2 Tbsp. olive oil
2 Tbsp. soybean oil
>*Heat in a skillet.*

1 8-oz. chicken breast
1 egg, beaten
Flour
>*Roll in egg, then flour and add to the skillet. Sauté on one side for about 4-5 minutes. Turn over.*

Juice of ½ lemon
>*Squeeze in.*

½ small onion, sliced
1 celery heart (available in specialty stores)
1 clove garlic
>*Add in and sauté 6-7 minutes.*

¼ cup white cooking wine
1 tsp. black pepper
1 tsp. dill
>*Add in, simmer 1-2 minutes.*

½ cup whipping cream
>*Add in, simmer 1-2 minutes.*

Remove chicken breast to a serving platter.
1 egg yolk
>*Break into the sauce, stir well, remove and pour on top of the chicken breast.*

Chicken Saganaki

1 8-oz. chicken breast
>*Charcoal broil or grill on flat top griddle.*

When chicken is almost done:
2 oz. Kefalograviera cheese
>*Place on top to melt. Place on a serving platter.*

1 tsp. soybean oil
1 Tsp. olive oil
½ tomato, chopped
>*Sauté in oil.*

1 tsp. Metaxa Brandy
>*Add in.*

¼ cup pesto sauce (see page 115)
>*Add in, heat gently to melt.*

Pour sauce on top of chicken breast.

Roasted Pepper Chicken

3 Tbsp. olive oil
3 Tbsp. soybean oil
1 8-oz. chicken breast
> *Cut chicken into strips, sauté 4-5 minutes.*

½ small zucchini, sliced
1 clove garlic, chopped
1 small yellow roasted pepper, sliced
1 small roasted red pepper, sliced
6 baby corns
> *Add in and sauté for 5-6 minutes.*

⅛ cup white cooking wine
1 tsp. black pepper
> *Add in and sauté 2-3 minutes.*

⅛ cup whipping cream
¼ cup Gorgonzola cheese, crumbled
> *Add in, heat gently for 1-2 minutes.*

¼ lb. cooked fetuccini
1 Tbsp. Romano cheese, grated
1 Tbsp. Parmesan cheese, grated
> *Add in, stir well.*

Blue Pepper Chicken

3 Tbsp. olive oil
3 Tbsp. soybean oil
> *Heat in a skillet.*

4 oz. chicken breast
> *Sauté 5-6 minutes until chicken is done. Remove from heat.*

1 large roasted red pepper
> *Open pepper and lay on a working surface.*

1 green chili
> *Place on top of pepper. Place chicken breast on top of that.*

1 Tbsp. blue cheese, crumbled
> *Put on top of chicken. Roll ingredients into pepper.*
> *Roll pepper in flour. Sauté until lightly brown on one side, turn*

¼ red bell pepper
¼ green bell pepper
4 mushrooms, sliced
1 clove garlic
> *Add in, sauté 5-6 minutes.*

1 Tbsp. red cooking wine
1 Tbsp. steak sauce
1 tsp. Worcestershire sauce
1 tsp. soy sauce
1 tsp. black pepper
> *Add in and simmer 3-4 minutes.*

Turkeys for the Thanksgiving Project, before and after they are cooked.

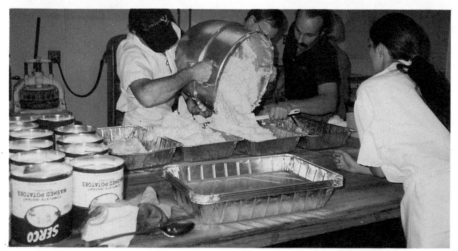

Volunteers help to prepare the foods for the needy on Thanksgiving.

Filling up the refrigerated trucks with the cooked bounty, getting ready to feed thousands of needy citizens.

Hundreds of cooked turkeys ready to be delivered to thousands of locations.

Volunteer drivers lined up early on Thanksgiving morning for a chance to take deliveries to various shelters and homes.

Some of our friends who helped every year on Thanksgiving…

Gary Mason

Phil Quartullo

Steve Ligidakis, Kathy Clarke, Joan Karros.

Dave Ludwitg, director of the Maricopa County Health Department.

Kate Wells, Lisa Ligidakis, Tawni Archer.

Many people brought their whole family to teach the children the glorious act of giving.

Planning the deliveries for the volunteer drivers.

THE BERMUDA TRIANGLE

*T*hat same year on October 3, 1995, I had opened the downtown restaurant called "Nick's on Central." The family that owned the San Carlos Hotel in downtown Phoenix was a long-time customer of my restaurants. Their children first started to visit the restaurant on McDowell and practically grew up with the restaurant. The father, Mr. Melikian, one day visited me at the restaurant on Indian School.

"You should be downtown because that is where the future is," he told me.

I told him I had no intention of moving anywhere. I didn't have the time or the funds to open another restaurant.

"Don't worry about that. Just come down and see me," he said.

The following day he called to invite me for lunch. I went down there mostly out of curiosity. The first time we talked and he took me on a tour of the hotel I was intrigued by its historical past. The ambiance of the hotel brought me back for a second invitation for lunch with the owners. We ate in the hotel restaurant where the lack of management was obvious. There had to be a reason why throughout the lunch hours in an area full of business offices there were only a handful of guests in the restaurant. Their dinner business was almost nonexistent. The idea grew in my head and as I learned more about the progress of downtown Phoenix, the more interested I became. The reasons that kept me intrigued in the San Carlos Hotel was first its history and then its European appearance.

I am a strong believer in preserving our history, and in the environment of the hotel my style of cooking would be a natural. We started talking about the possibilities and soon I was anxious to do the project. The owners of the hotel were going to help me with some of the expenses. It was that simple.

I signed a 10-year lease and the renovation of the restaurant began. Some people told me I was not doing the right thing. They thought that for a restaurant like mine which attracted mainly dinner guests it would not be proper for the downtown area. But I knew my customers. They would follow me anywhere. Others told me about the history of the restaurant space in the hotel and how many concepts it had gone through in the last ten years alone. But that didn't matter either. I believed in my concept.

Opening the restaurant was not easy, although the owners tried to help. There were other difficulties. We needed to remodel the place to bring it to a theme that would blend with the hotel's ambiance. It became a major job. My son Steven did most of the remodeling with the help of restaurant employees. I also spent a lot of time helping, running the restaurant on Indian School and trying to open this new restaurant. I was back to working 18 hours just like the old days. The opening of the new restaurant was costly too, about $60,000, and after the opening it cost much more as we discovered many items that were outdated and needed replacing. That's when the hotel owners washed their hands and left it up to me to take care of the problems. The fire system was outdated and some equipment was too old to work properly. All that cost thousands of dollars more.

But the grand opening celebration was a success. Almost 300 people showed up. We closed Monroe Street and put tables out on the street for people to sit. From day one that restaurant was a success story. Lunch crowds were endless and dinner was standing room only. The owners of the hotel were surprised by the crowds. "We never saw anything like this," they kept telling me.

The revenues of this new restaurant were much more than the Indian School restaurant at its best and this was only the beginning. I soon realized that my future was downtown.

After the Thanksgiving loss it was difficult to maintain the two restaurants. And then it was me, driving back and forth between the two places sometimes ten times a day trying to help overcome the difficulties. I was in a very delicate balancing act. I had split my crew into two parts and both kitchens were weak. When my customers started calling to find out which restaurant I would be at that day so they could come and see me, it was time for me to think seriously about what running those two restaurants was doing to me, my customers, and my beliefs. I was desperately trying not to lose control.

Sometime ago someone told me the restaurant downtown was like the Bermuda Triangle. That stuck in my mind but in the winter of 1995 I lived my own Bermuda Triangle. Between "Nick's Cuisine," the Thanksgiving fiasco, and "Nick's on Central," I felt I was sinking fast into a world I didn't want to be in.

At the beginning of 1996 I decided that enough was enough and closed the restaurant on Indian School Road. My decision was also influenced by the losses of the Thanksgiving Project. Hundreds of customers were disappointed to see "Nick's Cuisine" go, but I'd rather do that than disappoint them in the long run by the lack of service and commercialization of my cooking.

So, part of the triangle was gone. It was the other part, Thanksgiving, which ended up on a good note as I was chosen in 1995 to be a recipient of the City of Phoenix's humanitarian award. In a ceremony that was held at the Hyatt Hotel in downtown Phoenix, it was rewarding for me and meant so much more than other awards I had received before. I won the award against giant companies like American Express and it finally showed me someone recognized that ordinary people deserved attention in our community. I dedicated the award to all who helped me the last ten years on the Thanksgiving project. I wanted them to be proud for what they had done as I knew that night my children who were with me were proud of me.

story continues on page 184

The wisest is he who realizes that in respect of wisdom he is worthless.

— Plato

I will not throw away my span of life to purpose of searching after the impossible hoping in vain to find a perfectly faultless person.

— Plato

Nick's on Central

Letters from past Thanksgivings...

The following are some of the newsletters which I wrote in past years. I would like to share some of those thoughts with you.

Nick Ligidakis

Nick's CUISINE
OF SOUTHERN EUROPE

Nick In The News

3717 East Indian School Road . Phoenix, Arizona 85018 . (602) 955-5225 . WINTER 1993

MEMORIES OF THANKS
13,000 Thanksgiving Dinners Donated

Mid-morning on Thanksgiving Day, I sat in the far corner of the restaurant, the only spot that wasn't packed with bustling people. I looked around in amazement. Some were cooking turkeys, others were making gravy or mashed potatoes, and many others waited patiently for their turn to deliver food to needy families. More people were bringing in food donations and others were putting together dinner packages to be sent out.

I reflected back to Tuesday, when this three-day cooking marathon began. Then, what was happening right now seemed impossible. I tried to visualize everything that had happened since then, but the last 50 hours was something of a blur – a brilliant, beautiful blur.

Hundreds of people had gathered to feed thousands of less fortunate others. I should have been exhausted, but I felt great. The excitement of our mission had not let my legs get weary or my eyes heavy. I thought of the thousands of who would get a hot meal on this special day, and the words of Aristotle came to mind: "Democracy is the relationship of one to another." That relationship had blossomed fully over the last few days.

The skeptics had warned me that my project would be impossible to fulfill this year because of my financial problems. I told them to just watch. I had seen the compassion for people over the years past, and I knew I could count on my friends and hundreds of loyal customers.

The skeptics were laughing by Tuesday when I had only 60 turkeys to feed well over 10,000 people, but I was smiling and those who knew me best, like my kids, employees and close friends, were at ease. They knew it would be done.

As I sat in the corner of the restaurant I tried to remember when the storm of volunteers came. I could not point to the exact time but I knew it had been a forceful gathering. Our phone had never stopped ringing for the last 40-some hours, and people never stopped walking in with turkeys and other foods in their hands. The shifts of volunteers came and went as scheduled.

I looked on the mountain of turkeys that were piled up on the tables and felt relieved that this year's project would be so successful. This year's event was especially important because of the blows my business had been taking for the last years. It was important to prove that you can always get back on your feet and give to others even if you don't have as much as you used to. I still have more than many others. And I was happy, happy enough to get me going for another year.

As I was sitting in that corner, trying to go back over the last days' events, I was reminded of those vivid pictures that made the effort so worthwhile.

Like that little girl carrying a turkey that was almost bigger tan she was, and the school bus that pulled up to the restaurant after a long tour of collecting food. One of the kids gave me a can with a few pennies, dimes and quarters inside. "We collected this for you, too," he said proudly. I held the few coins in my hand and they looked like pieces of gold.

I watched a young disabled girl enter the front door. It took her a longtime to get to the front counter; she could hardly walk with that big heavy turkey. "I'm not supposed to walk," she said, "but I wanted to bring this myself." Happiness sparkled through her eyes, giving us a lesson for all to learn.

In my little corner, it was still kind of quiet, and I struggled to comprehend the events of the last few days. How many people had walked in, how many times had the phone rung, how many people had felt the true meaning of giving and receiving?

It was impossible to count. Impossible to remember. One thing was certain to stay with me forever, though. It was the spirit of the people that put the project together. The spirit had forever erased any skepticism of how powerful the compassion of giving to others is.

"Each man should give, whatever he has decided in his heart, to give not reluctantly nor under compulsion," the words of 2 co. 9:17, my greatest teacher, said in my head. Yes, I had seen that thought realized in the last few days, the priceless feeling of giving without expecting anything in return.

The restaurant was quiet now. A little remaining food littered the tables and volunteers were cleaning up the kitchen. Over 600 turkeys had reached over 270 locations and had fed well over 13,000 people. Now, volunteer drivers were coming back to report their stories with excitement in their voices. And somewhere deep inside I felt kind of guilty that we had to wait a full year to do this again, thinking that all those people would be hungry again tomorrow.

My employees came to pick up meals for their families, an annual tradition in our restaurant. It was almost over. I knew I should be home asleep, but the excitement would not let me go. I did not want to miss any of those last few precious moments.

Then that lady walked in, one of the last delivery volunteers. She walked straight up to me, held my face and kissed me on the forehead. "Thank you," she said. "I have everything I want, a big home, plenty of money and food, but today, I have found what was missing from my life. The true meaning of giving."

Yes, it was finally time for me to go. At home, I closed the door behind me, my small apartment quiet, and all the noise and commotion of the last few days left behind. I sat down to rest, but the power of the people's giving would not leave my mind.

My children came to visit me. I looked at them: Lisa, a beautiful young lady now, and Steve and Joe, big strong boys who had grown so tall. Where had all the years gone, I thought as they walked away. How fast life is moving. It reminded me that everything we do in life is meaningless unless it is focused to improve our relationship with one another, by bringing hope to the ones that have been discouraged by the irony of life. Then we can keep our dreams humble and the hope that together we can do better in life.

I looked around my home. I knew in that moment I had everything I wanted. I had the thing I had worked hard in life to achieve: the feeling that material things mean nothing, that the only thing that brings peace is fulfilling responsibilities and following beliefs, whatever the cost may be. Because beliefs are not just what we believe in, but the way we live.

Nick Ligidakis

Nick's CUISINE
OF SOUTHERN EUROPE

Nick In The News

3717 East Indian School Road • Phoenix, Arizona 85018 • (602) 955-5225 • WINTER/SPRING 1994

Friends Make Our Lives Rich

By early September of last year, people already were reminding me that Thanksgiving was just around the corner. But it seemed that just in my last newsletter, I was thanking people for 1992's successful feast. How could the year have gone by so quickly?

After feeding 13,000 less fortunate friends last year, everyone was very anxious to hear how many people were going to be fed in 1993. I was more concerned about *how* we were going to feed those thousands of people, and what would happen after the feast. Last year, it seemed that not enough people heard our community's cries for help – although a great many loyal friends and customers rallied to support our feast, I knew that this year, we would still have more mouths to feed.

I picked a number – 15,000 citizens – thinking that perhaps that huge number would startle people into realizing the tremendous need of people in our community. So many good people have been devastated by the ironies of life, and the simple dinner that had begun nine years ago as an act of kindness, now is a mission of huge proportions.

Some people don't understand why I continue to struggle and pull this off year after year. I have tried to analyze my own feelings as my motivations change through the years, and they are many.

The desire to stay humble. The need to be in touch with reality, even with its less beautiful side. The hope to draw strength by recognizing my own fortunate life. The virtue of giving hope to those less blessed. The pressures of guilt when we let other people down. The wish to offer a little balance in this society. The thrill of satisfaction and joy spurred by the true meaning of giving. The price of being an example to children. The ache to ease the pain that others suffer. The eagerness to provide heroes for our young ones to follow. The fear that our elders may not know that their only mistake has been to grow old and become forgotten by our busy society. The dream never to forget where I came from, and my own modest beginnings.

Looking back now, I can't help but wonder, do people really see the ills that have affected our society? Will people open their eyes, realize that they can help, and strive to make a difference?

That's why the number 15,000 was so important. It was big, but too small for a real solution unless others chose to help.

When we realized our goal to the media, some reporters asked me what my plan was to reach all the people whose assistance we needed. I spoke honestly: I had no clue how I was going to do it, but somehow, I had faith that it would happen.

That Monday before Thanksgiving, everything was calm, with most of our efforts going towards scheduling last-minute volunteers and wondering how in the world we were going to find enough turkeys to feed all our guests. At noon on Tuesday, the first volunteer arrived to begin preparing what few turkeys were available for stuffing. I needed well over 1,000 birds, and the donations simply were not coming in. By noon on Wednesday, we had only 350 turkeys. We called local supermarkets, looking to buy 200 turkeys just to keep our ovens running. Other volunteers were laboring to make tons of mashed potatoes, gravy, yams, cranberry sauce, stuffing, vegetables, breads and pies.

The supermarkets told us they could not sell that amount of turkeys to one buyer. We would pay any price we told them, it was for a noble cause, we insisted, but red tape is red tape, no matter what it's wrapped around. Time was too short to send buyers to multiple grocery stores, purchase the birds, thaw them and have them ready to serve.

Still, the calls came in with people asking to be included on our donation list. Volunteers came to me repeatedly, asking if we could add more names when our food supplies were so low. Yes, I said, we would find a way. Many people looked at me with disbelief, but others who had survived previous Thanksgivings, knew that as always somehow it would be accomplished.

Then, the media came to the rescue, with the unparalleled power of television, radio and newspaper. In all, our generous local media gave us more than an hour of air time, and a fistful of news clips to support our cause. Some people have said that such exposure generates our efforts – I say, if they knew how much work and anxiety each feast caused, they would know that no "publicity" could make up for it if our hearts were not in it.

Suddenly, volunteers came flooding in by the droves, laden with turkeys and trimmings. From then on, the pace was frantic. Cooked turkeys were piling up, and the Maricopa County Health Board was called in to help us find a way to store them at proper temperatures. I have never in my 25 years of restaurant management seen so many people work so hard to find solutions.

Ideas were exchanged rapidly – from shipping in dry ice, to renting walk-in refrigerators. Then, someone proposed leasing a refrigerated truck. We found such a truck, but we needed insurance. Thanksgiving eve, I located my insurance agent, only to find we also needed a License B truck driver to move the vehicle. We had no time. The restaurant was a mad house of food preparation, processing donations, TV cameras and phone calls struggling to solve our truck situation.

Finally, Zeb Pearce's Coors Beer located two trucks we could use. More red tape. First, we had to get clearance from the Liquor Board to park the trucks outside. The Board said it was not possible to receive clearance on such short notice when the office was closed, but we would not take no for an answer. Somebody listened, and finally, we received clearance on our fax machine. Shortly after, ABCO Foods called to say they were sending another truck. They arrived, and a team of friends washed them thoroughly inside and out.

The next steps were pure poetry – a human chain of dedicated workers – including a half dozen Health Department official – stretching out the restaurant door, through the parking lot and up the ramps of the humming, fog-misted trucks to store their fresh-cooked bounty. I took a moment to watch and wondered, how could anyone not be moved by all this?

At the same time, it was ironic. Our society has such a frantic lifestyle, and often the strain consumes people's true feelings and compassions. The struggle to pay our bills and survive has clouded our ability to love and help others. Tonight, that was different. People were struggling to help others. Those rich feelings help me through every year,.

By Thanksgiving morning, people were telling me to relax; that we had finally made it. The food was cooked, but still, it had to be delivered to more than 1,300 locations. Hundreds of volunteer drivers were lining up to deliver the food, and the complex assignment of directions this Valley-wide effort began.

Some people say I deserve credit for doing this every year. But it is not just me. So many valuable friends deserve recognition, too many to list in a four-page newsletter. My office manager, Kathy Karros, stayed up the entire three days with me, but throughout it all, I never saw fatigue in her eyes. Pam Del Ducca, a very busy entrepreneur herself, has returned year after year, exploiting her expertise to help my operation run as successfully as her businesses. Gary Mason, after spending countless hours pulling hundreds of turkeys from my ovens, cheerfully announced that now, he had to go home and cook for his own family. My friend Phil Quartullo returns year after year, as does Debbie Timmons. We experience that joy together, and that makes every year one to celebrate.

Suddenly, it was four o'clock Thanksgiving Day. The kitchen was being cleaned, and I still needed to visit my children for our own Thanksgiving dinner. As I drove there, I reflected on the thousands of people I'd seen with pure joy on their faces, and I felt proud. We had promised to give 15,000 people a little hope for the holidays, and the good citizens of Phoenix had disappointed no one.

That Thanksgiving, my daughter Lisa cooked her first turkey. My sons Steve and Joe made pies and appetizers. After seeing so much food over the last three days, I was sure I would not be able to eat. But that dinner was one of the best I had ever tasted, every morsel cooked with love. I sat with my family, and I realized how wonderful my life is.

Nick Ligidakis'

Nick in the News

Nick's Cuisine of Southern Europe	Nick's on Central
3717 E. Indian School Rd. • (602) 955-5225	202 N. Central Ave. • (602) 261-7899

WINTER 1995

Answers Without Questions

When I walked into the restaurant on Sunday, it was unusually quiet, strangely peaceful. I thought of the five days ahead, of the people that would come through the doors, the tons of food that would be cooked, the thousands of unfortunate friends that on Thursday, would receive home cooked meals and the joy of knowing that someone cared about them. I've experienced that feeling for the past ten years. It's so simple, but so difficult to explain – that beautiful act of giving and the unbelievable pleasure it brings. Plato describes it this way: "The good man, if he is temperate and just, is fortunate and is happy whether he is rich or poor…on the other hand, if he has great wealth and be unjust, he lives in misery." I thought of the years past, trying to count the many reasons why this project had grown so explosively since the first year when we fed 250 people. I knew I was going to be asked again and again, "Why." I have so many answers to give – hoping someone will listen, hoping someone will be touched. This project is reaching its highest level of its purpose now. After ten years, people finally are starting to understand that there is a tremendous need in our society, and that we are the ones who can cure it. When I read some of our past newsletters, I relive the memories of 1993 and 1994. I don't want to let the feelings go – life truly is about good memories. The only purpose of bad memories is to learn lessons, to learn how to find peace in your life.

Only the people who have worked side by side can understand the feelings, and they are my witnesses when I say that nothing in life gives satisfaction as the feeling of giving. Every other pleasure is temporary, and though it all seems of great importance at the time, eventually it wears out. But this feeling of giving becomes stronger as time goes by, and the images of people smiling and crying when they receive a plate of food can never leave your mind. Many people understand that material possessions bring only temporary pleasure – and mystery if they are misused. Socrates says: "When a man has health and wealth and a tyranny which lasts, and when he is preeminent in strength and courage and has none of the so-called evils which counter balance this good, but has only the injustice and the insolence of his own nature – of such one you are suspect, unwilling to believe that he is miserable rather than happy." I cannot think of any excuse to explain how our leaders – selected by the people – can allow citizens to sleep in the street and eat out of garbage cans. In this great country with its many riches and resources, old people are dying lonely, spending their golden years in grief and worrying how they will eat the next day. In this, the most powerful country that is trying to place law and order in the rest of the world, we let our children kill themselves in the streets.

American people are without homes or food. People are being born into despair, and we are doing nothing about it. As Plato said, "The citizens must indeed be happy and good, and the legislators will seek to make them so, but very rich and very good at the same time he cannot be, not at least in the sense that many speak of riches." Those are the ideas that we seem to have lost through the centuries. It seems we have reached the age of mistreated leaderships and abusive democracy. Maybe we expect too much from these politicians who seem incapable of understanding the suffering of humans.

And that is "why" my annual Thanksgiving feast exists. I think this project has changed some of those minds. Over the last decade, many came to help, and left determined to make a difference in our society. Others came to help with the wrong intentions, it's true, hoping to promote their ambitious careers. They left disappointed, since I will not cater to such selfish motives. Still others came to promote their companies and their products. I told them this was the wrong place for such nonsense. If people are not doing things strictly to help others, it defeats the purpose. Again, Aristotle speaks such trust: "And for all the rules, servants or ministers of the law, I give them the name not for the sake of novelty, but because I certainly believe that upon such service o ministry depends the well- or ill-being of the state."

And that, after all these years, and for all the years to come, is "Why."

Nick's Thanksgiving Project is an ongoing event.

If you would like to participate and help in any way,
please write to:

Nick Ligidakis
P.O. Box 388
Phoenix, AZ 85001

or call:
262-2610 or FAX: 252-4929

How Much Can A Mind Take

*N*ow I had to deal with my own triangle at Nick's on Central. I had to clean up after the aftermath of Thanksgiving and the closing of "Nick's Cuisine." I had to take care of bills that were left behind, and lawsuits of creditors that followed. We tried to talk to everyone who was anxious to be paid and to the ones who agreed, we started a payment plan. Others prosecuted.

I remember one court case in Tucson. After the court had made its decision, I would make payments on the amount owed. I went to my car so I could drive back to Phoenix but my car would not start. I tried again and again. I sat in the car and started thinking of the past 13 years and the marathon I had taken on. My mind was in pain trying to fit in all the memories of my fight for survival the past eight years. I wondered how much more my mind could take; the constant worry how to make it on a day to day basis, the focus of pleasing customers, the everyday planning of the restaurant operation, the employees, the bills. Problems I was never concerned with before. None of these things had bothered me in the past. My optimism was remarkable to many, but it took a car, in another city which would not start to give me time to sit back and think.

That was the first time the thoughts that I was consuming my mind with too much and surrounding my life with negative energy started to enter my mind. I had not given myself a chance to focus on other things in my life.

After I managed to start the car my mind was more determined than ever to fight for survival. But this time it was for survival of the mind which would free me from the destructions and allow me to bring my good energy back into focus.

But we never discover those things as long as we keep pounding our minds against the wall. The restaurant had become so much pressure and now I was beginning to feel it. It was not like the pressure I felt back in the days on McDowell where, despite the hard work and the difficulties, I was inspired to create and build up the concept I had imagined. Now it was all different. The constant pressure to survive was alarming my senses that something was wrong. The pressure was building up in my mind despite the fact that everything seemed to be moving in the right direction. The restaurant in downtown Phoenix was going to overcome all the problems of the past because our business was better than ever. Something was bothersome to me. Something would not let my mind relax and let me enjoy the success of this new restaurant.

If you see any possible way which evil can be explained other than pain or good as other than pleasure, you may still retract. Are you satisfied then at having a life of pleasure which is without pain?

— Socrates

FIGHT TILL THE END

*T*he news came suddenly in August, 1996. The hotel was sold to a new investment company. Everyone was excited as this new owner had plans to renovate the hotel to attract more guests. We all waited anxiously for them to take over and I was looking forward to building up my business with them for years to come.

On August 28th which was the second day the new owners took over the hotel, I got the biggest surprise of my life. As I went to open the restaurant I found the doors locked, the locks had been changed and there were signs on the doors stating the restaurant was now repossessed by the new ownership. They had found a loophole in my lease and took advantage of it. Their plans were to eventually take possession of all the spaces in the building and run business their way, it seemed that I was their first victim.

I met with them that same morning. They were very apologetic and told me they wanted nothing more than to have me running the restaurant. They assured me nothing would change in the operation, only from now on they would handle the financial details and technically I would be employed by them. A percentage of the profits from the restaurant would still belong to me except they would keep a small percentage from those profits. I felt that I was sitting in a big island of greed with these people. But I thought of my employees, my property, and Thanksgiving coming up and I figured I would fight until the end.

The restaurant re-opened the same day. The first month under the new management went smooth. The events that followed warned me of things to come. Their motives were not to take care of me as they had promised but to slowly turn the restaurant operation over to them and at the same time not interrupt the food service business in the hotel.

What do you expect from ones where money has become their God? I was perfectly willing in the beginning to adjust to their changes. My attorney advised me about lawsuits because he believed that the takeover of the restaurant was illegal. But I told him I would rather work with them and find a solution.

When they started to bring consultants and advisers to the restaurant I wanted to scream at them that it was unnecessary. I knew how to bring people in. Meetings came and went and my talking to them about my philosophy of business proved fruitless. It was obvious they wanted to do things their own way.

As weeks went by I was treated like an employee who was hired a few weeks ago. One day the first signs of disrespect to me was when they fired Kathy, my long-time manager who was the soul of the restaurant operation. I do not know if anyone could find a better employee who cared so much about the business and was devoted so deeply to our Thanksgiving project year after year.

After that incident the restaurant crew and the business started to follow the guidelines of the manual which described how to be robots and do our jobs. This was totally different from the concept I had dreamed 13 years ago; and after what I had put my mind and body through I was not about to surrender to this nonsense. I was not about to give in to the beliefs or to betray the concept that gave joy to thousands throughout the years. I felt used, mainly by Mr. Melikian, the ex-owner of the hotel, who's idea of bringing me to his hotel to open the restaurant was purely self-motivated. He always wanted to sell the hotel and with my restaurant present there, it was much more attractive to a buyer.

story continued on page 207

March 11, 1997

The first time I walked into Nick Ligidakis' restaurant and passed by the showcases of his famous desserts I was very impressed. I actually stayed for a long time as I admired with amazement. As I sat down for dinner he came over to greet our table and I told him how impressed I was by his wonderful display of desserts. He graciously smiled and thanked me. Looking back on that evening I never imagined I would be fortunate enough to have the joy and pleasure of knowing this man for who he truly is.

A man who possesses many qualities that most of us cannot find in *one* individual, are easily found in abundance inside Nick Ligidakis: wisdom, temperance, honesty, leadership, ambition, courage, justice and generosity. This man shows such effortless action in tasks that might seem complicated for some to complete. He shows modesty about his amazing achievements of success in his work, as well as his kind generosity in giving back to our community. He has a true love and passion for everything that he does. His accomplishments are completed unselfishly, without the expectation of anything in return such as fame or monetary gain.

He betrays such a simplistic view on life, yet he holds the complexity of the thoughts that run through his incredible mind. He has taught me that the experiences of pain in our life are necessary. For without pain, the future cannot hold pleasure. He has shared with me his thoughts through some of his own experiences regarding time passing us by as we sometimes get caught up in our busy daily lives. He has said, "Time is unforgiving" and we *must* realize this in order for us not to look back and feel as if we had missed the important values of life. For tomorrow arrives too quickly.

My life has been truly enriched by receiving the gift of knowing Nick.

Nick Ligidakis is the composer of the recipes that he creates and as the ingredients come together you can hear a "beautiful symphony."

Thank you, Nick.

Connie Damiani

Veal, Lamb, Steaks and other meats...

Mustard Lamb Fricassee

3 Tbsp. olive oil
3 Tbsp. vegetable oil
> *Heat in saucepan.*

3 lamb chops
> *Add in and brown well on one side and turn.*

1 Tbsp. sauterne wine
6 green onions chopped
6 artichokes, cut in pieces
1 small head of Romaine lettuce chopped
1 tsp. dill weed
½ tsp. black pepper
½ tsp. parsley
> *Add in and cook 9-10 minutes.*

Juice of ½ lemon
> *Add in and cook until lettuce is soft.*

1 cup whipping cream
1 tsp. Dijon mustard
> *Add in and simmer 2-3 minutes.*
> *Put lamb chops on a serving dish.*

1 egg yolk
> *Add to sauce and stir for a few seconds and pour sauce on lamb chops.*

Sir Wellington (see page 203)

Veal Mousaka

3 Tbsp. olive oil
3 Tbsp. soybean oil
> *Heat in saucepan.*

6 oz. veal, thinly sliced
> *Sauté for 3-4 minutes.*

½ cup onions sliced
6 mushrooms sliced
6 green onions chopped (use white part only)
1 clove garlic chopped
½ small potato thinly sliced
1 Tbsp. red cooking wine
> *Add in and sauté 6-7 minutes.*

2 cups of tomatoes in juice
½ tsp. cinnamon
½ tsp. nutmeg
> *Add in and simmer 4-5 minutes. Remove from heat.*

1 Tbsp. Romano cheese
1 Tbsp. Parmesan cheese
> *Add in.*

6 slices of eggplant
> *Grill until soft.*
> *Place ½ of the filling in a baking dish. Cover with eggplant and pour the rest of the filling on top.*

1 cup Kefalograviera cheese
> *Add this to the baking dish and bake at 425° for 25-30 minutes.*

Mustard Nut Veal

6 oz. veal slices
1 egg beaten
Flour
> *Dip veal in flour, then in egg and again in flour.*

3 Tbsp. olive oil
3 Tbsp. soybean oil
> *Place in saucepan and sauté veal until lightly brown on both sides.*

2 Tbsp. white cooking wine
> *Add in.*

5 mushrooms, thinly sliced
1 clove of garlic
3 asparagus spears, chopped
> *Add in and sauté until mushrooms are soft, about 4-5 minutes.*

1 Tbsp. hazelnuts, grated
Pinch of pepper
1 cup whipping cream
> *Add in and simmer 2-3 minutes.*

1 Tbsp. Dijon mustard
1 oz. sliced swiss cheese
> *Add in and stir until cheese is melted.*

Veal Skordato

2 slices of veal - about 4 oz. each
Place them on a working surface.

4 slices of ham
Place 2 pieces of ham on each piece of veal.

Clove of garlic, chopped
Place on top of ham.
Enclose ham and garlic in the veal slices.

1 Tbsp. chopped almonds
1 Tbsp. chopped walnuts
1 egg
Mix together.

Flour
Bread crumbs
Dip veal in flour, then in the nut mixture and roll veal in bread crumbs.

3 Tbsp. olive oil
3 Tbsp. soybean oil
Sauté veal on both sides until brown.
Place veal in a baking dish.
Sauté 4-5 slices of zucchini
Place on top of veal

½ cup whipping cream
Heat gently.

3 oz. Provolone
2 oz. Mozzarella
Add in and stir until cheese melts. Pour this mixture on top of veal.
Bake at 350° for 20 minutes.

Roast Leg of Lamb (see page 245)

Veal Melintzana

2 thin slices of veal
2 thin slices of eggplant
1 clove of garlic, chopped
1 artichoke heart (not marinated), chopped

> *Lay one veal slice on a working surface and place one slice of eggplant on top of it. Place garlic and artichoke*
> *on top of eggplant. Cover with the other slice of eggplant and then with the other slice of veal.*

Flour
1 egg, beaten
Breadcrumbs

> *Roll the stuffed veal on flour, then dip it in the egg and coat well with breadcrumbs.*

3 Tbsp. olive oil
3 Tbsp. soybean oil

> *Heat in a a sauce pan. Place veal in and brown well, about 3-4 minutes for each side.*

½ onion, chopped
1 clove garlic, chopped

> *Add in.*

1 Tbsp. white cooking wine

> *Add in and sauté until onions are soft, 3-4 minutes.*

8 oz. tomatoes in juice

> *Add in crushing the tomatoes.*

6 whole cloves
2 whole cinnamon sticks
2 bay leaves
⅛ tsp. ground cinnamon
⅛ tsp. ground nutmeg
⅛ tsp. black pepper

> *Add in and simmer 9-10 minutes. 1 serving.*

Wine brings out the flavor of foods. It helps to bind sauces so you can do away with butter. Wine gives enough flavor to foods so you can omit salt altogether. Wine stimulates the appetite because of the alcohol and it also helps the digestion.

Cooking wines are young, but respectable wines. Wine has been used in cooking since the ancient times by the Greeks and Romans. Joan of Arc liked to soak bread in wine mixed with water and at times she ate nothing else except that.

Veal Stuffed Zucchini

2 medium zucchinis

> *Boil in water until soft, about 5-6 minutes.*
> *Cut zucchinis in halves horizontally and clean out pulp. Save ¼ of the pulp.*
> *Place the zucchini shells in a small casserole with hollow side up.*

3 Tbsp. olive oil
3 Tbsp. soybean oil

> *Heat in saucepan.*

10 oz. veal, chopped

> *Add in. Sauté 2-3 minutes.*

8 mushrooms, sliced
10 green onions, chopped
1 small onion chopped

> *Add in. Sauté until soft.*

1 clove garlic
¼ of the zucchini pulp

> *Add in. Simmer 3-4 minutes.*

1 Tbsp. white cooking wine
⅛ tsp. Greek oregano
⅛ tsp. sweet basil
⅛ tsp. black pepper
1 tsp. grated Romano
1 tsp. grated Parmesan

> *Add in and simmer 2-3 minutes. Place filling on top of zucchini shells.*

2 cups soft Ricotta cheese

> *Cover the filling with this.*

½ lb. Feta cheese

> *Place on top of Ricotta.*

1/8 tsp. whole thyme

> *Sprinkle on top of cheese. Bake at 425° about 30 minutes. 2 servings.*

Gyros Platter (see page 202)

Filo Veal

3 Tbsp. olive oil
3 Tbsp. soybean oil
> *Heat gently in a saucepan.*

6 oz. veal, sliced
Flour
> *Dip veal in flour and place in the saucepan and sauté 2-3 minutes.*

4 baby pearl onions, peeled
½ potato, peeled and sliced
½ carrot, sliced
⅛ cup sugar peas
> *Add in and sauté 3-4 minutes.*

½ tsp. black pepper
Juice of ½ lemon
> *Add in and sauté 2-3 minutes.*

4 sheets of Fillo dough
> *Brush with olive oil and place them one on top of the other.*
> *Discard liquid from the saucepan and place the veal in the middle of the fillos then place the vegetables on top of the veal.*

2 oz. Kaseri cheese
> *Place on top of vegetables.*
> *Fold the Filo over to enclose all ingredients.*
> *Place in an oiled baking pan and bake at 375° for about 20-25 minutes.*

Lamb Kallithea

3 4 oz. lamb chops
> *Grill for 4-5 minutes on both sides, until they are browned well.*

3 Tbsp. olive oil
3 Tbsp. soybean oil
> *Heat in a saucepan.*

5 mushrooms, sliced
1 tomato, cubed
4 green onions, chopped
1 clove garlic, chopped
> *Add in and sauté for 4-5 minutes*

⅛ cup white cooking wine
Juice of ½ lemon
Pinch of each: black pepper, parsley, basil, oregano, thyme, rosemary
> *Add in and sauté 2-3 minutes longer.*

1 Tbsp. Parmesan cheese
> *Add in.*
> *Place lamb chops on a serving platter and pour the vegetables over the meat.*

Feta Lamb

3 Tbsp. olive oil
3 Tbsp. soybean oil
3 lamb chops (approximately 4 oz. each)
> *Brown well on both sides.*

½ Tbsp. red cooking wine
> *Add in.*

½ cup red onions, chopped
½ cup onions, chopped
2 artichoke hearts
1 clove garlic
> *Add and simmer for about 6-7 minutes.*

1 tomato, chopped
½ tsp. black pepper
½ tsp. oregano
½ tsp. mint leaves
> *Add and simmer for 5-6 minutes.*

4 oz. Feta cheese
> *Add and simmer until cheese is melted.*

Roman Artichoke Lamb

3 4oz. lamb chops
Boiling water
> *Boil chops for about 5 minutes.*

3 Tbsp. olive oil
3 Tbsp. soybean oil
> *Heat in saucepan. Place chops in and sauté 2-3 minutes.*

6 green onions, chopped
2 artichoke hearts
> *Add in and simmer 2-3 minutes.*

1 Romaine lettuce, chopped
> *Add to the sauce pan.*

½ tsp. dill weed
½ tsp. parsley, chopped
⅛ tsp. black pepper
Juice of ½ lemon
> *Add in, cover and simmer 4-5 minutes.*

½ cup whipping clean
> *Add in. Remove chops to a plate.*

Yolk of 1 egg
> *Add to the saucepan. Stir well and pour sauce over chops. 1 serving.*

Country Lamb Chops

3 Tbsp. olive oil
3 Tbsp. soybean oil
> *Heat in a saucepan.*

3 4oz. lamb chops
> *Place in the sauce pan and sauté until light brown, 3-4 minutes on each side.*

1 Tbsp. red cooking wine
> *Add in.*

6 pearl onions
6 oz. okra
4 oz. eggplant chopped
2 oz. garbanzo beans (canned)
> *Add in and sauté 6-7 minutes.*

6 sun-dried tomatoes
1 clove garlic
> *Add in.*

1/8 tsp. whole rosemary
Pinch of black pepper
> *Add in and sauté 2-3 minutes*

1 cup juice of a can of whole tomatoes
> *Add in. Simmer 6-8 minutes. 1 serving.*

Steak Stefado

3 Tbsp. olive oil
3 Tbsp. soybean oil
16 oz. New York tenderloin steak, cubed
> *Sauté in a skillet for 3-4 minutes.*

12 pearl onions
> *Add in and sauté until onions are soft, 3-4 minutes.*

1 lb. whole plump tomatoes
> *Crush with juice and add in.*

2 cinnamon sticks
¼ tsp. ground cinnamon
12 whole cloves
2 cloves garlic, chopped
6 whole black peppercorns
2 bay leaves
¼ tsp. whole rosemary
⅛ tsp. whole thyme
⅛ tsp. ground black pepper
> *Add in and simmer 15 minutes.*

1 Tbsp. wine vinegar
> *Add in, cover and simmer 25 minutes. 2 servings.*

Greco Roman Steak

3 Tbsp. olive oil
3 Tbsp. soybean oil
>*Heat in a heavy skillet.*

2 8oz. New York cut sirloin steaks
>*Add in and sauté on both sides until brown, 3-4 minutes each side.*

6 sun dried tomatoes
1 Tbsp. capers
2 cloves garlic
>*Add in and sauté 2-3 minutes.*

1 Tbsp. red cooking wine
>*Add in.*

⅛ tsp. basil
⅛ tsp. oregano
>*Add in.*

¼ cup Feta cheese
>*Add in and stir to melt.*
>*Place steaks on platter and spoon sauce over them. 2 servings.*

Baked Seafood Steak

3 Tbsp. olive oil
3 Tbsp. soybean oil
>*Heat in a sauce pan.*

12 oz. fillet mignon steak
>*Add in and sauté 2-3 minutes on each side.*

½ lb. mushrooms, sliced
6 asparagus, chopped coarsely
1 clove garlic
½ cup bay shrimp
½ cup snow crab meat
>*Add in and sauté 3-4 minutes.*

1 Tbsp. white cooking wine
⅛ tsp. whole rosemary
⅛ tsp. thyme
Pepper to taste
>*Add in to the sauce pan.*
>*Place steak in a small baking dish and pour sauce over steak.*

10 slices of swiss cheese
>*Layer on top of steak.*
>*Bake in 375° oven for 10 minutes. 2 servings.*

Southern Steak

3 Tbsp. olive oil
3 Tbsp. soybean oil
> *Heat in a fry pan.*

2 8 oz. New York tenderloin steaks
> *Add in and sauté gently, 4–5 minutes on each side.*

6 pepperoncinis, chopped thickly
8 sun dried tomatoes
1 Tbsp. capers
4 green chilis, sliced
1 Tbsp. garlic chopped
7-8 whole black peppercorns
Pinch of black pepper
Pinch of whole thyme
> *Add in and sauté 4–5 minutes.*

1 tsp. red cooking wine
> *Add in and stir well.*
> *Serve over fresh cooked pasta or rice pilaf. 2 servings.*

Mushroom Steak

1 10 oz. New York tenderloin steak
> *Grill for 4–5 minutes.*

3 Tbsp. olive oil
3 Tbsp. soybean oil
> *Heat in a sauce pan. Add steak to pan.*

6 mushrooms, sliced
1 small zucchini, sliced
> *Add in and sauté for 3–4 minutes.*

⅛ cup red cooking wine
1 tsp. black pepper
> *Add in and sauté 4–5 minutes.*

Traditional Greek

1 10 oz. New York tenderloin steak
> *Grill on both sides until done to likeness.*

Juice of 1/2 lemon, squeezed over steak
Pinch of each: oregano, thyme, rosemary
> *Sprinkle on top.*

Baby Corn Steak

1 10 oz. New York tenderloin steak, cut into 6 strips
3 Tbsp. olive oil
3 Tbsp. soybean oil

> *Heat in a sauce pan.*
> *Add the steak to the sauce pan and sauté for 4-5 minutes until steak is lightly browned.*

⅛ cup red cooking wine

> *Add in.*

1 small roasted red pepper, cut in strips
½ green bell pepper, sliced
6 baby corns
½ small onion, sliced
3 green onions, chopped
1 clove garlic, chopped
¼ tsp. chili powder
¼ tsp. cayenne pepper
½ tsp. black pepper
¼ tsp. paprika

> *Add in and sauté for 7-8 minutes longer, until vegetables are soft.*

¼ cup of whipping cream

> *Add in, stir well and heat for 1-2 minutes.*

Steak Metaxa

1 8 oz. fillet mignon steak, butterflied
3 Tbsp. olive oil
3 Tbsp. soybean oil

> *Heat in a skillet, add steak and sauté until the steak is brown on one side 3-4 minutes.*
> *Turn steak to other side.*

⅛ cup white cooking wine

> *Add in.*

½ onion, sliced
4 green onions, chopped
1 clove garlic, chopped
1 tsp. orange peel, grated

> *Add in and sauté 5-6 minutes.*

½ oz. Metaxa brandy

> *Add in and simmer 1-2 minutes.*

1 tsp. black pepper
¼ cup whipping cream
½ tsp. nutmeg
1 tsp. Dijon mustard

> *Add in and stir well. Heat for 1-2 minutes.*
> *Serve sauce over the steak.*

Peppery Steak

3 Tbsp. olive oil
3 Tbsp. soybean oil
1 8 oz. fillet mignon steak, cut into 6 strips
> *Heat in a skillet, add steak in and sauté until brown, 4-5 minutes.*

⅛ cup red cooking wine
> *Add in.*

1 Tbsp. black olives, sliced
1 Tbsp. green olives, sliced
1 small green pepper, sliced
1 small red pepper, sliced
½ small onion, sliced
½ small red onion, sliced
4 mushrooms, sliced
1 clove garlic, chopped
> *Add in and sauté, 4-5 minutes.*

1 tsp. soy sauce
1 tsp. Worcestershire sauce
1 tsp. steak sauce
1 tsp. black pepper
> *Add in and sauté 3-4 minutes.*

1/2 tomato, cubed
> *Add to the skillet, until just warm.*

Peloponnese Souvlakia

1 8 oz. New York tenderloin steak, cut into 4 pieces
4 large mushrooms
1 small onion, quartered
1 small red pepper, cut into 4 pieces
> *Thread steak on to a large skewer, alternating the vegetables with the steak.*

½ cup olive oil
¼ cup red wine vinegar
1 clove garlic, chopped
Juice of half of lemon
Pinch of each: black pepper, parsley, basil, oregano, thyme, rosemary
> *Mix in a bowl.*
> *Grill skewers of meat and vegetables, brushing frequently with the oil mixture.*

Pork Williams

3 Tbsp. olive oil
3 Tbsp. soybean oil
3 4 oz. pork chops
> *Sauté chops 3-4 minutes on each side.*

½ onion, chopped
4 green onions, chopped
> *Add in and sauté until onions are soft, 4-5 minutes.*

¼ cup pecan pieces
1 red apple, thinly sliced
> *Add in and sauté 4-5 minutes.*

1 Tbsp. white cooking wine
⅛ tsp. black pepper
> *Add in and simmer 2-3 minutes.*

1 cup whipping cream
> *Add in and simmer 2-3 minutes.*

2 Tbsp. sour cream
> *Add in.*
> *Remove pork chops to a serving plate.*
> *Mix sauce well and pour over chops.*

Celery Pork

3 Tbsp. olive oil
3 Tbsp. soybean oil
> *Heat in a sauce pan.*

3 4 oz. pork chops
> *Add in and sauté 3-4 minutes on each side.*

Juice of 1/2 lemon
> *Add in.*

1 marinated heart of celery, sliced. (available in specialty shops).
1/2 onion, sliced
1 clove garlic, chopped
> *Add in and sauté 5-6 minutes.*

1 tsp. black pepper
1/4 cup whipping cream
> *Add in and heat 1-2 minutes.*
> *Remove pork chops to a serving platter.*

1 egg yolk
> *Add in to the skillet and stir well over low heat, remove immediately.*
> *Pour over chops.*

Sausage Souvlakia

1 Italian mild sausage
1 Portuguese sausage
1 French sausage
1 small onion, quartered
1 small red pepper, quartered

Thread sausages and vegetables alternately on to a large skewer.

½ cup olive oil
¼ cup red wine vinegar
1 clove garlic, chopped
Pinch each of: black pepper, parsley, basil, thyme, oregano, rosemary

Mix in bowl.
Grill skewers of meat and vegetables, brushing frequently with the oil mixture.

Southern Style Ribs

2 slabs of baby back ribs, cut into desired pieces

Place in a small pot of boiling water.

1 Tbsp. each of: basil, oregano, rosemary

Bring to a boil, add the spices, reduce heat and cook for about 15 minutes.
Remove ribs. Remove the skin from the inside of the slabs.
Place in a baking pan and bake at 375° for 15 minutes.
Remove and brush with BBQ sauce and bake for 15 minutes longer, brushing frequently with the BBQ sauce (see page 202).
Place ribs on a serving platter and pour BBQ sauce over them.

Southern Style Ribs

Beer Based Barbeque Sauce

2 Tbsp. olive oil
> *Heat in a heavy pot.*

2 onions, finely chopped
3 cloves garlic, chopped
> *Add in and simmer for 4-5 minutes.*

1½ tsp. ginger root, finely chopped
1 small (28 oz.) can of plum tomatoes, finely chopped (save juice)
> *Add in and simmer 4-5 minutes longer.*

½ can beer
Juice from the tomatoes
> *Add in.*

1 tsp. cayenne pepper
1 Tbsp. chili powder
1 tsp. oregano
1 Tbsp. BBQ spice
1½ cups chili sauce
¼ cup dark brown sugar
⅓ cup sherry wine
⅓ cup soy sauce
1 Tbsp. prepared horseradish
1 tsp. paprika
> *Add in and stir well. Simmer for about 1 hour until sauce starts to thicken.*

Gyros Platter

1 Tbsp. soybean oil
8 slices of Gyros meat (see page 244)
> *Grill Gyros meat until done. (Frying in a pan is also optional)*

2 7-inch flat Pita Bread
> *Brush lightly with soy bean oil. Warm, gently on a hot top or in the oven. Cut each Pita into 8 pieces. Arrange on one end of a serving platter and place cooked Gyros meat on top. On the other end arrange:*

2 slices of tomatoes
¼ red onion, sliced
6 Kalamata olives
3 peperoncinis
¼ cup Feta, crumbled.
> *In the middle of the platter, pour ½ cup of yogurt sauce. (see page 113)*

Sir Wellington

2 Tbsp. olive oil
2 Tbsp. soybean oil
> *Heat in a sauce pan.*

6 oz. tenderloin steak, cut into small pieces.
> *Add in and sauté 3-4 minutes.*

⅛ cup white wine
> *Add in.*

6 green onions, chopped
6 mushrooms, sliced
1 clove garlic, chopped
½ tsp. prepared horseradish sauce. (see page 113)
¾ cup Swiss cheese
Pinch of black pepper
> *Add in and sauté until mushrooms are soft.*
> *Place one 6" x 12" puff pastry dough on a working surface and add filling to the center. Fold filling in and with fork seal the pastry. Bake at 425° for 25-30 minutes.*

Loukanikon Gemisto

3 Greek-style sausage
> *Place in a baking dish and bake in 350° oven for about 6-7 minutes. Cut sausage lengthwise to form a pocket*

3 oz. Kefalograviera cheese
> *Stuff into the pockets of the sausage.*

12 slices bacon
> *Wrap the sausages with the bacon, using 4 strips for each sausage. Secure bacon with toothpicks.*

3 Tbsp. olive oil
> *Heat in a skillet. Add sausages to the skillet and sauté 6-7 minutes.*

⅛ cup white cooking wine
> *Add in.*

½ small red pepper, sliced
½ small onion sliced
4 mushrooms, sliced
1 tsp. black pepper
> *Add in and sauté 6-7 minutes.*

Lemon Peel Veal

3 Tbsp. olive oil
3 Tbsp. soybean oil
>*Heat in a skillet*

6 oz. veal, thinly sliced
1 egg
Flour
>*Dip in egg then in flour. Sauté for 2-3 minutes on one side. Turn over.*

⅛ cup white cooking wine
Juice of ½ lemon
½ small onion, sliced
½ small zucchini, sliced
1 Tbsp. capers
1 tsp. green peppercorns (in a can, packed in water)
4 sun-dried tomatoes, chopped
½ tomato, cubed
½ tsp. lemon peel, ground
>*Add in and saute 6-7 minutes.*

1 tsp. rosemary
1 tsp. thyme
1 tsp. black pepper
>*Add in, sauté 1-2 minutes.*

Horiatiko Pesto Lamb

3 Tbsp. olive oil
3 Tbsp. soybean oil
>*Heat in a skillet.*

3 4-oz. lamb chops
>*Add in and sauté 3-4 minutes on one side, then over.*

⅛ cup red cooking wine
Add in.
½ small red onion
½ small red pepper
1 tsp. black olives, sliced
½ tomato, cubed
½ cup spinach, chopped
>*Add in and sauté 6-7 minutes.*

½ cup Feta Pesto sauce (see page 115)
1 tsp. Dijon mustard
>*Add in and stir well for 2-3 minutes.*

Black Bean Steak

1 10-oz. N.Y steak

Charcoal or grill until about medium rare.

3 Tbsp. olive oil
3 Tbsp. soybean oil

Add the steak in (if charcoal or grill is not available, you can sauté the steak).

⅛ cup red cooking wine

Add in.

½ red onion, sliced
1 tomato, cubed
1 clove garlic, chopped

Add in and sauté for 4-5 minutes.

2 Tbsp. black beans (canned)
½ tsp cayenne pepper
½ tsp. paprika
½ tsp. chili powder
½ tsp. mustard powder

Add in and sauté 3-4 minutes.

Wild Steak

3 Tbsp. olive oil
3 Tbsp. soybean soil

Heat in a skillet.

1 10-oz. N.Y. steak

Cut in 5 pieces, add in and sauté 5-6 minutes.

⅛ cup red cooking wine

Add in.

4 pearl onions (canned)
6 wild onions (available in jars at specialty shops)
1 clove garlic

Add in and sauté 4-5 minutes.

6 plum tomatoes (canned)
1 cinnamon stick
2 bay leaves
Pinch of nutmeg
Pinch of cinnamon
6 whole cloves
1 tsp. oregano
1 tsp. black pepper
1 tsp. rosemary

Crush tomatoes in. Add rest of ingredients. Simmer 7-8 minutes.

Roman Bean Steak

3 Tbsp. olive oil
3 Tbsp. soybean oil
Heat in a skillet.
1 10-oz. N.Y. steak
Cut into 5 pieces and sauté 4-5 minutes.
⅛ cup white cooking wine
Juice of ½ lemon
Add in.
½ small onion, sliced
2 oz. ham, chopped
2 green onions, chopped
½ small romaine lettuce, chopped
Add in and sauté for 7-8 minutes.
1 tsp. black pepper
1 tsp. dill
1 tsp. thyme
2 Tbsp. caneli beans (or other white beans)
Add in and sauté 2-3 minutes.
¼ cup whipping cream
1 tsp. Dijon mustard
Add in and heat gently 1-2 minutes.
Yolk of 1 egg
Break in, stir well and remove from heat.

Village Steak

3 Tbsp. olive oil
3 Tbsp. soybean oil
Heat in a skillet.
1 10-oz. N.Y. steak, cut in 6 pieces
Sauté until lightly brown.
⅛ cup white cooking wine
Add in.
½ red bell pepper, sliced
5 mushrooms, sliced
1 small zucchini, sliced
1 clove garlic, chopped
Add in and sauté 6-7 minutes.
½ tsp. black pepper
½ tsp. basil
½ tsp. oregano
½ tsp. thyme
½ tsp. rosemary
Add in and sauté 3-4 minutes.

TRUE FREE SPIRIT IS UNTAMED

I wanted to wait until Thanksgiving so I could do the project, and after that, I made up my mind I was not going to stay here under these circumstances. I had nothing else to prove to anyone. The thousands who believed in my work proved as an example. The popularity of the creativity of my work had reached the stage of huge proportions. One could come into the restaurant every day for the next two years and not have the same meal. There were that many choices on the menu! One could come into the restaurant every day for the next six months and not have the same dessert! People liked that.

The restaurant's guests brought their friends and proudly showed them the amazing menu and took them on a tour around the seven dessert cases with their dazzling array of desserts so they could point out their favorites. Everyone was intrigued by the endless selections of coffees and teas. Guests read the history of the restaurant from the articles displayed on the walls. Everyone's imagination was captured by the tastes of the foods and the charisma of the restaurant from the very first time. I could see the pleasure in their eyes, especially when new guests were first introduced to me.

But now the concept of the restaurant was slowly being taken away by the new ownership of the hotel. My customers sensed the changes. They stood behind me with their support and said to me that "without you we will not come back here."

When my employees sensed I was not planning to stay under the present circumstances, they started to open up to me. My kitchen crew was nervous. They felt that without my presence in the restaurant they would be lost. Some of the kitchen employees had been with me from 8 to 12 years. I had taken them from washing dishes and trained them to become cooks and bakers. I was their security because I had taught them an art. Only now they were not sure if they could do it without me there.

Leslie was one of my long-time servers when she learned of my plans to leave. She said, "When I started working for you four years ago, I was afraid and intimidated by people. You have taught me how to stand up for myself." I felt good knowing that some people looked up to me.

Sean was another server who was not going to stay. He was upset with the new ownership and how they were ruining the business. "I was always afraid to grow older, but after being around you, now I can't wait be 50 years old," he told me one day.

"Fifty years old is a wonderful age to be because you know who you are and you have the ability to make decisions which are beneficial to your life," I told him.

Many other servers moved me with their support. Some of them said "I don't want to stay here. Nobody can give the character which you have given to this restaurant. We will follow you to your next restaurant."

Mark was a new server. He had trusted me with some of his difficulties and I tried to advise him about a few subjects. "I was so intimidated by you when I first met you, but now I look up to you. You have changed my attitude about life and my way of thinking about my problems," he told me.

People assured me to retain my free, untamed spirit. For people who have made money, their God did not realize the greed of the few causes suffering of the many and must realize that a spirit true to itself must remain untamed.

I had been used for the second time in such a short period. I had to move on with my life and leave the destruction behind. This time I had been used by the new owners of the hotel. They used me like a bridge to cross over their troubled waters and once they had done that, they were ready to burn the bridge.

This, of course, is typical of the corporate world. There is no compassion for human feelings. Once they have used you, they are ready to throw you away. My intuition warned me about the things to come.

I have always tried to search for the good in an experience and any lesson I could learn from it. I was not bitter because others were trying to use my ability to accomplish their own end. In fact, this reinforced my confidence! Now I could only learn a lesson on where to let my ability be exposed. I don't understand how people can get so lost in materialism to the extent they are blind to the fact that they are hurting innocent bystanders. How can their conscience permit them to step on others beliefs and ideals?

Sometimes there are people who do not allow anyone to step on them because their spirit is free and untamed!

story continues on page 239

Wisdom is the supreme part of happiness. Great words of prideful men are ever punished with great blows, and, in old age teach the chasted to be wise.
— Sophocles

For many unworthy men are rich, while good men are poor. But we will not barter with them, our worth for their wealth, since the one stands even unshaken, whereas riches pass now in to one man's hands, now in to another's.
— Solon

Seafood and
Seafood Pasta...

Clam Linguini

3 Tbsp. olive oil
3 Tbsp. soybean oil
> *Heat lightly in a sauce pan.*

½ cup baby clams
1 clove of garlic
> *Sauté on low heat for 4-5 minutes.*

¼ cup white cooking wine
¼ cup clam juice
> *Add in and cook for 3-4 minutes.*

½ tsp. oregano
½ tsp. parsley
½ tsp. thyme
½ tsp. basil
½ tsp rosemary
¼ tsp. black pepper
4-5 hot pepper flakes
> *Add in and cook for 4-5 minutes.*

¼ lb. of fresh linguine, slightly undercooked
> *Add in and cook until all juice is absorbed by the pasta.*

1 tsp. Romano cheese
1 tsp. Parmesan cheese
> *Add in and mix well.*

Red Clam Linguini

3 Tbsp. olive oil
3 Tbsp. soybean oil
> *Heat in a sauce pan.*

½ cup baby clams
1 clove garlic
> *Sauté on low heat 4-5 minutes.*

¼ cup white cooking wine
⅛ cup clam juice
1 cup whole tomatoes in juice, crushed
> *Add in and cook for 5-6 minutes.*

½ Tbsp. each of: oregano, thyme, basil, rosemary, parsley
¼ tsp. black pepper
4-5 hot pepper flakes
> *Add in and cook 4-5 minutes*

¼ lb. of fresh linguini, slightly undercooked
> *Add in and cook until all juice is absorbed by the pasta.*

1 tsp. Romano cheese
1 tsp. Parmesan cheese
> *Add in and mix well.*

White BBQ Grouper

8 oz. grouper, fillet
Flour
1 egg beaten
> *Dip fillet in egg and then in flour.*

3 Tbsp. olive oil
3 Tbsp. soybean oil
> *Heat in sauce pan. Brown fillet 2-3 minutes on each side.*

⅛ cup white cooking wine
> *Add in.*

1 small red onion, chopped
1 small red pepper, chopped
> *Add in and simmer 4-5 minutes.*

1 clove garlic, chopped
> *Add in and simmer 2-3 minutes.*

1 cup whipping cream
⅛ tsp dry mustard
⅛ tsp BBQ spice
⅛ tsp whole rosemary
⅛ tsp whole thyme
⅛ tsp black pepper, ginger
> *Add in and stir.*

Pinch of cayenne pepper
> *Simmer 2-3 minutes. 2 servings.*

Shrimp Broccoli Linguini

3 Tbsp. olive oil
3 Tbsp. soybean oil
> *Heat in a skillet.*

½ cup broccoli, chopped
1 cup bay shrimp
1 clove garlic
> *Add in and sauté for about 4-5 minutes.*

⅛ cup white cooking wine
1 tsp. black pepper
> *Add in and sauté 2-3 minutes*

¼ lb. linguini, cooked
¼ cup Mitzithra cheese, grated
> *Add in and stir well.*

Peppercorn Calamari

3 Tbsp. olive oil
3 Tbsp. soybean oil
> *Heat in a sauce pan.*

8 small squid, cleaned and cut into thin rings
> *Place in sauce pan and sauté for about 6-7 minutes.*

6 green onions, chopped. Discard the green part.
> *Add in and sauté until onions are soft, 4-5 minutes.*

1 Tbsp. white cooking wine
> *Add in and stir well.*

2 cups whole plump tomatoes in juice, crushed
> *Add in.*

5 red jamaican peppercorns
5 black jamaican peppercorns
2 bay leaves
6 whole cloves
Pinch of black pepper
¹⁄₁₆ Tbsp. red pepper flakes
¹⁄₁₆ Tbsp. basil
¹⁄₁₆ Tbsp. rosemary
> *Add in and simmer 10 more minutes.*

½ lb. cappellini pasta (fresh preferred)
> *Cook in boiling water for 3 minutes. Place pasta in a serving bowl and toss with half of the sauce. Pour remainder of the sauce on top. 2 servings.*

Coconut Fried Shrimp (see page 219)

Red Seafood Linguini

3 Tbsp. olive oil
3 Tbsp. soybean oil
1 cup clams, chopped
½ cup scallops, chopped
½ Tbsp. garlic in oil, chopped
> *Sauté for 5-6 minutes.*

1 Tbsp. white cooking wine
> *Add in.*

1 cup of whole tomatoes in juice, crushed
> *Add to the sauce pan.*

⅛ tsp. black pepper
⅛ tsp parsley
⅛ tsp basil
⅛ tsp oregano
⅛ tsp thyme
⅛ tsp whole rosemary
Pinch of red pepper flakes
> *Add in and simmer for 9-10 minutes.*

1 tsp. Romano cheese
1 tsp. Parmesan cheese
> *Add in and stir well.*

½ lb. Linguini (fresh preferred)
> *Cook in boiling water 3 minutes if fresh. (7-8 minutes if dry). Place pasta in a serving bowl and toss with half of the sauce. Pour remainder of the sauce on top. Makes 2 servings.*

Crab Agnolotti

3 Tbsp. olive oil
3 Tbsp. soybean oil
> *Heat in a sauce pan.*

6-7 medium mushrooms, sliced
> *Add in and sauté 3-4 minutes.*

¼ cup green peas
Add in and sauté 2 minutes more.
¼ cup snow crab meat
> *Add in and sauté 3-4 minutes.*

1 Tbsp. white cooking wine
Pinch of black pepper
> *Add in and sauté 2-3 minutes.*

1 cup heavy whipping cream
> *Add in and simmer 3-4 minutes.*

2 cups agnolotti
> *Cook in boiling water 6-7 minutes.*

1 Tbsp. Romano cheese
1 Tbsp. Parmesan cheese
> *Add in and toss well. Makes 2 servings.*

Dijon Snapper or Sea Bass and Nuts

1 8-oz. snapper fillet (sea bass may be substituted)
Flour
1 egg, beaten

> *Dip fillet in egg and then in flour.*

3 Tbsp. olive oil
3 Tbsp. soybean oil

> *Heat in a sauce pan. Brown snapper 3-4 minutes on each side.*

8 green onions, chopped

> *Add in and sauté 4-5 minutes.*

1½ cups whipping cream

> *Add in.*

1 Tbsp. each of: pecan pieces, chopped hazelnuts, sliced almonds

> *Add in.*

1 Tbsp. Dijon mustard

> *Add in. Remove snapper. Stir sauce for a few seconds. Pour sauce over fish. Makes 1 serving.*

Broccoli Sole

8 oz. fillet. Scrod may be substituted.
Flour
1 egg beaten

> *Dip fillet in egg and then in flour.*

3 Tbsp. olive oil
3 Tbsp. soybean oil

> *Heat in a sauce pan. Brown fish 3-4 minutes on both sides. Remove to serving platter.*

1 cup broccoli florets
6 green onions, chopped

> *Add in and sauté 5-6 minutes.*

1 clove garlic
⅛ cup snowpeas

> *Add in and sauté 2-3 minutes.*

⅛ cup sliced almonds
Pinch of black pepper

> *Add in and simmer 2-3 minutes.*

1 cup whipping cream

> *Add in and simmer 2-3 minutes.*

⅛ cup mild yellow Cheddar cheese, shredded

> *Add in. Stir sauce until cheese is melted and pour this sauce on top of fish. Makes 1 serving.*

Baked Cashew Seafood

3 Tbsp. olive oil
3 Tbsp. soybean oil
> *Heat in a sauce pan.*

½ cup celery, chopped
10 green onions, chopped
> *Add in and sauté 2-3 minutes.*

1 cup clams, chopped
½ cup baby shrimp
½ cup crabmeat
1 clove garlic, chopped
> *Add in and simmer 4-5 minutes.*

⅛ cup cashew nuts, chopped
Pinch of black pepper
⅛ tsp. whole rosemary
⅛ tsp. sweet basil
> *Add in and simmer 2 minutes.*

1 cup whipping cream
⅛ cup Romano cheese, grated
⅛ cup Parmesan cheese, grated
> *Add in and simmer for 2-3 minutes. Pour mixture in a small casserole.*

½ lb. Provolone cheese, shredded
¼ lb. Mozzarella cheese, shredded
> *Spread on top of casserole. Bake in a 425° oven about 25 minutes. Makes 2 servings.*

Capellini Tonato

3 Tbsp. olive oil
3 Tbsp. soybean oil
> *Heat in a heavy skillet.*

1 small red onion
> *Add in and cook until soft.*

4 oz. fresh tuna, cut into small pieces
2 small tomatoes, peeled and chopped
> *Add in and sauté 5-6 minutes.*

1 Tbsp. black olives, sliced
1 clove garlic, chopped
⅛ cup white cooking wine
> *Add in and simmer on low heat 2-3 minutes.*

1 tsp. sweet basil
1 tsp. rosemary
1 tsp. parsley
> *Add in and simmer 3 minutes.*

1 Tbsp. capers
> *Add in. Remove from heat. Stir well and pour sauce over ¼ lb. cooked capellini (angel hair pasta).*

Corinthian Sea Bass

3 Tbsp. olive oil
3 Tbsp. soybean oil
> *Heat in a sauce pan.*

Flour
1 egg, beaten lightly
8 oz. sea bass fillet
> *Dip the sea bass in egg and flour and place in the pan. Sauté for about 4-5 minutes. Turn the sea bass to the other side.*

½ small onion, chopped
2 cloves of garlic, chopped
1 Tbsp. black olives, sliced
> *Add to the pan as soon as you turn the sea bass.*

⅛ cup white cooking wine
> *Add in.*

6 oz. plum tomatoes, crushed.
> *Add to the pan.*

½ tsp. parsley
⅛ tsp black pepper
⅛ tsp basil
⅛ tsp oregano
⅛ tsp thyme
⅛ tsp rosemary
> *Add in and simmer 8-10 minutes.*

Sun Dried Sea Bass

3 Tbsp. olive oil
3 Tbsp. soybean oil
> *Heat in a sauce pan.*

8 oz. sea bass
Flour
1 egg, beaten
> *Dip sea bass in egg and then in flour and place in sauce pan.*
> *Sauté 4-5 minutes on each side.*

1 Tbsp. white wine
5 sun dried tomatoes
1 tsp. capers
> *Add in.*

1 clove garlic
1 small tomato, chopped
Pinch of black pepper
½ tsp. white rosemary
½ tsp. basil
> *Add in and simmer 5-6 minutes.*

Goat Shrimp

8 large shrimp
> *Cleaned, washed, deveined, butterflied.*

¼ cup sun dried tomatoes, chopped thinly
½ cup Feta cheese
> *Mix well and stuff shrimp with this mixture.*

32 strips of bacon
> *Wrap shrimp making sure they are wrapped well.*

½ cup olive oil
½ cup soybean oil
> *Heat in a heavy skillet. Sauté shrimp well on both sides until bacon is cooked well. About 10 minutes.*

Juice of ½ lemon
Pinch of black pepper
Pinch of sweet basil
Pinch of Greek oregano
Pinch of whole thyme
1 clove of garlic, chopped
> *Add in. Sauté 5 minutes longer.*

Lobster Tortellini

3 Tbsp. olive oil
3 Tbsp. vegetable oil
> *Heat in a sauce pan.*

4 green onions, chopped
½ clove garlic
6 water chestnuts
> *Add in and sauté 2-3 minutes.*

1 Tbsp. almonds, sliced
1 cup broccoli flowerettes
½ cup peas
¼ cup lobster meat
¼ cup scallops
1 Tbsp. Sauterne cooking wine
> *Add in and cook 6-7 minutes.*

½ cup whipping cream
> *Add in and cook 1-2 minutes.*

2 cups tortellini, cooked
½ cup Romano cheese
½ cup Parmesan cheese
> *Add in and stir well.*

Basmati Seafood

3 Tbsp. olive oil
3 Tbsp. soybean oil
>*Heat.*

½ onion, thinly sliced
1 clove garlic, chopped
2 artichoke hearts, sliced
6 green onions, chopped
6 mushrooms, sliced
4 asparagus, cut in pieces
½ red pepper, sliced
1 Tbsp. capers
>*Add in and sauté 3-4 minutes.*

½ cup clams
1 cup small shrimp
½ cup scallops
4 shrimp, cut in pieces
¼ cup crabmeat
⅛ cup lobster meat
2 cups clam juice
1 cup white cooking wine
1 tsp. each of: black pepper, rosemary, basil, thyme, parsley
2 plum tomatoes, crushed
½ cup tomato juice
1 cup basmati rice
>*Add all in and simmer 10 minutes or until rice is done. Add a little water if too dry.*

½ cup Feta cheese, crumbled
¼ cup Romano cheese
¼ cup Parmesan cheese
Add in and stir gently until cheese melts.

There are over 20,000 species of fish. Fish has been eaten by mankind since the beginning of time. It satisfies the need for protein.

Preserving fish started as far back as when fire was used. The Babylonians' diet consisted of dried fish. The ancient Greeks ate a lot of tuna marinated in oil.

Today, Japan and Africa consume the most preserved fish in the world.

Linguini Pesce

3 Tbsp. olive oil
3 Tbsp. soybean oil
>*Heat in a saucepan*

5 mushrooms, sliced
3 asparagus spears, cut in pieces
1 cup of Bay shrimp
½ cup of crabmeat
1 clove of garlic, chopped
>*Add in and sauté for about 5-6 minutes.*

⅛ cup white cooking wine
1 tsp. black pepper
½ tsp. basil
½ tsp. rosemary
>*Add in and sauté 3-4 minutes.*

½ cup whipping cream
>*Add in. Heat gently for 1-2 minutes.*

¼ lb. cooked linguini
¼ cup grated Romano
¼ cup grated Parmesan
>*Add in, mix well and serve.*

Coconut Fried Shrimp

8 large shrimp (21-25 size)
>*Peel but leave the tail intact. Butterfly the shrimp, by slicing the back.*

Flour
>*Wash the shrimp and roll them in the flour.*

3 eggs, beaten
>*Roll the floured shrimp in the egg.*

Shredded coconut
>*Roll the shrimp in the coconut, making sure they are covered well with coconut.*

Canola oil
>*Deep fry the shrimp at 350° about 3-4 minutes until coconut is golden brown. Shrimp will cool quickly. Serve with coconut fry bananas. Cut the bananas in large pieces and use the same above method to coat and fry them.*

Feta Shrimp

3 Tbsp. olive oil
3 Tbsp. soybean oil
Heat in a sauce pan.

8 large shrimp, peeled
Flour
Dip the shrimp in flour and place them in the sauté pan. Sauté 1-2 minutes.

Juice of ½ lemon
Squeeze in.

½ small onion, sliced
2 green onions, chopped
1 clove garlic, chopped
Add in and sauté 5-6 minutes until onions are soft.

⅛ cup white cooking wine
Add in.

6 plum canned tomatoes
Crush them in a bowl and add in.

Pinch of each: black pepper, parsley, basil, thyme, oregano
Add in and simmer 3-4 minutes.

⅛ cup Romano cheese
⅛ cup Parmesan cheese
Add in and stir well and place the mixture in a baking dish.

¼ lb. Feta cheese, crumbled
Place on top of the mixture.

Rosemary
Sprinkle a little on top of the Feta cheese. Bake in a 375˚ oven for 15 minutes.

Tiger Tail (see page 227)

Shrimp Athena

8 large shrimp (21-25 size), peeled
3 Tbsp. olive oil
3 Tbsp. soybean oil
> *Heat in a skillet.*

2 eggs, beaten
> *Dip shrimp in the egg.*

Flour
> *Roll shrimp in the flour. Place them in the skillet and sauté for 2-3 minutes.*

Juice of ½ lemon
> *Add in.*

½ small onion, sliced
3 green onions, chopped
1 clove garlic, chopped
> *Add in and sauté for 5-6 minutes until onions are soft.*

⅛ cup white wine
> *Add in.*

6 plum tomatoes (canned)
> *Crush tomatoes in a bowl and add them in.*

Pinch of each: black pepper, parsley, basil, oregano, thyme, rosemary
> *Add in and simmer for 5-6 minutes.*

1 tsp. Romano cheese
1 tsp. Parmesan cheese
> *Add in and stir well.*

Back when simplicity was a way of life, among the many things that made our lives less complicated were small eateries. They were on almost every corner. Memories are preserved in the minds of people who were fortunate enough to frequent such places because they were rewarded with wholesome foods.

Today we search the streets to find such treasures and when we do they seem like a hidden oasis among a sea of chain restaurants.

The simple way to enjoy fresh homemade foods has become complicated by the commercialism of dining. Tempting aromas of cooked foods have been swallowed up by plastic foods. So much emphasis is been put in the ambiance that the food takes a back seat.

Our minds are hungry for real food and our palates cannot be abused any longer. For some of us food is not a remedy for hunger but a pleasant way of life. What a pity that our grandchildren will miss those magical aromas of food! Some day we will tell them that there were such places where we understood that simple is better!

Calamari Provencale

8 small calamari tubes
2 eggs, beaten
Flour

> *Dip the calamari in the egg and then in the flour.*

½ cup olive oil
½ cup soybean oil

> *Heat in a skillet until very hot. Add the calamari and fry until golden brown, 4-5 minutes.*

Juice of ½ lemon

> *Add in and remove from heat.*

1 Tbsp. olive oil
1 Tbsp. soybean oil

> *In another skillet heat gently.*

5 mushrooms, sliced
1 tomato, cubed
3 green onions, chopped
1 clove garlic, chopped

> *Add in and sauté until mushrooms are soft.*

⅛ cup white cooking wine

> *Add in..*

Pinch of each: black pepper, basil, oregano, thyme, rosemary

> *Add in. Add the calamari to the vegetables and sauté 3-4 minutes longer.*

1 tsp. Romano cheese
1 tsp. Parmesan cheese

> *Add in and stir well.*

Artichoke Sole

1 8-oz. fillet of sole
1 egg, beaten
Flour

> *Dip fillet in egg and then in flour.*

3 Tbsp. olive oil
3 Tbsp. soybean oil

> *Heat in a skillet and sauté the sole fillet 2-3 minutes on each side. Place sole on a serving platter.*

5 mushrooms, sliced thinly
4 artichoke hearts, sliced
3 green onions, chopped

> *Add to the skillet and sauté until mushrooms are soft, 4-5 minutes.*

⅛ cup white cooking wine
½ tsp. black pepper

> *Add in.*

⅛ cup whipping cream

> *Add in and heat 1-2 minutes.*

1 egg yolk

> *Break yolk in the skillet and stir well. Remove from heat immediately. Pour sauce over the sole fillet.*

Scallops Plaki

12 lb. scallops
3 Tbsp. olive oil
3 Tbsp. soybean oil

Heat oil in a sauce pan and add scallops. Sauté 2-3 minutes.

½ small onion, sliced
1 small carrot, sliced
1 tomato, cubed
1 clove garlic, chopped
1 Tbsp. raisins
1 Tbsp. pine nuts

Add in and sauté 4-5 minutes.

⅛ cup white cooking wine
½ tsp. black pepper
½ tsp. basil
½ tsp. parsley
½ tsp. rosemary
1 cup clam juice

Add in and sauté 3-4 minutes.

⅛ lb. capellini pasta, slightly undercooked

Add in and simmer until the pasta is cooked and all the liquid is absorbed.

Pinch of black pepper
Pinch of parsley
Pinch of basil
Pinch of oregano
Pinch of thyme
Pinch of rosemary
Add in and simmer for 5-6 minutes.

Glyfada Dover Sole (see page 228)

Bloody Mary Seashells

4 jumbo pasta shells, cooked
> *Place in a small baking dish.*

⅛ cup lobster meat
¼ cup crabmeat
1 egg
½ cup Ricotta cheese
½ cup Mozzarella cheese, shredded
¼ cup Provolone cheese, shredded
> *Mix well in a bowl and stuff the pasta with this filling. Place excess filling on top of shells.*

3 Tbsp. olive oil
3 Tbsp. soybean oil
> *Heat in a sauce pan.*

1 Tbsp. celery, chopped
½ small red pepper, sliced
1 clove garlic, chopped
½ small tomato, cubed
> *Add to the sauce pan and sauté 3-4 minutes.*

1 Tbsp. white cooking wine
2 Tbsp. Vodka
⅛ cup clam juice
1 tsp.l black pepper
1 tsp. basil
1 tsp. rosemary
> *Add in and simmer 3-4 minutes. Pour on top of lobster filling and bake at 375° for about 20-25 minutes.*

Out of the talented great chefs of ancient Greece, there were only a few who were famous in the whole country. Those few specialized in cooked seafood. One of them was Nereus from the Island of Chios who created a wonderful mixed fish soup and a famous broth of conger eels. Another one was Alkis from the Island of Rhodes who created masterpieces of roasted fish. Then was Anexagoras, a culinary poet who followed Alexander and his army. He cooked famous pots of fish.

Another poet, philosopher and cook was Archestratus, who created many recipes from seafood. One of them was fish wrapped in fig leaves and cooked on fire. Archestratus was the first to believe in fish being barely cooked. Some new cooking styles today have adopted this way of cooking fish. Archestratus was very thin according to the standards back then. He died from complications of stomach ulcer.

Green Lobster Manicotti

2 sheets of green lasagne (see pages 45-46) approximately 20 in. x 12 in.

Lay on a working surface.

⅛ cup lobster meat
¼ cup crabmeat
1 egg
½ cup Ricotta cheese
½ cup Mozzarella cheese, shredded
¼ cup Provolone cheese, shredded

Mix well in a bowl. Divide the mixture in 2 parts. Place each part on the end of each pasta sheet and roll. Place manicotti in a small baking dish.

3 Tbsp. olive oil
3 Tbsp. soybean oil

Heat in a saucepan.

1 Tbsp. celery, chopped
½ small carrot, sliced
½ small red pepper, sliced
1 clove garlic, chopped
1 tsp. pine nuts
½ tomato, cubed

Add to the sauce pan and sauté 3-4 minutes.

1 Tbsp. white cooking wine
2 Tbsp. vodka
⅛ cup clam juice
1 tsp. black pepper
1 tsp. basil
1 tsp. rosemary

Add in and simmer 3-4 minutes. Pour on top of manicotti. Bake at 375° for 20-25 minutes.

What is the meaning of food? To many it is a daily luxury celebrating the glorious tastes of culinary gifts. To unfortuate others it is an endless struggle to provide nourishment for their bodies.

Many have it in abundance.
Others need it to survive.

For some it is an act of indulgence with guilty calories and, sadly, unappreciated pleasure. To unfortunate others hunger has taken away all other pleasures of life and has become an act of survival.

To some of us where food is an art and success is measured by how to create pleasant tastes for a perfect meal, food is more meaningful. It is a source of life, not only to some of us, but to every human on earth who cannot be denied the simple pleasure that many of us take for granted.

Marine Scallops

12 oz. scallops

Place in a small baking dish.

1 clove garlic, chopped
1tsp. black pepper
1 Tbsp. butter
1 tsp. parsley
1 tsp. oregano
1 tsp. thyme
2 Tbsp. white cooking wine

Place on top of scallops. Bake in a 375˚ oven for about 15 minutes.

2 Tbsp. butter

Heat gently in a sauce pan.

½ cup toasted bread crumbs
1 tsp. parsley

Add in and heat for 2-3 minutes. Remove scallops from oven, and pour liquid into the sauce pan with the heated bread crumbs. Mix well and then pour the bread crumb mixture on top of the scallops. Bake at 375˚ about 15 minutes until the bread crumbs are lightly browned.

Baked Clam Linguini

2 cups of red clam sauce (see page 210)
¼ lb. linguini, cooked
1 Tbsp. capers
1 Tbsp. Romano cheese, grated
1 Tbsp. Parmesan cheese, grated

Place all ingredients in a bowl and mix well. Place in a baking dish and bake at 375˚ about 10 minutes.

Tuna Souvlaki

8 oz. tuna, cut into 4 pieces
½ red pepper, cut in half
4 mushroom caps
4 slices of zucchini

Thread tuna and vegetables on to a skewer. Grill, basting with the following:

3 Tbsp. olive oil
3 Tbsp. soybean oil
1 Tbsp. red wine vinegar
Juice of ½ lemon
1 tsp. black pepper
1 tsp. basil
1 tsp. rosemary

Brochette of Scallops

18 large scallops
> *Thread scallops on to 3 wooden skewers, 6 on each skewer.*

Flour
2 eggs, beaten
Bread crumbs
> *Dip skewers in flour, then in the egg and then in bread crumbs.*

3 Tbsp. olive oil
3 Tbsp. soybean oil
> *In a sauce pan sauté the skewers until browned, about 7-8 minutes. Place on a serving platter.*

3 Tbsp. butter
2 green onions, chopped
1 clove garlic, chopped
> *Heat gently in a sauce pan for about 2-3 minutes.*

¼ cup white cooking wine
¼ cup whipping cream
1 tsp. black pepper
> *Add in to the sauce pan and heat for about 5-6 minutes until sauce thickens. Pour sauce over the scallops.*

Tiger Tail

2 Lobster tails, approximately 6 oz. each
> *Cut the lobster shell on top, and pull the lobster meat away from the shell without separating it from the shell. The meat should be attached to the shells.*

1 clove garlic, chopped
¼ cup chicken livers
½ cup soy sauce
1 tsp. ginger
½ cup white cooking wine
> *Mix in a bowl. Place lobster tails in the bowl with the lobster side in the sauce. Marinate for 10-15 minutes. Place lobster on a working surface. Slice lobster meat to become butterflied. Place ½ of the chicken livers in the middle of the lobster meat.*

16 strips of bacon
> *Wrap bacon around the lobster meat being certain to enclose the livers. Secure bacon with tooth picks. Place both tails, standing up in a baking dish with a little water. Bake at 375° for about 25-30 minutes, until bacon is cooked.*

Glyfada Dover Sole

1 whole Dover sole
2 Tbsp. olive oil
2 Tbsp. soybean oil

Heat in a large skillet. Sauté the sole until done. Approximately 7-8 minutes on each side.
Remove sole from the skillet. With a small knife remove the bones from the ends of the fish.
This can be done by forcing the bones out with the knife. After removing the head, pull the middle bone of the fish sideways. It should come out easily enough. (If not, the fish was not cooked enough)
Slice the top fillet of the fish lengthwise and pull the two slices to the side.

3 Tbsp. olive oil
3 Tbsp. soybean oil

Heat in a saucepan.

2 green onions, chopped
⅛ cup bay shrimp
⅛ cup crab meat

Add in and sauté 4-5 minutes.

Juice of ½ lemon
1 tsp. black pepper
1 tsp. Parsley

Add in and sauté 2-3 minutes. Place bottom part of the sole in a small baking dish. Pour the filling in the middle of the fish, then cover with the top two slices. Bake in a 375° oven for about 10 minutes. Sprinkle top with 2 Tbsp. sliced almonds.

Aegean Sea Bass

1 whole Sea Bass, approx 2 lb. Cleaned and deboned.

Cut the fish from the bottom to create a pocket.

12 Kalamata olives, pits removed
½ cup of Feta cheese, crumbled

Stuff the pocket of the fish. Place fish in a baking dish.

2 Tbsp. olive oil
4 Tbsp. water

Add to the baking dish.

8 pear tomatoes (canned)

Crushed around the fish. Add a little of the tomato juice.

1 clove garlic, chopped
1/2 small onion, sliced

Arrange around the fish.

1 tsp. black pepper
1 tsp. basil
1 tsp. rosemary

Sprinkle in the baking dish. Bake at 375° for about 30-35 minutes, basting fish occasionally with the juice from the baking dish.

Smelts Milanese

12-14 smelts
Flour
> *Roll the smelts in flour.*

4 Tbsp. olive oil
4 Tbsp. soybean oil
> *In a sauce pan fry the smelts for about 6-7 minutes.*

½ lemon
> *Squeeze the juice on the fish. Place the smelts in a baking dish.*

2 cups Marinara sauce (see page 115)
> *Pour on top of smelts.*

2 oz. mozzarella, shredded
> *Sprinkle on top. Bake at 375° for about 15-20 minutes.*

Shrimp Basil Fettuccine

8 large shrimp (21-25 size)
> *Peel and wash.*

Flour
> *Dip shrimp in flour.*

3 Tbsp. olive oil
3 Tbsp. soybean oil
> *Sauté shrimp for about 7-8 minutes.*

Juice of ½ lemon
1 Tbsp. white cooking wine
½ tomato, chopped
> *Add in and sauté 4-5 minutes.*

½ cup Feta Pesto sauce (see page 115)
> *Add in and stir until warm.*

¼ lb. fettuccine, cooked
1 tsp. Romano cheese
1 tsp. Parmesan cheese
> *Add in and stir well.*

FOR SHRIMP BASIL AGNOLOTTI:
> *Substitute the fettucine with 12 cooked agnolotti pasta (half moon egg pasta stuffed with spinach filling)*

Seafood Rotini

3 Tbsp. olive oil
3 Tbsp. soybean oil
> *Heat in a sauce pan.*

6 large shrimp, peeled and washed
8 large scallops
> *Add in and sauté 5-6 minutes.*

½ small red pepper, sliced
4 mushrooms, sliced
½ cup broccoli, chopped thickly
6 Chinese pea pods
1 clove garlic, chopped
> *Add in and sauté 7-8 minutes longer.*

⅛ cup white cooking wine
1 tsp. black pepper
> *Add in.*

¼ lb. rotini pasta, cooked
> *Add in.*

¼ cup mytzithra cheese, grated
> *Add in and stir well.*

Garlic Shrimp On The Shell

3 Tbsp. olive oil
3 Tbsp. soybean oil
> *Heat in a sauce pan.*

18-20 small shrimp (35-40 size)
> *Place in the sauce pan and sauté for 7-8 minutes.*

Juice of 1/2 lemon
1 clove garlic, chopped
1 Tbsp. white cooking wine
> *Add in and sauté 3-4 minutes longer.*

4 Tbsp. Italian dressing (see page 112)
> *Add in and sauté 2-3 minutes. Remove shrimp.*

¼ lb linguini, cooked
1 tsp. Romano cheese, grated
1 tsp. Parmesan cheese, grated
> *Add to the sauce pan and heat for 2-3 minutes Place pasta on a serving platter and arrange shrimp on top.*

Scallops Krassata

3 Tbsp. olive oil
3 Tbsp. soybean oil
> *Heat in a sauce pan.*

12 scallops
> *Add in and sauté for 4-5 minutes.*

4 mushrooms, sliced
3 artichoke hearts, sliced
1 tsp. capers
1 clove garlic, chopped
2 green onions, chopped
1 small roasted red pepper, sliced
> *Add in and simmer 7-8 minutes.*

⅛ cup white cooking wine
1 tsp. black pepper
½ tsp. basil
½ tsp. parsley
½ tsp. rosemary
> *Add in and simmer 4-5 minutes.*

Salmon Under Green

1 8-oz. salmon fillet
> *Grill on both sides until done. Place on a serving platter.*

3 Tbsp. olive oil
3 Tbsp. soybean oil
> *Heat in a saucepan.*

3 green onions, chopped
½ green pepper, sliced
3 asparagus spears, cut in pieces
½ cup chopped spinach
> *Add in and sauté 4-5 minutes.*

Juice of ½ lemon
1 Tbsp. white cooking wine
> *Add in.*

1 tsp. black pepper
1 tsp. dill
½ cup whipping cream
> *Add in and simmer 1-2 minutes.*

1 egg yolk
> *Break in, stir well and remove from heat. Pour sauce over salmon.*

Ahi Tuna or Swordfish Pomodori

1 8-oz. Ahi tuna or swordfish fillet
> *Grill until fish is done. Place on a serving platter.*

5 sun-dried tomatoes
> *Grind in a food processor.*

3 Tbsp. feta cheese
> *Add in and mix well.*

3 Tbsp. Italian dressing (see page 112)
> *Add in and mix well. Pour sauce over fish.*

Southern Salmon

1 8-oz. salmon fillet
> *Grill until done and both sides. Place on a serving platter.*

3 Tbsp. olive oil
3 Tbsp. soybean oil
> *Heat in a saucepan.*

¼ small red onion, sliced
1 tsp. capers
1 tsp. black olives, sliced
½ tomato, chopped
> *Add in and sauté 4-5 minutes.*

1 Tbsp. white cooking wine
4 sun-dried tomatoes (grind in a food processor)
1 Tbsp. Feta cheese
¼ cup Feta Pesto sauce (see page 115)
½ tsp. basil
½ tsp. rosemary
½ tsp. black pepper
> *Add in and simmer 3-5 minutes over gentle heat. Pour sauce over salmon.*

In the older days salmon was a common catch in many parts of Europe. Now it is a rarity to find salmon in many parts of Europe, especially in the Loire and the rivers of southern England. There is salmon fishing in Ireland, Scotland and Norway, but the pollution of the rivers made salmon catching very difficult. The Atlantic salmon is also slowly disappearing because of overfishing. The Pacific salmon is still plenty, but its quality is inferior to others. The Canadian salmon is one of the best with its true salmon pink color, and besides the lakes of Canada and the rivers of the Atlantic it is also found in the springs of California and swims up to Alaska.

Salmon has the reputation of a wanderer because it travels constantly. Salmon contains vitamins A and D and is high in protein and phosphorus.

Spinach Pesto Calamari

2 large calamari tubes (about 6″ long)
½ cup Feta Pesto sauce (see page 115)
½ cup spinach, chopped
¼ cup rice, cooked

>*Mix well. Stuff the calamari.*

1 egg, beaten
Flour

>*Dip the calamari in egg. Then roll in flour.*

3 Tbsp. olive oil
3 Tbsp. soybean oil

>*Heat in a skillet. Add calamari and sauté on both sides until lightly brown, about 8-10 minutes.*

Juice of ½ lemon

>*Squeeze over calamari.*

½ small onion, sliced
½ tomato, chopped
1 Tbsp. capers

>*Add in and sauté 5-6 minutes.*

⅛ cup white cooking wine
1 tsp. black pepper
½ cup Feta Pesto sauce (see page 115)

>*Add in and simmer 2-3 minutes.*

Clams in Zucchini

1 zucchini

>*Cut off both ends and discard. Boil in water for about 4-5 minutes. Cut in half lengthwise, scoop out the middle to form 4 zucchini shells. Place them on a serving platter.*

4 slices Canadian bacon

>*Lay them on top of the zucchini shells.*

2 Tbsp. olive oil
2 Tbsp. soybean oil

>*Heat in a skillet.*

3 green onions, chopped
1 small zucchini, chopped
1 cup baby clams

>*Add in and sauté 5-6 minutes.*

⅛ cup white cooking wine
1 tsp. black pepper
1 tsp. basil
1 tsp. rosemary
½ cup Mytzithra cheese, grated

>*Add in and simmer 2-3 minutes. Pour on top of Canadian bacon. Bake in 375° oven 10-12 minutes.*

FOR EGGPLANT MYTZITHRA:
> *Use the preceeding recipe only substitute the zucchini for eggplant.*

Scalloped Sole

2 fillets of sole (about 5 oz. each)
> *Lay one fillet in a small baking dish.*

3 Tbsp. olive oil
3 Tbsp. soybean oil
> *Heat in a skillet.*

6 large scallops
¼ small onion, sliced
¼ cup spinach, chopped
1 clove garlic
> *Add in and sauté 5-6 minutes.*

1 tsp. Parmesan
1 tsp. black pepper
Juice of ¼ lemon
> *Add in and sauté 1-2 minutes. Place filling on top of the sole. Cover filling with the second fillet of sole.*

½ cup clam juice
½ cup white cooking wine
> *Pour in the baking dish. Bake in a 375° oven for about 20-25 minutes. Remove from oven. Pour juice from baking dish into a saucepan. Add 2 Tbsp. butter and heat until melted. Add 1 egg yolk and stir well. Remove from heat and pour over stuffed sole.*

Scallops Fettuccine

3 Tbsp. olive oil
3 Tbsp. soybean oil
> *Heat in a skillet.*

½ cup baby clams
½ cup scallops
1 clove garlic
> *Add in and sauté 4-5 minutes.*

⅛ cup white cooking wine
1 tsp. black pepper
1 tsp. parsley
1 tsp. basil
1 tsp. oregano
1 tsp. thyme
1 tsp. rosemary
> *Add in and sauté 2-3 minutes*

½ cup clam juice
¼ lb. fettuccine, cooked
> *Add in and sauté 2-3 minutes.*

Sole in Fillo

2 fillets of sole, approximate 5 oz. each
3 Tbsp. soybean oil
3 Tbsp. olive oil

Heat oil in a skillet and sauté sole for about 2-3 minutes. Remove sole.

4 fillo dough sheets

Lay one on top of the other after brushing them with olive oil. Place one piece of the sole in the middle of fillo. In the same skillet add:

¼ cup spinach, chopped
3 green onions

Sauté for 4-5 minutes.

1 Tbsp. white cooking wine
2 Tbsp. Feta cheese
12 white grapes
½ mango, sliced
1 tsp. black pepper
1 tsp. parsley

Add in and heat for 1-2 minutes. Place filling (discard any liquid) on top of sole. Cover with the other piece of sole. Fold filo to enclose the stuffed sole in. Place in a baking dish. Bake at 375° for 20-25 minutes.

Grapeleaf Seabass

1 8-oz. seabass

Grill on both sides until done. Place on a serving platter.

½ cup grapeleaf pesto (see page 70)
¼ cup Italian dressing (see page 112)

Mix well together and pour on top of seabass.

Shrimp Asparagus in Pastry

1/2 cup asparagus puff filling (see page 73)
1/2 cup bay shrimp

Mix together.

3 puff pastry squares (5″ x 5″)

Place on a working surface. Divide filling into 3 parts. Place in the middle of each pastry. Wet the edges of the dough, fold dough over and seal with a fork. Bake in a 450° oven for 15-20 minutes.

Spinach Shrimp Fettuccine

8 large shrimp (21-25 size), peeled
Flour

Dip the shimp in the flour.

3 Tbsp. olive oil
3 Tbsp. soybean oil

Heat in a saucepan. Add the shrimp and sauté 3-4 minutes.

Juice of ½ lemon
1 Tbsp. white cooking wine
½ cup spinach, chopped
½ tomato, chopped

Add in and sauté 3-4 minutes.

½ cup Feta Pesto sauce (see page 115)
¼ lb fettuccine, cooked
1 Tbsp. Romano cheese, grated
1 Tbsp. Parmesan cheese, grated
1 tsp. black pepper

Add in and simmer 2-3 minutes.

Shrimp on Fillo

1 fillo crust (see page 221)

Place in a baking dish.

2 Tbsp. cream cheese
2 Tbsp. Feta cheese

Place in the midele of the fillo and bake in 350° oven 10-12 minutes.

3 Tbsp. olive oil
3 Tbsp. soybean oil

Heat in a skillet.

8 large shrimp (21-25 size), peeled
Flour

Dip shrimp in flour then add to skillet and sauté 3-4 minutes.

3 green onions, chopped
¼ small onion, sliced
1 clove garlic

Add in and sauté 4-5 minutes.

Juice of ½ lemon
2 Tbsp. white cooking wine

Add in.

1 cup Marinara sauce (see page 115)
1 tsp. Romano cheese
1 tsp. Parmesan cheese

Add in and simmer 3-4 minutes. Remove fillo from oven and pour the shrimp filling in the middle of it.

Shrimp Marinara

8 large shrimp (21-25 size), peeled
Flour

Roll shrimp in flour.

3 Tbsp. olive oil
3 Tbsp. soybean oil

Heat in a skillet and add shrimp. Sauté for 5-6 minutes.

Juice of ½ lemon
1 Tbsp. white cooking wine
1½ cups Marinara sauce (see page 115)
1 Tbsp. Romano cheese, grated
1 Tbsp. Parmesan cheese, grated

Add in and simmer 2-3 minutes.

Calamari Ouzeri

½ cup olive oil
½ cup soybean oil

Heat in skillet.

8 small calamari tubes   (breaded in buttermilk pancake mix (see page 66), and then dipped in flour

Sauté in a skillet until calamari is golden brown.

⅛ cup white cooking wine
2 Tbsp. ouzo

Add in.

½ small onion, sliced
½ red pepper, sliced
½ green pepper, sliced
1 clove garlic, chopped
1 small tomato, cut into small pieces
4 peperoncini peppers, cut into pieces
1 Tbsp. capers

Add in and sauté 7-8 minutes.

1 tsp. black pepper
1 tsp. oregano
½ cup Feta cheese

Add in and sauté 2-3 minutes longer.

I was sitting with my daughter Lisa one day as I was finishing this book in January, 1997, We were talking about the book when she told me she was hungry. I prepared this dinner.

Shrimp Ravioli

3 Tbsp. olive oil
3 Tbsp. soybean oil
8 large shrimp (21-25 size) peeled and dipped in flour
½ small onion, sliced
Sauté in a skillet for 5-6 minutes.
1 clove garlic, chopped
Juice of ½ lemon
Add in and sauté 3-4 minutes longer.
6 plum tomatoes (canned), crushed
1 Tbsp. white cooking wine
1 tsp. black pepper
1 tsp. parsley
1 tsp. basil
1 tsp. rosemary
1 tsp. oregano
1 tsp. thyme
Add in and simmer 4-5 minutes.
¼ lb. ravioli, cooked (prefer spinach pasta with cheese filling)
Add in and simmer 1-2 minutes.
2 Tbsp. Romano cheese, grated
2 Tbsp. Parmesan cheese, grated
Add in and stir gently. Remove from heat after 1-2 minutes.

Cooking is a ritual act for chefs who create new tastes of foods. It is also a ceremony to chefs who follow a long tradition to recreate dishes according to a certain criteria of their customs. In any of the above cases the dish should not be prepared according to the guests' specifications. It would be ridiculous to ask an Italian chef to microwave some macaroni and cheese or to ask a Chinese chef to prepare the duck rare.

Cooking is like any other art. It is left to the imagination and the custom of the chef, and it is entirely his or her business to prepare the dish. Their imagination and tradition will never fail to satisfy the guest's taste and broaden his or her knowledge to the taste of the dish.

THE CHOICE BETWEEN
MATERIALISM AND IDEALISM

On the night before Thanksgiving, 1996, I felt a cloud of sadness in my senses. I tried to sleep, but every few minutes I woke up thinking I had to go back to the restaurant and finish the cooking of turkeys, gravy, and mashed potatoes. A couple of times I caught myself trying to get dressed, only to realize it was just a dream.

I walked around the house trying to convince myself I was tired and needed to go back to sleep, but every time I tried that I saw hundreds of turkeys roasting in the big rotating oven, hundreds of volunteers helping to prepare meals for the needy, and then there were the faces of those who were waiting for meals. Those faces passed by the hundreds through my mind: old, sick, poor and the abused; the sadness on their faces was so vivid that it seemed real and was disturbing. Some of those faces were familiar, others I had never seen before.

My mind was running out of control and I knew then that my happiness and harmony was in jeopardy. I got out of bed and played some videos from past Thanksgivings. I watched the years pass and the glorious times of giving. In my mind I relived the difficult memories of how we put this project together. In every one of the past ten years the project came through. I had given my heart and soul, and most of the time the project had drained me financially. Tonight, none of this mattered at all. On my mind was the fact that I had let thousands of people down. The volunteers who participated in this project would not have a chance to experience that joy this year. The hungry would go without food on a day we celebrate by giving thanks for the food we eat; and I had let myself down as well.

Tears ran from my eyes. My vision for a better world, free from hunger, hate, abuse and discrimination was a blurred picture. I felt I was being pushed over the edge by the materialistic world, the ones who thought they could step on anyone with their powerful attorneys and their corporate funds. I knew I was not going to let that happen to me. I felt the boot of that materialistic world right above my head, ready to step on and crush my ideas and beliefs; ready to disturb my mind and life. How could I look in the mirror tomorrow and feel good about myself? It would be meaningless. Idealism comes through happiness and harmony in life does not come with the price you pay but with the deeds you do.

That night I tried to find comfort in the fact that I did try to put the project together this year. But from trying, to actually doing it, is a big difference. I can only blame myself for the failure, even though all along I was led to believe that the project would be on for this year as usual. It was a strange feeling for sure, because for once I did not have the final word. It was up to the new investment company to decide the faith of the Thanksgiving Project.

I was asked by the owners of the investment company to write a proposal about the project. I did that, and in the proposal I clarified that the company would not have to bear any cost. I proposed to feed 10,000 people. Donations and funds for such a small project could be easily raised as we had plenty of time. Meetings came and went and I was told the proposal was presented to the stockholders and we were waiting for an answer. Meanwhile I started to get ready. I called people that had helped me before and started to organize. After all, this was a new location and I had to figure out how everything was going to work. Phone calls to the press were made and a press release prepared asking for help with donations and volunteers. There were only three weeks left before Thanksgiving.

At my next meeting with the owner of the investment company I got the news, "We're not going to be able to help with your Thanksgiving Project. We must keep the doors open for business," she said! I looked at her, not sure if she was joking, and when I realized that she was not, told her, "There will be no business the week of Thanksgiving, all my customers know we traditionally close to do this project."

"No, no. We can't do that. We can't afford to close. We must stay open," she replied.

I left and as I was going down the stairs I tried to imagine the stockholders who had made that decision. How could they only be concerned about money and be out of touch with the needs of our society? I tried to figure out why they didn't want to do the Thanksgiving project. As I pointed out to them, it would be to their advantage because everyone in the media would be reporting this act of kindness and it would help their image in the community. I was completely puzzled about their not wanting anything to do with the homeless.

As I was attending a meeting with the downtown business people, the main issue was how to keep the homeless away from their businesses. It then dawned on me that the homeless was also another reason for them to refuse. They didn't want them coming near the hotel. I was upset at the thought that we must look down to the ones in need so we could build up our own image. Granted, many of the transients could be bothersome to the customers and inappropriate if standing in front of our door, but this was, after all, Thanksgiving. It was just one day of the year.

I went back to the owner of the corporation. I explained the way the project worked. In years passed, "We cook the foods here, then we take it to their homes. No one ever comes to the restaurant," I said. But her mind was made up and she would not listen.

"Fine, then I'll look for a commissary elsewhere so I can do a small Feed the Hungry project," I said.

"No, we need you here to build up the business," she answered.

As I walked away I didn't even bother to look back. "You aren't going to tell me what to do," I said through my teeth. The frustration was building up inside me. I could not understand what was the big deal of taking some time off and feeding a few thousand needy people!

I went to my office and started to make calls to find a kitchen big enough to do the project. There were only 10 days left. I went to my kitchen and talked to the cooks. Some of them had been with me for many years. It felt like they were part of my family. I thought of them being without jobs and my thoughts of walking away from that environment. I realized that I still had responsibilities here.

I took a walk outside. I thought about courage which has always been my strongest virtue. I did not feel too courageous at that moment. The words of Socrates came to mind..."Courage is not diving in a well without water." Of course not, that's stupidity. Was my situation here the same? Maybe I had to display wisdom in order to make sense of all the pain I was going through.

I remembered talking to my friend from India. "Pain is part of life, but suffering is an option," she told me the Sikhs believe.

I was kind of confused. Courage would make me unwise, and wisdom would make me uncourageous. What a choice! But in either case I had to stop the suffering.

I decided to be patient. I tried to organize a last-minute chance to do a small Thanksgiving project but there was just not enough time. On the night before Thanksgiving I was still suffering and the confusion continued on into the next day when I went to the restaurant to prepare dinner specials for the customers, something I'd have never done before! I felt out of place and as I counted the customers who came for dinner on my fingers, I knew being there was a total mistake. I left for my son Steven's home where he had prepared Thanksgiving dinner for our family. That gave me comfort. Afterwards, I went back to the restaurant. There was so much food left over I packaged 11 dinners to symbolize my 11th Thanksgiving for the hungry and gave it to one of my servers. "Go out and find 11 very hungry people and pass the dinners to them," I asked. Then I went home and the questions started again in my mind. It was the most miserable Thanksgiving day for me. One of the saddest days of my life.

That night was when I decided to prepare my letter of resignation. In that letter I asked to assure employment for six of my long-time kitchen employees and in return I would allow them to use my name and a small part of my menu for six months. I also listed the reasons why I wanted to no longer to be there. That letter was hand-delivered on December 1, 1996 and included a 30-day notice so the transition would be smooth and not interrupt their business.

Afterwards I felt great. My choice between materialism and idealism was clear and I felt proud and good about myself. I gained back my spirit and my energy as I felt the oppressive boot of that plastic world move away from my head. My only thoughts about the corporation was the desire to get them involved in society, to invest some of their wealth back into the community because the more people we helped, the healthier our community would become, and so will our prosperity. The spiritual reward is priceless.

For this one corporation and others who think like them, that they are indestructible because of their wealth, I'd like to quote something from Plato. "The good man, if he is temperate and just, is fortunate and is happy whether he is rich or poor. On the other hand, if he has great wealth and is unjust, he lives in misery."

And that misery hit the restaurant immediately. As soon as the press reported my resignation, business dropped to less than half and as time went by only some lunch business was sporadically in evidence. Dinner business became practically nonexistent.

What a price to pay, plus the stigma that this corporation was not willing to help our community in their time of need. I am personally going to make this experience my mission...to see that this corporation named "Biltmore Holdings," is going to get involved in the future with the community that made them who they are. And to have other hotels like them have a change of heart. I will invite them to watch me because I already have made my commitment for 1997. This Thanksgiving I will provide food for 25,000 needy citizens.

And as for the "San Carlos Hotel," a landmark in the downtown Phoenix area which was built in 1928, a place I was so anxious to be a part of preserving, I would like to see it be a landmark of giving in the years to come. Now I know the conscience of the ones who thought they could crush anyone's ideas who did not agree with them. They can see the price to pay is heavy. I'm sure their money can cover the heavy losses of the restaurant since my absence. But their minds came a little closer to the reality of the real world: a world which just a block away sleeps the homeless on cold sidewalks and in alleys where they dig in garbage cans for their daily bread.

As for me, I feel the victory of the spirit in my heart. The hundreds of phone calls and the letters I have received assure me the majority of society still has compassion for the needy, and the spirit to make people better and well.

I am happy that I had used both courage and wisdom to make my decision.

story continued on page 261

Until philosophers are kings or the kings and princes of this world have the spirit and power of philosophy, and political greatness and wisdom meet in one, and those commoner natures who pursue either to the exclusion of the other compelled to stand aside, cities and human race will never rest from their evil and then only will this our state have a possibility of life and behold the light of the day.

— Plato

Specialties...

Gyros

6 lbs. ground beef
2 lbs. ground lamb
2 small onions, grated
Juice of 2 lemons
5 cloves garlic, chopped
3 eggs
½ lb. cornmeal

> *Mix well.*

1 Tbsp. basil
1 Tbsp. black pepper
1 Tbsp. oregano
2 Tbsp. parsley
¾ Tbsp. mint leaves
¾ Tbsp. thyme
½ Tbsp. cumin
½ Tbsp. ground mustard

> *Add to the meat mixture and mix well.*

This recipe will make approximately 10 lbs. of gyros. Divide into two parts. Place each part in a large plastic bag. Press the mixture to form an almost square block about 2″ thick. Place it in the freezer and when ready to use, slice the gyros meat and grill it with vegetable oil. (You can also slice the remaining gyros and freeze it in bags.)

Eggplant Mozzarella

2 slices eggplant

> *Cut into halves. Bread (see page 66) it and fry to golden brown.*

1 cup Meat Sauce (see page 116)

> *Place in a small baking dish. Lay the eggplant on top.*

1 Tbsp. Romano cheese
1 Tbsp. Parmesan cheese

> *Sprinkle on top of eggplant.*

1 cup Meat Sauce

> *Pour on top.*

4 oz. Mozzarella cheese, shredded

> *Place on top. Bake in 425° oven about 20 minutes.*

Eggplant Parmigiana

1 small carrot, chopped
½ celery stalk, finely chopped
3 cups Marinara Sauce (see page 115)
Mix in a bowl.
2 pieces eggplant, cut in halves
Bread* (see page 66) and fry until golden brown. Place half the filling in a small baking dish. Lay the eggplant on top.
1 Tbsp. Romano cheese
1 Tbsp. Parmesan cheese
Sprinkle on top. Pour rest of filling on top of eggplant.
4 oz. Mozzarella cheese
Place on top. Bake in 425° oven for 20-25 minutes.

Roasted Leg of Lamb

1 leg of lamb, approximately 10-12 lbs. with bone in
Place in a roasting pan, bone end down.
1 cup olive oil
Rub the leg with oil.
Juice of 2 lemons
Rub over the leg.
4 cloves garlic, chopped
Place it all over the lamb leg.
2 Tbsp. oregano
2 Tbsp. thyme
2 Tbsp. basil
2 Tbsp. black pepper
2 Tbsp. rosemary
Mix in a bowl and cover the leg with it. Refrigerate overnight. When ready to bake, place a little water in the roasting pan about 1"-1½" high).
10 small potatoes, peeled and cut in half
Place in the pan around the lamb.
1 lb. butter
2 cups white cooking wine
Heat in a saucepan until butter is melted. Pour over the lamb and potatoes. Bake in 375° oven for 35-40 minutes, basting with the juice from the pan. Turn oven down to 275° and bake for 3-3½ hours, basting occasionally. Serve with Mushroom Rice Pilaf (see page 118).

Stuffed Potatoes

2 potatoes, cut in half lengthwise

> *Scoop out the middle, leaving the shells. Fry the shells in canola oil until golden brown.*

2 oz. gyros meat (see page 244)
8 small slices jalapeño peppers
1 Tbsp. black olives
1 roasted red pepper, cut in half

> *Mix in a bowl. Place each half of the roasted red pepper on the inside of the two shells. Divide the filling into two parts. Place each part on top of the roasted pepper. Cover with the two remaining shells. Now you have two potatoes with the filling enclosed inside. Bread the potatoes using breading method on page 66 and deep fry in canola oil for about 5-6 minutes. Cut the potatoes in half (not lengthwise) and serve.*

Peperoni Tirato

2 roasted red peppers

> *Cut on one side and open. Lay one on a working surface.*

½ cup Ricotta cheese
1 Italian sausage, cooked and sliced
2 oz. Mozzarella cheese, shredded
2 oz. Provolone cheese, shredded

> *Mix in a bowl. Place on top of the pepper. Wrap the other pepper around it. Bread the pepper using the breading method on page 66. Fry in canola oil for about 5-6 minutes. Place in a baking dish and bake in 375° oven for 10-12 minutes.*

Kanela Duck (see page 248)

Stuffed Grapevine Leaves

Method of preparing on page 74. Stuffed with rice, see page 74.

WITH GROUND BEEF:
3 Tbsp. olive oil
> *Heat in a saucepan.*

1 onion, finely chopped
4 green onions, finely chopped
2 Tbsp. dill
2 Tbsp. mint
> *Sauté for 3-4 minutes.*

2 fresh tomatoes, chopped fine
1 tsp. pepper
> *Add in and sauté for 2-3 minutes. Place filling in a mixing bowl.*

½ lb. ground beef
1 cup rice
> *Add to the bowl and mix well. To prepare, use the method on page 74.*

WITH GROUND LAMB:
> *Substitute the ground beef with ground lamb. Eliminate the tomato. To prepare, use the method on page 74.*

BAKED WITH YOGURT:
> *In a baking dish place 6 dolmades (see page 74). Top them with 2 cups Yogurt Sauce (see page 113). Sprinkle the top with 1 Tbsp. pine nuts and bake in 350° oven for 15 minutes.*

> *To serve the grapevine leaves, place on a plate and serve with Yogurt Dressing (see page 113) or with Egg-Lemon Sauce (see page 119).*

Lamb and Co. In Foil (see page 248)

Kanela Duck

½ cup olive oil
1 duck, cut in half

> *Sauté until duck is lightly brown.*

12 pearl onions

> *Add in and brown onions. In the bottom of a cooking pot place 6-7 rosemary sticks. Pour ¼ cup olive oil in. Place in duck, cut end down and add onions.*

16 oz. tomatoes in juice, crushed
8 oz. tomato paste

> *Mix together and place in pot.*

2 cloves garlic, chopped
½ tsp. black pepper
½ tsp. rosemary leaves
½ tsp. whole black pepper
½ tsp. ground cinnamon
10 cloves, whole
4 cinnamon sticks
4 bay leaves

> *Add in. Cover and simmer over low heat for about 2 hours.*

⅛ cup red wine vinegar

> *Add to pot about halfway through cooking. Makes 4-5 servings.*

Lamb and Co. In Foil

12 oz. lamb leg meat
6 oz. tenderloin steak
4 oz. pork chop
½ cup olive oil

> *Sauté meats in oil.*

1 Tbsp. red cooking wine

> *Add in.*

8 pearl onions

> *Add in.*

2 cloves garlic
½ tsp. black pepper
½ tsp. parsley
½ tsp. basil
½ tsp. oregano
½ tsp. thyme
½ tsp. mint

> *Add in. Place lamb in a piece of foil. Place 2 oz. kefalograviera cheese on top of lamb. Sprinkle juice of 1/2 lemon over it. Place the rest of the filling on top. Enclose filling into foil. Place it in a pan with a little water on the bottom. Bake for 11/2 hours a 375°.*

Stuffed Italian Rolo

1 cup spinach, chopped
1 cup Ricotta cheese
½ small onion, chopped
4 mushrooms, chopped
4 slices ham, chopped
½ tsp. nutmeg
1 egg
1 Tbsp. Romano cheese, grated
1 tsp. black pepper

> *Mix well in a bowl.*

1 pasta sheet (see pages 45-46) approximately 12˝ x 12˝

> *Place filling on one end of the sheet and roll to enclose filling. Place in a baking dish.*

3 Tbsp. olive oil
3 Tbsp. soybean oil

> *Heat in a saucepan.*

½ small onion, chopped
1 clove garlic, chopped

> *Sauté for 4-5 minutes.*

8-9 plum tomatoes (canned), crushed

> *Add in.*

1 Tbsp. black pepper
2 Tbsp. white cooking wine
Pinch of nutmeg
½ cup whipping cream
2 Tbsp. pine nuts

> *Add in and simmer 4-5 minutes. Pour over the pasta roll, bake at 375° for about 20-25 minutes.*

True ham comes from the upper thigh of the pig. Commercialized hams come from other parts of the pig, especially the shoulder. The consumer cannot tell the quality by looking at it because it is disguised by browning the outside with bursts of heat after it was brushed with flavor oils and artificial colors. Only genuine braised ham is delicious but is very expensive.

Arborio Chicken

3 Tbsp. olive oil
3 Tbsp. soybean oil
8 oz. chicken breast, cut into pieces
> *Sauté in a large saucepan 5-6 minutes.*

4 mushrooms, sliced
1 clove garlic
½ red onion, sliced
1 Tbsp. sweet peas
½ celery rib, sliced
3 asparagus spears, cut into pieces
1 tomato, cubed
> *Add in and sauté 5-6 minutes until onions are soft.*

½ cup white cooking wine
1 tsp. black pepper
1 tsp. oregano
1 tsp. rosemary
1 tsp. capers
1 tsp. Worcestershire sauce
> *Add in.*

2 cups chicken broth (see page 135)
1 cup arborio rice
> *Add in and simmer until rice is cooked. Add more chicken broth if needed.*

Duck is the first poultry to be domesticated in yards. The Chinese did it by taming them and hatching the eggs. Duck is the pride of Chinese cooking. For centuries Chinese have tried to perfect their duck recipes. Duck provides less meat than chicken. The duck's breast lean fillet is becoming a delicacy, hence the high price. You must be careful with duck because the older it is the more fat it contains and it becomes very difficult to cook.

Chinese cooks prepare the best duck dishes in the world. One of the best recipes is roasted duck which is cooked over fire of fruit trees (apricot, pear, vine). The cook must be very skillful to prepare this recipe because the color of the roasted duck must remain pale and also prevent the duck from catching fire from its own juices.

Cous Cous Calamari

3 Tbsp. olive oil
3 Tbsp. soybean oil
> *Heat in a large saucepan.*

12 small calamari tubes, cut in half
½ cup baby clams
> *Add in and sauté 3-4 minutes.*

¼ cup white cooking wine
> *Add in.*

3 green onions, chopped
½ small red onion, sliced
½ small red pepper, sliced
8 black peppercorns
1 clove garlic, chopped
4 peperoncini peppers, chopped
1 Tbsp. capers
> *Add in and sauté 6-7 minutes until onions are soft.*

8 plum tomatoes (canned), crushed
½ cup of the juice of the tomatoes
3 bay leaves
1 tsp. black pepper
1 tsp. basil
1 tsp. rosemary
Pinch of red pepper flakes
½ tsp. cumin
> *Add in and simmer 3-4 minutes.*

2 cups clam juice
1 cup cous-cous
> *Add in and simmer until cous-cous is cooked (add more clam juice if needed).*
> *Add 1 Tbsp. Parmesan cheese when almost done.*

Cous-cous is classified as pasta. It is made of wheat, millet or sorghum and is crushed rather than ground. First mention of cous-cous was in the 16th century when it was highly regarded in Provence and along the Ligurian coast.

Orzo Lamb

3 Tbsp. olive oil
3 Tbsp. soybean oil
> *Heat in a large saucepan.*

4 small lamb chops
> *Brown lightly on both sides.*

1 cup eggplant, chopped
> *Add in and sauté 3-4 minutes.*

½ **red pepper, sliced**
½ **cup okra, cut in pieces**
8 pearl onions, cut in half
1 clove garlic
¼ **cup black beans (cooked)**
4 sun-dried tomatoes, in pieces
> *Add in and sauté until vegetables are soft.*

8 plum tomatoes (canned), crushed
½ **cup of the juice from the tomatoes**
1 tsp. black pepper
1 tsp. parsley
1 tsp. basil
1 tsp. oregano
1 tsp. thyme
1 tsp. rosemary
½ **tsp. mint leaves**
> *Add in and simmer 4-5 minutes.*

2 cups chicken broth (see page 135)
1 cup orzo
> *Add in and simmer until orzo is done (add more chicken broth if needed).*

1 Tbsp. Romano cheese
1 Tbsp. Parmesan cheese
> *Mix in when almost done.*

Orzo is pasta which resembles rice. It cooks like pasta and is very popular in Italy and Greece (Manestra).

Kota Manestra

3 Tbsp. olive oil
3 Tbsp. soybean oil
8 oz. chicken breast, cubed

Sauté in a large saucepan for about 4-5 minutes.

1 small zucchini, sliced
3 artichoke hearts, sliced
1 tomato, chopped
1 clove garlic
1 Tbsp. capers

Add in and sauté for 5-6 minutes.

¼ cup white cooking wine
1 tsp. black pepper
1 tsp. oregano
4 plum tomatoes (canned), crushed
¼ cup juice from the tomatoes

Add in and simmer 2-3 minutes.

2 cups chicken broth (see page 135)
1 cup orzo

Add in and simmer until orzo is done (add more chicken broth if needed).

¼ cup Feta cheese
1 Tbsp. Romano cheese
1 Tbsp. Parmesan cheese

Add in a few minutes before orzo is done.

The Greeks have enjoyed shellfish and crawfish since the Archaic times. Oysters, sea urchins, crabs, mussels, shrimp and prawns were found on the rocky coastlines of Greece.

The old Athenians used to vote by writing the name in a oyster shell.

The Romans had a great passion for oysters. Oysters and mussels have been a part of many great recipes since the Ancient times. They were very popular also in the Renaissance. In fact, Oysters Rockefeller is a recipe from the early 18th century.

Rice Kabia

3 Tbsp. olive oil
3 Tbsp. soybean oil
> *Heat in large skillet.*

4 oz. chicken breast, cut in pieces
1 Italian sausage, cooked and sliced
6 large shrimp, peeled
½ cup baby clams
> *Add in and sauté until chicken is browned, about 4-5 minutes.*

¼ cup white cooking wine
> *Add in.*

4 mushrooms, sliced
¼ cup okra, cut in pieces
3 green onions, chopped
1 clove garlic, chopped
½ small red pepper, sliced
1 Tbsp. capers
3 artichokes, sliced
1 small tomato, chopped
½ small zucchini, sliced
2 Tbsp. garbanzo beans (cooked)
> *Add in and sauté 5-6 minutes.*

4 plum tomatoes (canned), crushed
¼ cup juice from tomatoes
1 tsp. black pepper
1 tsp. parsley
1 tsp. basil
1 tsp. rosemary
> *Add in and simmer 2-3 minutes.*

2 cups chicken broth (see page 135)
1 cup long grain rice
> *Add in and simmer until rice is cooked (add more chicken broth if needed).*

Rice will improve the health of the people who eat it and it will also influence their character, especially in countries of rice growers where they do not remove the husk which is rich in vitamin B.

Most of the world's rice production comes from China and Japan. the general belief is that rice was initially grown in North China, but there is evidence that the cultivation of these grains have been imported from Mesopotamia in earlier times.

Grain Bean Basmati

3 Tbsp. olive oil
3 Tbsp. soybean oil

Heat in a large skillet.
4 oz. chicken breast, cut in pieces
1 Italian sausage, cooked and sliced

1 cup cooked ham, cubed

Add in and sauté 4-5 minutes.

2 small tomatoes, chopped
4 mushrooms, sliced
½ small onion, sliced
½ small red pepper, sliced
½ cup celery, chopped
6 okra, cut in pieces
1 clove garlic, chopped
6 whole cloves

Add in and sauté 5-6 minutes.

¼ cup white cooking wine
½ tsp. steak sauce
½ tsp. worcestershire sauce

Add in.

⅛ cup butter beans
⅛ cup borgoli beans
⅛ cup lentils
⅛ cup white beans
1 tsp. black pepper
1 tsp. parsley
1 tsp. thyme
1 tsp. rosemary
1 tsp. oregano
1 tsp. basil
2 bay leaves

(All the beans must be cooked or can be canned.) Add in and simmer 2-3 minutes.

1 cup basmati rice
2 cups chicken broth (see page 135)

Add in and simmer until rice is done (add more chicken broth if needed).

Basmati rice is regarded to be among the best in the world. It is mainly grown in India. It is not easily found because most of this rice does not reach urban markets. The situation of rice growing in India is not as good as it is in China because irrigation is unreliable and can only produce about two crops a year.

Kapari Beefteki

16 oz. ground beef
> *Divide into equal parts, flatten, and form into oblong burgers*

¼ cup Feta cheese
> *Crumble and place on top of one burger.*

1 Tbsp. capers
> *Place on top of Feta cheese. Cover the capers with the second burger. Press down to seal the Feta and capers inside.*

3 Tbsp. olive oil
3 Tbsp. soybean oil
> *Heat on a flat top griddle (or in a skillet). Fry beefteri until both sides are done.*

½ small red onion
> *Grill until soft (you can do it on the same surface). Place on top of beefteri.*

1 Tbsp. Feta cheese
> *Sprinkle on top of onions. Cover and cook for a few minutes longer until Feta is soft.*

Kreatopita

1 filo crust (see page 221)
> *Place in a baking dish.*

2 oz. Kefalograviera cheese, sliced
> *Place in the middle of the crust.*

3 Tbsp. olive oil
3 Tbsp. soybean oil
> *Heat in a saucepan.*

6 oz. meat from lamb chops, cut into pieces
4 oz. rib eye steak, cut in strips
> *Add in and sauté 6-7 minutes.*

Juice of ½ lemon
2 Tbsp. red cooking wine
> *Add in.*

8 pearl onions (you can use canned)
1 clove garlic
> *Add in and sauté 3-4 minutes.*

1 tsp. black pepper
½ tsp. parsley
½ tsp. basil
½ tsp. oregano
½ tsp. thyme
½ tsp. rosemary
½ tsp. mont leaves
> *Add in and sauté 3-4 minutes. Place mixture on top of filo crust.*

1 roasted red pepper, cut in strips
> *Arrange on top of meat mixture. Bake in 375° oven 10-12 minutes.*

Gorgonzola Roasted Peppers

1 cup spinach puffs filling (see page 69)
¼ cup Ricotta cheese
> *Mix well.*

2 large roasted red peppers
Flour
> *Stuff them with the filling. Roll peppers in flour.*

3 Tbsp. olive oil
3 Tbsp. soybean oil
> *Heat in a saucepan. Sauté until golden brown. Arrange on a serving platter.*

1 Tbsp. whipping cream
4 Tbsp. gorgonzola cheese, crumbled
> *Heat gently until the cheese is melted. Pour over the peppers.*

Turkey Pastichio

6 oz. turkey meat from a cooked turkey breast, thinly sliced
3 Tbsp. olive oil
3 Tbsp. soybean oil
> *Heat in a saucepan.*

½ small onion, sliced
1 clove garlic, chopped
> *Add in and sauté 3-4 minutes. Add in the turkey and sauté 2-3 minutes.*

1 Tbsp. white cooking wine
> *Add in.*

5 plum tomatoes (canned), crushed
1 tsp. pepper
¼ tsp. parsley
¼ tsp. oregano
¼ tsp. basil
> *Add in and sauté 3-4 minutes.*

½ tsp. cinnamon
1 Tbsp. Romano cheese
1 Tbsp. Parmesan cheese
¼ cup whipping cream
2 cups mostaccioli pasta, cooked
1 Tbsp. Ricotta cheese
> *Add in and simmer for 3-4 minutes. Place in a baking dish.*

2 Tbsp. whipping cream
½ cup Provolone cheese, shredded
> *Heat until cheese melts and pour over top of baking dish. Bake 375° for 12-15 minutes.*

Grilled Vegetable Mousaka

3 Tbsp. olive oil
3 Tbsp. soybean oil

Heat in a skillet.

6 thin slices eggplant

Sauté until eggplant is soft. Place on a paper towel to absorb oil. (For eggplant and the other vegetables of this dish, you can use a flat griddle, if available, to cook the vegetables.)

6 thin slices of potato

Add to skillet and add more oil if necessary. Sauté until potatoes are soft. Remove and place on a paper towel.

½ small zucchini, sliced
4 mushrooms, sliced
1 clove garlic, chopped
½ small onion, sliced

Add in and sautéuntil vegetables are soft.

⅛ cup white cooking wine

Add in.

4 plum tomatoes (canned)
½ tsp. cinnamon
½ tsp. nutmeg

Add in and simmer 4-5 minutes. Place half of the vegetable sauce in a baking dish. Layer the eggplant and potatoes on top.

1 tsp. Romano cheese
1 tsp. Parmesan cheese

Sprinkle on top. Add the rest of the sauce on top.

2 Tbsp. whipping cream
4 Tbsp. Mozzarella cheese, shredded

Heat until cheese melts. Bake at 375° for 12-15 minutes.

Rice arrived in western Europe around the 4th century B.C. Theophrastus, a spiritual student of Aristotle, mentioned "oryzon," an exotic plant around 300 B.C.

The health benefits of rice were praised since the early days. A Greek doctor, Dioscorides Pedanius, expressed interest of the virtues of rice water in digestive disorders around the 1st century A.D.

Sea Snail Fettuccine

3 Tbsp. olive oil
3 Tbsp. soybean oil
  Heat in a skillet.

8 large snails
8 large scallops
6 large shrimp, peeled
  Add in and sauté 4-5 minutes.

⅛ cup white cooking wine
  Add in.

3 green onions, chopped
4 mushrooms, sliced
1 tsp. capers
1 clove garlic
1 tsp. black olives, sliced
1 small tomato, cubed
  Add in and sauté 6-7 minutes.

1 tsp. black pepper
¼ lb. fettuccine, cooked
  Add in and simmer 2-3 minutes.

1 Tbsp. Romano cheese, grated
1 Tbsp. Parmesan cheese, grated
  Add in and stir well.

People have been eating flour since many centuries B.C. But it was the Greeks who made baking bread a true art. One of the most famous bakers was Theanos, who was praised by both Plato and Aristophanes.

Manuscripts from Athens in the 3rd century A.D. revealed over 75 different kinds of bread even back then! At first bread was baked into molds, but then the Greeks invented the bread oven which could be pre-heated and became the model for culinary use.

Some of the breads that were baked in Greece at that time were: "syncomiste" (dark bread), "phaios" (whole meal bread), "steptice" (loaf bread), "blosmilos" (square bread), "semidalite" (wheat bread), "hemiarton" (crescent-shaped bread), and "agoraios" (loaves). There were also several types of cakes made as well as wedding cakes.

Antigyros (white gyros)

4 lbs. ground turkey
4 lbs. ground chicken
1 lb. ground duck
3 eggs
Juice of 2 lemons
2 onions, finely chopped
1 lb. cracker meal
Juice of ½ orange
6 mushrooms, finely chopped
4 artichoke hearts, chopped
3 cloves garlic, chopped
2 Tbsp. black pepper
¼ cup celery, chopped
1 Tbsp. oregano
1 tsp. basil
1 tsp. rosemary
1 Tbsp. Dijon mustard
2 tsp. cumin
½ tsp. cinnamon
½ tsp. nutmeg
½ tsp. ginger

Mix all ingredients well. Makes approximately 12 pounds of white gyros meat. Divide into two parts. Place each part in a large plastic bag. Press the mixture to form an almost square block, about 2" thick. Place in the freezer. When ready to use, slice the white gyros. Grill slices in vegetable oil. (You can also slice the remaining meat and freeze in plastic bags.)

In old China when people were hungry, some of them went begging for food. If their effort to find food was fruitless, most resulted in stealing chickens. To elude the authorities, the thieves would dig a hole in the ground and bury the chicken, then they would light a fire on top of the hidden chicken and sit around the fire pretending they were keeping warm. Many hours later the chicken would be roasted underneath the fire.

From that idea the famous recipe of beggars chicken was inspired. The chicken is stuffed with various filings then wrapped in lotus leaves and covered with clay and baked. The taste and tenderness of the chicken is unforgettable.

AND THEN IT WAS CHRISTMAS

*I*n my quest to find the meaning of Christmas, I realized the whole world comes to a stop so celebration can take place.

The materialistic way of celebrating this special day always bothered me. I felt pity in my heart thinking that a pretty wrapped box would be opened by someone who would pretend to be happy. But it really would be just a blur of happiness. A brief smile and a plain "thank you" and next year there would be expectations for even bigger and better gifts. This game we are playing, who will buy more gifts, will never let us grow. We will remain children, expecting gifts in boxes forever.

I thought of this day when the world stops and what it meant to me. It was that same day many years ago that I, as a newborn, had seen the light of life for the first time and placed a smile on my parents hearts forever. I thought, well, what a special day to be born on!

But as I grew older the meaning of Christmas puzzled me. I felt this day had more meaning in life than also being my birthday. Until one year the joy of birth became a lesson of death. I was flying back home on Christmas day to see the man I had admired most in my life for the last time, I tried to figure out the meaning of this and if there were any gifts or material things that could replace the death of my father and the times I had missed with him.

He felt so much joy, years ago,
    on my birthday.
I felt so much pain, years later,
    on his death.
What was this lesson of joy and sadness?

After his death, years came and passed with mixed feelings in my heart. Very few could see the pain as I made sure the children and the ones very dear to me had a gift to open at Christmas. But at the same time I saw people pretending to be happy at Christmas parties and others stressing out trying to buy the right gift for the people they saw once a year.

I was ready to give up my quest for the meaning of Christmas as I heard constant complaints from almost everyone on how this day had completely lost its meaning. Very few remembered that on this day the birth of Christ must symbolize the search for peace on earth, the quest of freedom for our souls away from excess material things that have complicated our lives. No matter what religion, race, or color, at least this day marked the birth of someone who died for his passion to spread kindness to the world and must motivate us to do the same and not find excuses to be happy or sad because of a gift.

Gifts brought happiness to children
    who have received them,
and sadness to the ones who did not.
This day brought smiles to people
    who were sitting around the warm fires in their homes,

and terror to others' minds who had to sleep in the snow on the streets.

Thousands celebrated the birth of Christ. Thousands cried for the dead in their war-torn countries. There were adults with happy faces sitting around tables full of food, yet there were children dying from hunger. I kept asking myself, "What is this day of Christmas all about?"

I read the Bible to understand. I asked people to explain, but everyone had a different explanation which came in a box with pretty wrapping.

I kept thinking this riddle that puzzled me would never be solved until one day just before Christmas, the answer came unexpectedly.

It was a few days later that I handed in my resignation and had freed my mind of the torture I had put my feelings through. I remember a phrase, "wisdom is the supreme part of happiness." It was almost Christmas and I felt wiser than ever. My senses, my actions, and my thoughts were in total control. In a way I never thought possible. The birth and the death were just emotional roads to prepare me for the rest of the way. I was in total control of my destiny, something I had searched for in books and teachings all my life. Yet it was so simple to understand. It was not an event or in a box. It was not even a tree or streets decorated with lights!

It was a feeling!

And all other things paled in the power of this extraordinary sense.

Now, I was in control. I was laughing at the years of struggles and misunderstandings. I felt pity for those who believe the supreme road to happiness lies in money and power. Those things surrounded me for the last three months and I could not stand being there. I felt out of place in all the meetings that bored me so much with all the talk of building wealthy empires. That was blinding their minds, preventing them from seeing clearly the simple and meaningful things in life.

I know it because the only way I could see it clearly was when I decided to leave behind the worries of the business and the arguments of the possessions. I wanted to go somewhere to be productive for myself as well as society. In my frustration for the answer that would complete my harmony and peace I left everything behind without a second glance and took nothing but a few dollars. I had started 13 years ago, now I had so much more. Thousands of people believed in me. I had a mature mind, a giving heart, and a reputation that could open any door for my work. Above all, I had family that never worried about my ability to survive. Only my decision to leave the environment that was clouding my mind made me see this feeling.

It was love, love for freedom of mind to choose who or what you give your heart to. I had lost the love for my work in the last three months, and wanted it back. I had lost faith in people who did not understand my need of helping our community to get better. I wanted to get away from those people. It's funny how things work out sometimes!

The death of the business I had made my universe for the last 13 years created the birth of the feeling that I had forever been searching for.

We think of the love in our hearts as fires burning and bells ringing. We think of beautiful songs and breathtaking sunsets. We think of beautiful forests and wide blue seas, but it is not just that. That is only the pretty wrapping of the box.

The need to free my mind and myself was obvious. That will end my misery and make me more appreciative. On Friday, December 13th, 1996, after an argument I had with the owner of the corporation, I walked out from the restaurant and never looked back. As I stepped outside, my senses stopped. I was peaceful. Nothing else mattered. The feeling was so powerful it infused me with total control. The feeling I found in the freedom of mind was addictive and I knew I could not live without it. Finally at Christmas of 1996, I had found what I wanted. It was so simple. It was in front of me all the time!

Now that life has come full circle, I must move on and start again the next pages of my life, and do things prosperous for myself and others without letting it consume my freedom of mind.

The past 13 years were full of feelings and lessons. I gave birth to an art that I never knew I possessed. I made thousands of friends with my cooking and baking, and a few enemies from my business decisions. It gave me the opportunity to blossom by learning from the experiences that went with it. I put smiles on people's faces and gave hope to tens of thousands who realized some people still cared. I made people believe anything is possible once you put your mind to it. My only hope is that this last Thanksgiving was not a disappointment to a lot of people because I could only feed 11 for my 11th Thanksgiving.

Thirteen years seems like a lifetime. So much hard work, worries, sleepless nights, and struggle to survive. Was it all meaningless? I don't think so. I feel it was worth it and if not for the notoriety my work received, for the fact I have seen my children grow closer to me and I now earn their respect of believing we do not have to live in a world we disagree with. We must live in our own world and make it what we like…

So the trip of the last 13 years was worth it and I'm gratified. Just like that trip on the Island of Thassos many years ago, I am ready to take that trip again. Only this time I am going to slow down and enjoy the scenery…

Those who render no service either by word or deed, who can not help city or people in the time of need, ought to be stopped, even if they have riches in abundance, above all they are insolent as well as inefficient.

— Socrates

There are so many things that I can do without.

— Socrates

Doing fundraising dinners for Thanksgiving with my friends, chefs Laurie Vacha and Erasmo Kamnitzer.

On Thomas Road, raising funds for the hungry with Laurie, Erasmo and our crew.

Breakfast...

Cream Toast

8 slices French baguette
> *Place on a working surface.*

6 oz. cream cheese
¼ cup grated walnuts
> *Mix well in a bowl. Divide into four parts and spread on top of the 4 slices of bread. Cover with the remaining 4 slices so you can make a sandwich.*

3 eggs
1 Tbsp. heavy cream
Pinch of nutmeg
Pinch of cinnamon
> *Place in a bowl and mix with a fork. Dip the four sandwiches in the egg batter. Grill well on both sides using 4 Tbsp. canola oil. Place on a serving platter.*

3 Tbsp. apricot jam
2 Tbsp. orange juice
> *Heat gently in a saucepan. Stir well and place on top of the cream toast.*

Crab Puffs

2 eggs, fried
> *Place in a mixing bowl.*

2 Tbsp. cream cheese
3 oz. crabmeat
> *Mix well with eggs.*

4 puff pastry dough squares 5″ x 5″
> *Place on a working surface and wet the edges with a little water. Divide the crab filling into four parts. Place each part in the middle of each pastry dough, fold the dough into triangles and with a fork, seal the edges gently. Bake in 425° oven about 15-20 minutes until puffs are golden brown.*

½ cup heavy cream
> *Heat gently in saucepan.*

1½ oz. Swiss cheese, grated
> *Add in and stir to melt.*

Pinch black pepper
1 tsp. lemon juice
> *Add in and stir well. Arrange puffs on a serving platter and pour sauce on top.*

NOTE: In all the pancake recipes we are use buttermilk pancake mix to save time since other ingredients are added to the mix (milk, eggs). The taste does not differ from that made from scratch. If you prefer to make the mix from scratch, here is the recipe:

Mix 2 eggs, beaten well with ¾ cup milk and ¾ cup buttermilk. Add in 2 Tbsp. baking powder and 2 cups sifted flour. After mixing well, add 1 Tbsp. vegetable oil.

Cheese Brioche

4 slices of brioche bread, cut into triangles (see page 40)
4 eggs
1 Tbsp. heavy cream
Pinch of nutmeg
Pinch of cinnamon

Beat well in a bowl. Dip brioche into the egg batter and grill in canola oil. After you turn the bread the first time, place on slice of Swiss cheese on each slice of bread. Let it melt.

Stuffed Brioche

4 slices of brioche bread, cut into triangles (see page 40)
4 eggs
1 Tbsp. heavy cream
Pinch of cinnamon
Pinch of nutmeg

Mix well in a mixing bowl. Dip bread into batter and grill in canola oil.

4 slices ham
4 slices turkey

Grill to just hot. After you turn your bread the first time, place one slice each of the ham and turkey on top of the bread. When the bread is done, cover the ham and turkey with the rest of the slices.

Strawberry Cream

2 oz. cream cheese
1 oz. strawberry jam
4 strawberries, chopped

Mix well in bowl.

4 puff pastry dough squares

Place on a working surface. Divide filling into four parts and place in the middle of the dough. Wet the edges with a little water. Fold over into triangles. Seal gently with a fork. Bake in a 425° oven for about 20-25 minutes or until golden brown.

½ oz. strawberry jam
3 strawberries, chopped
1 Tbsp. sliced almonds
1 Tbsp. heavy cream

Heat gently in a skillet. Arrange strawberry cream on a serving platter. Pour sauce over the top.

Whole Wheat Cream

8 slices of 9 grain whole wheat bread, sliced out of small rolls
> *Lay on a working surface.*

6 oz. cream cheese
1 Tbsp. grated hazelnuts
> *Mix well in a bowl. Divide in 4 parts and place on top of the 4 slices. Cover with the rest of the bread.*

3 eggs
1 Tbsp. heavy cream
Pinch of cinnamon
Pinch of nutmeg
> *Mix in a bowl with a fork. Dip the 4 sandwiches and grill on both sides well in 4 Tbsp. canola oil. Place on a serving platter.*

3 Tbsp. strawberry jam
4 strawberries, chopped
2 peach halves, chopped
1 Tbsp. heavy cream
> *Heat gently in a skillet. Pour over whole wheat toast.*

Raspberry Stuffed Toast

8 slices of a French baguette
> *Lay them on a working surface.*

6 oz. cream cheese
6 raspberries
¼ cup raspberry jam
> *Mix well in a bowl. Divide into 4 parts and place each portion on top of 4 bread slices. Cover with the rest of the bread slices.*

3 eggs
1 Tbsp. heavy cream
Pinch of nutmeg
Pinch of cinnamon
> *Place in a bowl and mix with a fork. Dip the four sandwiches in the egg batter and grill on both sides well using 4 Tbsp. canola oil. Place on a serving platter.*

3 Tbsp. orange jam
1 Tbsp. sliced almonds
1 Tbsp. heavy cream
> *Heat gently in a skillet and pour over the raspberry stuffed toast.*

Blue Cakes

1 egg

Beat well in a bowl.

4 cups milk

Add in and mix well with a fork.

¼ cup blueberries
1 Tbsp. blueberry jam
3 cups buttermilk pancake mix

Add in and mix well. Adjust thickness if necessary by adding more pancake mix. Spoon the mixture on a griddle with canola oil and grill the pancakes until brown on both sides.

Buttermilk Pancakes

1 egg

Beat well in a bowl.

4 cups milk

Add in and mix with a fork.

3 cups buttermilk pancake mix

Add in and mix well. Adjust thickness if necessary. Spoon the mixture onto a griddle with canola oil and grill the pancakes until brown on both sides.

Strawberry Pancakes

1 egg

Beat in a mixing bowl.

2 cups milk

Add in and mix well.

1 cup buttermilk pancake mix

Add in and mix well. This batter should be thinner than regular pancake batter. Pour onto a griddle using 4 Tbsp. canola oil then pour the batter in a way to make a short line. You will make 2 lines with the batter. After one side is grilled, turn the pancakes over and spoon 1 Tbsp. cream cheese on each pancake.

2 tsp. strawberry jam

Place 1 tsp. on each pancake.

4 strawberries, chopped

Place 2 on each pancake. Fold the pancakes over to enclose the filling and grill until brown. Place on a serving platter.

1 Tbsp. strawberry jam
½ Tbsp. heavy cream

Heat gently in a skillet. Pour on the middle top of the pancakes.

Ham Stuffed Pancakes

1 egg
> *Beat well in a bowl.*

2 cups milk
> *Add in and mix well.*

1 cup buttermilk pancake mix
> *Add in and mix well. This batter should be thin.*

4 Tbsp. canola oil
> *Pour onto griddle then pour the batter in a way to make 2 short lines. After cooked on one side, turn over. Place in the middle of each pancake:*

2 slices ham
2 slices Swiss cheese
> *Fold the pancakes to close in the filling. Grill well on both sides. Place 1 slice Swiss cheese on top and let it melt.*

Peach Cream Cakes

1 egg
> *Beat in a bowl.*

2 cups milk
> *Add in and mix well.*

1 cup buttermilk pancake mix
> *Add in and mix well. This batter should be thin.*

4 Tbsp. canola oil
> *Pour into a griddle and pour batter in a way to make 2 short lines. After grilled on one side, turn pancakes over.*

2 peach halves, chopped
2 Tbsp. cream cheese
> *Place them on top of the pancakes, dividing equally. Fold the pancakes over to enclose the filling and grill well on both sides. Place on a serving platter.*

2 Tbsp. apricot jam
1 Tbsp. orange juice
> *Heat gently in a skillet. Pour on the middle top of the pancakes.*

Nine Grain Pancakes

1 egg
> *Beat in a bowl.*

4 cups milk
> *Add in and mix well.*

2 cups nine grain cereal
1 cup buttermilk pancake mix
> *Add in and mix well. Adjust thickness as necessary. Spoon the mixture onto a griddle using 4 Tbsp. canola oil and grill on both sides until golden brown.*

Use the same method, but make the pancakes smaller
1 cup honey
⅛ cup water
Pinch of cinnamon
> *Heat gently in a skillet. Pour over the pancakes.*

Green Grain Cakes

1 egg
> *Beat in a mixing bowl.*

1½ cups milk
> *Add in and mix well.*

½ cup buttermilk pancake mix
1 cup nine grain cereal
> *Add in and mix well.*

½ cup spinach, chopped (can be frozen)
½ cup broccoli, chopped (can be frozen)
3 asparagus spears, chopped (can be frozen)
¼ cup Feta cheese, crumbled
> *Add in and mix well. Spoon onto a griddle using 4 Tbsp. canola oil and grill until golden brown.*

Potato Feta Cakes

1 egg
> *Beat in a mixing bowl.*

1½ cups milk
> *Add in and mix well.*

1½ cups buttermilk pancake mix
> *Add in and mix well.*

¼ cup red onions, chopped
½ cup Feta cheese, crumbled
1 large potato, cooked, peeled and shredded
½ tsp. black pepper
> *Add in and mix well. Adjust thickness as necessary. Spoon onto a griddle using 4 Tbsp. canola oil. Grill until golden brown.*

Ricotta Crab Cakes

1 egg
> *Beat in a mixing bowl.*

1½ cups milk
> *Add in and beat well.*

1½ cups buttermilk pancake mix
> *Add in and mix well.*

½ cup broccoli, chopped (can be frozen)
½ cup Ricotta cheese
¼ cup crabmeat, chopped
> *Add in and mix well. Adjust thickness as necessary. Spoon onto a griddle using 4 Tbsp. canola oil. Grill until golden brown.*

Golden Grilled Potatoes

4 Tbsp. canola oil
1 small onion, sliced
8 mushrooms, sliced
1 red pepper, sliced
2 potatoes, cooked, unpeeled and sliced
½ tsp.. black pepper
> *Pour oil on griddle and add ingredients. Grill until onions are soft, approximately 5-6 minutes.*

Egg Saganaki

2 5″ x 5″ puff pastry dough squares
> *Bake in 425° oven 10-12 minutes. Place on a serving platter. Meantime do the following:*

2 slices approximately 3″ x 4″ Ketalograviera cheese
1 egg
> *Beat well.*

Flour
> *Dip cheese in the egg and then in the flour.*

4 Tbsp. canola oil
> *Heat in a saucepan. Fry cheese on both sides. Place on top of pastry dough.*

4 slices tomatoes
> *Heat them in the saucepan. Place on top of cheese.*

2 eggs, basted
> *Pour each egg on top of each pastry dough square.*

Lobster on Pastry

2 5″ x 5″ puff pastry squares
> *Bake in a 425° oven for 15 minutes. Place on a serving platter.*

4 Tbsp. canola oil
> *Heat gently in a skillet.*

4 slices tomatoes
> *Heat in the skilled and place on top of the dough (2 on each square).*

4 oz. of lobster meat
> *Sauté in the skillet for a few minutes. Place on top of the tomatoes (approximately 2 oz. on each square).*

4 asparagus spears
> *Sauté in the skillet for a few minutes. Place on top of the lobster meat (2 on each square).*

2 eggs
> *Bring water to a boil and break the eggs in the water. Poach for about 1 minute. Spoon the eggs out and place them one on each pastry square.*

2 Tbsp. heavy cream
1 oz. Swiss cheese, shredded
Pinch of black pepper
Few drops of lemon juice
> *Place in a skillet and heat gently until the cheese melts. Pour on top of the eggs.*

Eggs Sfoliata

2 5″ x 5″ puff pastry squares
> *Bake in 425° oven for about 15 minutes. Place on a serving platter.*

4 Tbsp. canola oil
> *Heat gently in a skillet.*

4 slices tomatoes
> *Heat gently and place on top of the pastry dough (2 tomatoes on each square).*

2 artichoke hearts, chopped (not marinated)
> *Sauté in the skillet and place on top of tomatoes (1 on each square).*

4 slices Canadian bacon
> *Sauté in the skillet and place on top of the artichokes (2 slices on each square).*

2 eggs
> *Bring water to a boil. Break the eggs in the water, poach them for about 1 minute. Place them on top of the Canadian bacon (1 on each square).*

2 Tbsp. heavy cream
1 oz. Swiss cheese, shredded
> *Heat gently to melt the cheese. Pour over eggs.*

Cinnamon Logs

3 slices brioche bread (see page 40)
> *Cut each piece into 4 pieces.*

3eggs
> *Beat well in a bowl.*

1 Tbsp. heavy cream
Pinch of nutmeg
Pinch of cinnamon
> *Add in and beat well.*

6 Tbsp. canola oil
> *Pour on a hot griddle. Dip bread slices in the egg batter and place them on the griddle. Grill well on all sides.*

½ cup honey
2 Tbsp. water
Pinch of cinnamon
> *Heat gently in a saucepan. Dip grilled slices of bread in it and place them on a serving platter. Pour remaining honey on top of the logs.*

Brioche French Toast

3 slices of brioche bread (see page 40)
> *Cut into triangles.*

3 eggs
1 Tbsp. heavy cream
Pinch of nutmeg
Pinch of cinnamon
> *Beat well in a bowl. Dip bread in the batter and grill on a hot griddle using 4 Tbsp. canola oil.*

Country Eggs

3 eggs
> *Beat well in a bowl.*

4 slices tomatoes, chopped
2 oz. Feta cheese, crumbled
> *Add in the bowl and mix well.*

4 Tbsp. canola oil
> *Heat in a skillet and fry the egg mixture, stirring occasionally until eggs are done.*

The respect for wildlife made ancients not break eggs. Very few recipes are found with eggs in ancient Greece. The incubator was invented by Romans for hatching eggs in quantity. Now farming of chickens allows us to use eggs without harming reproduction.

Baked Egg Sub

2 eggs
> *Place in a bowl and mix well.*

1 oz. Mozzarella cheese, shredded
1 oz. Provolone cheese, shredded
1 oz. Feta cheese
1 oz. Ricotta cheese
> *Add in the bowl.*

4 Tbsp. canola oil
> *Heat in a skillet.*

4 mushrooms, sliced
> *Add in and sauté for 1-2 minutes. Add the egg mixture and fry until eggs are done.*

1 8″ (approximately) sub roll
> *Slice one of the sides to create a pocket. Spoon in the egg mixture. Bake the sub in a 375° oven for about 6-7 minutes.*

Morning Steak

4 Tbsp. canola oil
1 6-oz. rib eye steak
> *Sauté the steak until done to your likeness. Place on a serving platter.*

1 Tbsp. canola oil
2 eggs
> *Heat oil in frying pan. Break the eggs in and cover. Cook for 2-3 minutes until eggs are basted. Place on top of the steak. Serve with Golden Grilled Potatoes (see page 273).*

Omelettes

All of the following omelets are made with 3 eggs. For best results eggs should be at room temperature. Place ½ tsp. heavy cream in bowl with eggs and beat well. Make sure the cooking surface is hot. Use about 4 Tbsp. canola oil. Place filling in the middle, fold the eggs over and then cover it until done.

CALIFORNIAN:
½ avocado, sliced
2 slices Cheddar cheese
4 strips bacon, cooked

ATHENIAN:
1 oz. Feta cheese, crumbled
1 artichoke heart (not marinated)
1 oz. crab meat, cooked and chopped

TOMATO PESTO:
⅛ cup Feta Pesto sauce (see page 115)
3 slices tomatoes, chopped
1 oz. Feta cheese, crumbled

ROMAN:
⅛ cup green pepper, sliced and grilled
⅛ cup Italian sausages, cooked and chopped
2 slices Canadian bacon, chopped and grilled

THREE CHEESE:
2 slices Swiss cheese
2 slices Provolone cheese
2 slices Cheddar cheese

Fritatas

Use 3 eggs and the same method as the omelets (see page 276). Only in this case you will mix the filling with the eggs and pour onto a hot surface, cover and cook. When done it will look like an open omelet.

SFOUGATO:
4 oz. ground beef, grilled
4 slices tomatoes, chopped
⅛ cup sliced onions, grilled
⅛ cup Mitzithra cheese, grated

ISLAND:
2 oz. crabmeat, grilled and chopped
3 asparagus spears, cooked and chopped
¼ cup broccoli, cooked and chopped
2 slices Swiss cheese, chopped

NICK'S:
1 oz. Feta cheese, crumbled
4 strips bacon, cooked and chopped
1 artichoke heart, chopped
1 heart of palm, chopped
4 or 5 french-fried potatoes, cooked and chopped

VEGETABLE:
⅛ cup broccoli, cooked and chopped
⅛ cup spinach, cooked and chopped
⅛ cup cream cheese
⅛ cup Mitzithra cheese, grated

Notes...

HIPPOCRATES

Hippocrates, the father of medicine, was the first to write about the respect of foods, especially the foods which grew from the earth.

The old Greek doctor had many theories about the benefits of foods which nurse our bodies and those theories have been confirmed from science throughout the centuries. Just before the 4th century B.C., Hippocrates wrote:

"For that of medicine would not have been invented at first...if when men are indisposed, the same food and other articles of regimen which they ate and drink when in good health were proper for them, and if no others were preferable to these....I hope not even the mode of living and nourishment enjoyed at the present time by men in health would have been discovered, had a man been satisfied with the same food and drink as satisfy an ox, a horse and every animal except man. For example, the productions of the earth, such as fruits, weeds and grass...from this necessity it appears to me that they would search out the foods befitting their nature...fashioning them to the nature and powers of man and considering that the stronger things nature will not be able to manage if administered, and that from such things pain, diseases and death would arise. But such a nature could manage, that from them food, growth and health would arise...experimenting with food they baked or boiled, after mixing many other things, combining the strong and uncompounded with the weaker components, to adapt all to the constitution and power of man."

Today, we must understand what Hippocrates was saying, we can prevent illness and become stronger by the way we eat.

According to Plato, Hippocrates was a contemporary of Socrates. Hippocrates was a practitioner and a teacher of medicine. He traveled from city to city. But mostly he practiced and taught the art of medicine in Athens which was the mecca of the great sophists and rhetoricians.

Hippocrates is the father of medicine. Today, all doctors take the Hippocratic Oath before practicing medical duties. The oath first originated from his famous medical school of Cos.

Hippocrates was born in 460 B.C. and died in old age, in approximately 375 B.C. in Larissa. The last account for his tomb was in the early 3rd century A.D.

Galen, legislator of medicine, believed that the "best physician is also a philosopher." He wrote that Hippocrates was the ideal physician "who with purity and with holiness lived his life and practiced his art."

Galen's library burned during the fire in Rome in 191 A.D. Little of his writing is known now. Galen died shortly after that at the turn of the century.

COPYCATS

It happens all the time!

Copyright violations have been abused since the dawn of time. We can hear it in music. We can see it in movies, paintings, clothes, writings and all other arts. We even notice it from people who in their effort to impress us are using someone else's humor and wisdom.

Copyrights are widely abused in cooking also. Of course, it's flattering if someone uses your idea for entertainment and it is satisfactory to be someone else's inspiration to broaden their ideas. We all have been touched by someone's genius in our life.

To purposely copyright someone for personal gain is a disrespect to the artist's work. What kind of people imitate others? I believe they are the ones who lack imagination and are without dignity. Not everyone is fortunate to possess imagination but everyone should have the dignity to ask and respect the permission of the artist who has devoted endless hours to create the work.

Copyrights, supposedly, are protected by laws. Once you have filed your original work with the Library of Congress, you should be protected. The 1976 Copyright Act gives the owner of copyright the exclusive right to authorize others for the use of his or her work in literary, dramatic musicals, artistic and all other original work.

But people motivated by greed are trying to invade someone else's work. To a true artist this is an insult. It has little to do with money. Granted, every artist has every right to be rewarded. It is the frustrating idea that someone will take your original work and abuse it for personal gain.

The following lines are a part of a write-up by Miss Elin Jeffords, one of the most well-known food critics in the Phoenix area:

Page 10 – Tribune Newspapers, TGIF, August 11, 1995

Nick Ligidakis' influence felt at Euro Cafe

By Elin Jeffords
Tribune correspondent

...A young server brought us menus. Listing close to 200 items, it immediately recalled Nick Ligidakis' Golden Cuisine menu. To digress slightly, Ligidakis is somewhat of a legend locally, both for his selfless charitable involvement and his very idiosyncratic restaurant. He prides himself on his culinary creativity, his huge menu, his enormous portions, his ultra-rich pastries and the fact he prepares everything from scratch. He has an immensely loyal following, and, I quickly deduced from the many references to him on Euro's menu, an acolyte named Romeo has done a spin-off. (Another is Mike's golden Crust in Glendale.)...

Miss Jeffords went on to be very critical of the food that was served to her in that restaurant. To the point that I was greatly bothered because my creations were abused. Both of these men mentioned in the write up have worked for me and went on to open restaurants. For me the knowledge of wrongdoing followed by an apology would have been enough satisfaction. There are others who try to mimic. Some blandly tell you right to your face that they will use your work.

When the new ownership bought the San Carlos Hotel and after the owner learned of my plans for leaving the restaurant and that my name, recipes and menus would go with me because they are copyrighted, to my surprise she turned to me and said, "We bought the hotel and all that comes with the property." I mean, how bold is that?

Copycats are not always negative. For example, I know of at least a dozen restaurants which have imitated my Thanksgiving Project to feed the hungry. And that is a great thing.

I didn't know Nick Ligidakis very well, but through dinners and desserts eaten in a few of his restaurants, I came to appreciate and admire him tremendously. I tried to catch his eye a few times while he was working in his kitchen or just wandering through his restaurants, but only once or twice did he happen to look up and return my gaze, and, just for a second, smile.

Smiling is something I didn't see Nick do very often. He was always so intent on what he was creating at the time. I understood that, and accepted his aloofness as just plain being busy. Now that I have finished "our" first book together, and am in the middle of the second, I am privileged to work with him, learn about him, and, maybe just a little, understand him. Plus, he smiles a lot more now.

This book is a tremendous effort for anyone to undertake, and I am proud to be a part of its development and accomplishment. Of course, Nick deserves all the credit. All I did was offer a few suggestions here and there, type it, and revise it, and revise it, and revise it... It's a great book, and it was written and imagined by a great man.

To everyone, enjoy this work. Though some of us may have been in similar shoes as Nick has been with either business or family, there is one difference. Nick is honestly the man portrayed here, everychapter and every recipe of it.

Thank you, Nick, for this opportunity, and for our continued long and meaningful friendship.

Debra N. Ross, 1997

THOUGHTS

I started writing this book in the summer of 1993. I was on my way to Greece for vacation. The flight from Phoenix to Athens via New York is a long one. I always like to write so I made use of my plane flight. My idea for this book is simply to tell a story of someone who started a small business from nothing without even the belief of one person of my dream. Then, there were one or two persons who became fans of my cooking and soon there were thousands, tens of thousands who would enjoy my cooking and respect the concept of not only taking but also giving.

To me, success is not measured on how rich a person's bank account is, but how much people believe in you and your art. I did not know how this book would end, but that was the exciting part. I wanted this book to end as a great success story of a boy from Greece who made it big in America. It just sounded good for an ending, I guess.

But the ending took an unexpected twist. The ending even surprised me! The biggest surprise was how good it felt to finally sit back and catch up with the things I had neglected all these years in my struggle to survive: my family, my sanity, myself, even the writing of this book was put on the back burner for years. Even though I wanted to preserve my recipes, there was not enough time in my days or enough energy in my mind.

On that trip in the summer of 1993 I was determined to someday finish this project. I was just hanging around in the JFK Airport in New York. I arrived there from Phoenix and was waiting for my flight to Athens.

"Hello, Mr. Ligidakis," I heard a voice saying. I turned around and saw a gentleman talking to me.

"Hello, sir," I replied. I was confused as to how this man knew my name.

"I love your restaurant," he said.

I was relieved to hear that because it answered my question where this man knew me from. We talked for a while. He was traveling from Phoenix to Israel and was waiting for his flight to Tel Aviv.

I walked to the little airport store to get a newspaper. As I was standing in line, a lady who was walking by looked at me and smiled.

"You are from Phoenix," she said.

"Yes, I am." I replied.

"You are that person who has a restaurant and feeds the hungry every Thanksgiving," she said.

I was really puzzled of how people knew of my restaurant. Aafter all, I was in New York, on the other end of the country. She told me that she never had been in the restaurant, but saw it on the T.V. news. She promised she would visit the restaurant when she was back in Phoenix. She went on to catch her flight.

I sat in a chair at the New York airport and thought that this was very odd that two people within a few minutes, would know my restaurant in Phoenix. I started thinking of more people who I had met through the business. A person who once picked up a calzone said, "I am going to San Diego to see my wife. She told me not to come unless I had a Nick's calzone with me."

Another person drove straight from Houston and said, "I wanted to get here before you closed so I could have your manicotti," he said.

There was a girl who was going to have a baby and was worried what to eat in the hospital and asked me if I would deliver her food.

One morning I went to open the store at 7:00 a.m. and this couple was waiting outside. "We have been waiting here since 6:00. We are going out of town. Will you make us some dinners to take with us?" they asked.

"I was in Napal for a month. There were only six Americans there. We started to talk about restaurants back home and to my surprise I found another person that I had something in common with. He was a frequent guest of Nick's. We talked for hours about his food, and we got homesick." When that story was told to me I realized how small the world is.

Someone from Chicago took 48 loaves of bread with her on her way back.

Another woman from Dallas wanted 48 cinnamon rolls to freeze.

Wayne has moved to Minnesota but every time he comes to Phoenix he makes me prepare 16 pizzas and he takes them back frozen.

I can fill pages with memories. I was determined to preserve some of the memories and all the recipes. I am glad I waited until now to finish my book because I would not have been able to share all the years of memories and wisdom I have collected over time. Besides, until recently I would not have known how it all would have ended.

What the press is saying about Nick, his cooking, and his charity work…

Cook Finds Himself In Tight Spot

Kitchen makes every inch count

By Dorothee Polson
The Arizona Republic

Table No. 3 is known as the Torture Table at the Golden Cuisine Restaurant, 5024 E. McDowell.

Torture because the table is square against a refrigerated case and displays more than two dozen dazzling desserts, such as After Death Cake, amaretto fruitcake, Jack Daniel's pudding and baklava.

But if you sit at table No. 3, and have the willpower to tear your eyes from Sweet Chocolate Death (layers of cake, meringue, chocolate mousse and chocolate icing) and look beyond, you can watch owner Nicolaos Ligidakis cooking in a very tiny kitchen.

How tiny is it?

It is so small that there is room for only one person in the cooking area.

It is so small that standing between his range and his preparation counter, Nick can reach both. Within a step is his refrigerator, freezer and pizza oven.

That's small.

Yet from this cramped, one-cook space, Ligidakis bakes all the desserts, cooks the 220 items on his menu, prepares about 100 takeout orders daily, and serves more than 240 sit-down meals every day in a dining room that seats 38 people.

"It is a matter of kitchen organization," Ligidakis said. "I used my engineering background to plan for everything to be within reach of my fingertips."

The walls provide the storage, with open shelves built to the ceiling holding grape leaves, capers, hearts of palm and other exotic supplies.

Crowded into a corner of the kitchen, I watched for two hours as Nick swiftly prepared lunch orders. At one point he was working on two submarine sandwiches, two pita sandwiches, chicken Kapama, a Golden Salad, a monumental pizza and a herculean calzone (turnover) – all at one time.

"That's nothing," a waitress whispered as she squeezed past me.

At dinner he is often working on 30 orders at a time."

Everything is cooked from scratch and to order. Yet Ligidakis never looks at an order ticket, never consults a recipe – he has created most of them – never uses a timer, and, so far, has not been known to make a mistake.

"It is all in my head" is the way he explains it.

When he bought the tiny takeout pizzeria in 1984, it was grossing about $36,000 a year.

"Now I do that much in a month," he said.

His story is the American Dream: the penniless immigrant who toils tirelessly and makes his fortune from the kitchen of his homeland.

"The customers liked my pizza and kept coming back, bringing friends.

"I started creating new recipes: first lasagna, then sandwiches, then Greek and Italian specialties. I never stop thinking of new dishes.

"I taught myself how to bake. I had never baked in my life; now I turn out 80 cakes a week plus other desserts. I create a new one almost every week.

"Now 90 percent of my business is repeat customers," he said.

In Greek tavernas the kitchen is as busy as the dining room. Customers may go into the kitchen and peer into the pots to see what's cooking before they make their selections.

"My kitchen is too small for that, but it is important to me that people can see into my kitchen and watch me cook if they want to," Ligidakis said. "I feel of my place, this is Europe."

"Never, in my wildest dreams, did I ever plan to have a restaurant," he said.

An engineering graduate, Ligidakis was a professional soccer player in his native Greece when he was recruited to play soccer in the United States. But the sports promoters ran out of money, and the team of young Greek athletes was left stranded in Chicago. That was in 1969, when he was 24 years old.

"I had no money and could speak no English," Nick recalled. "Fortunately, there is a big Greek community in Chicago. I got a job in a Greek bakery, then in a Greek restaurant; but in management, not cooking.

"My father had owned a taverna (small cafe) in Greece for 35 years and was famous as a chef. We kids never worked in his restaurant, but we great up knowing good food."

Things went well for Nick in Chicago, but by the time he got to Phoenix, he had only $52 and nowhere to live.

"I saw this small place, the Golden Pizzeria, for sale," he said. "The banks wouldn't even talk to me, but I had friends who loaned me a down payment. I went $50,000 into debt, worked 18 hours a day, seven days a week for a year and half. I slept on an air mattress in the kitchen.

"I had never made pizza in my life, so I read books and studied about it. First thing I did was throw out the microwave oven."

Golden Cuisine has outgrown its premises. It will close July 3 and reopen Sept. 1, three doors down, in the same shopping strip. There will be a huge commissary for Ligidakis' new enterprises, including a wholesale line of Golden Boy feta dressing and other sauces. The commissary also will prepare desserts and sandwich ingredients for his new, franchised fast-food chain, Pita Stop. The first Pita Stop will open July 15 at Tri-City Mall.

The new Golden Cuisine will feature a pasta maker's kitchen with a glass front so guests can watch. The entry will be a spacious retail deli area. There will be much more storage space.

"But the dining room will be only a bit bigger, not for more seats, but for more comfort," Ligidakis said.

And the kitchen?

"Same size as before," he said. "The original plan works perfectly. There is no need to make it bigger."

Table No. 3 still will be the Torture Table, set against a display of more new desserts than ever. And between them there will be a view of the dinky kitchen with the former soccer player-engineer at work. Cooking.

Best Pizza / East Phoenix

The Valley's News and Arts Journal

1984

Golden Pizza
5024 E. McDowell

Golden Pizza's fresh, delicious pies are done right, from the crust on up. The sauce is think and spicy; the good-quality cheese is lavishly applied; the Italian sausage is homemade; the vegetables are crisp. There's even a wider than usual choice of add-on items, including banana peppers, Canadian bacon and pineapple. In addition to its supreme pie, Golden Pizza serves an excellent calzone and an unusual and savory version of Buffalo wings.

DESTINATIONS OF THE SOUTHWEST

Nick Ligidakis'
Golden Cuising of Southern Europe

*6 mi. E. at 5024 E.
McDowell Road
275-9223
L.D. Sun. reserved
D only. Closed Mon.
Closed July 15-Aug. 15
Moderate*

Phoenix, Arizona – The pizza, pastas, and southern European specialty dishes served here are outstanding. In addition, some of the most tantalizing and novel desserts in the Southwest are displayed in deli cases along one side of the tiny dining room. How about cinnamon stick cake, for example? It's an epicurean extravaganza of cinnamon, walnuts, honey, orange zest, and whipped cream, with a baklava crust. Sunday dinners, by reservation only, are worth a special trip. This out-of-the-way culinary haven is a tribute to the chef/owner's skills, innovative spirit, and dedication to freshness and the use of quality ingredients.

Restaurant Owner Considers A Finished Meal A Failure

By Dave Eskes
The Phoenix Gazette
Friday, March 27, 1987

SCOTTSDALE – Publisher Brad Steiger spoke of Nick Ligidakis' Golden Pizzeria with a reverence customarily reserved for Michelangelo's statue of "David."

"I was picking up some photos at Image Craft," he began, "when I got the hungries. So I stopped by Nick's for a small sandwich.

Steiger had never been in Nick's. As he recalled the transforming experience, his voice rose.

"A small sandwich? It was a turkey sub – it was incredible!"

Ligidakis has become something of a cult figure to East Valley residents. Especially those at the Motorola plant across from his tiny restaurant on 50th Street and McDowell.

The former soccer player has a simple, Spartan motto: "If you finish your meal, I have failed."

Ligidakis seldom fails. His calzones, for example, are hubcap-size and fill an entire plate. Doggy bags are the rule, not the exception.

Which suits his customers fine. In the tradition of Henry VIII, they firmly believe a bulging stomach is at least as important as a meal's presentation.

Presentation, after all, can loosely be interpreted as the act of setting the plate on the table.

Steiger became so impressed with Ligidakis (who does most of the cooking) and his victuals that he collaborated on a cookbook with with the chef.

Called "Nick's Creative Cooking Made Easy," it contains 160 original creations, ranging from appetizers to soups and entrees, to breads and desserts.

In it, you will find everything from fish roe salad to fried milk. But most recipes are staples such as Eggplant Mousaka, Veal Skordato and Stuffed Eggplant Leaves. And most use common ingredients.

"Nick's Creative Cooking" is a local production, with black and white photos of Ligidakis hard at work, while his customers chow down around crowded tables.

It is liberally sprinkled with testimonies as fervent as those at tent meetings. Included among them are:

"The Fettuccini Formaggi is a pasta and cheese love's heaven! Nick's special touches put me on Cloud Nine!" Kristie.

Or, "Being a connoisseur of fine foods and dining, I look to each experience as an adventure." Sincerely, Glen.

Then, an unashamedly biased, "Nick Ligidakis, a great cook and an excellent father...I recommend Chicken Picata..." Steve Ligidakis.

The affable Ligidakis is not exactly an unknown quantity. He has been reviewed numerous times and appeared on the "Cookin' With Rita" show on KPHO-TV (Channel 5) a few months ago.

He will appear on "Cookin' With Rita" again, at 8 a.m. April 4.

"He just seems to put things together," Steiger said. "I suggested he *had* to write things down. Panic was the motivator. They had to be preserved."

Ligidakis is excited for quite another reason.

"I hope customers cook my recipes," he said. "It takes the heat off me, and they won't have to wait to be seated."

PEOPLE PLUS — Marathon man

By Dave Eskes
The Phoenix Gazette
Thursday, November 24, 1988

For **Nick Ligidakis**, it's been just another day...and night...and day.

Ligidakis, owner of Golden Cuisine on McDowell Road, is accustomed to working like a slave on a Roman galley.

After all, the affable ex-soccer player from Greece offers a menu the size of "War and Peace" and does most of the cooking himself.

This year – the third year in a row – he cooked Thanksgiving dinner for the homeless at the Central Arizona Shelter.

And he cooked for 1,000 hungry people – twice as many as last year.

Wednesday, Ligidakis and his wife, **Karen**, closed the restaurant at 2 p.m. and, with a handful of friends, prepared 75 turkeys.

They did it all from the kitchen of Golden Cuisine, which makes a walk-in closet look like a suite at the Biltmore.

Ligidakis didn't know how many potatoes he's use. Or yams. Or cranberries. Or vats of dough for rolls.

He doesn't work that way.

"I can cook about 16 turkeys at one time," he said. "The pizza oven holds eight, and the two smaller ovens about four each."

"I don't really plan. But, you know, that's the way I like to work."

Ligidakis financed the project, which cost $4,500, from sales of his cookbook, "Nick's Creative Cooking Made Easy," and out of his own pocket.

It's his way of saying thanks.

ZAGAT ARIZONA RESTAURANT SURVEY

Golden Cuisine of Southern Europe
5024 E. McDowell Road (50th St.), Phoenix, 275-9246

This tiny hole-in-the-wall is a cult favorite among locals; dynamo chef-owner Nick single-0handedly bakes luscious desserts and prepares from scratch Mediterranean-inspired creations; portions are obscenely large, prices low and service comes with a smile.

Pita eatery helps put stop to burger blues

By Carrie White
Tribune writer

The Pita Stop may not be a fancy enough choice for a first date.

But you won't want to miss it the second time around.

The dishes can get a bit sloppy. But boy, are they good. And fresh. And, for this type of establishment, they are a delightful alternative to the burger blues.

The Pita Stop is in perhaps an unlikely location – the west end of the second floor of Tri-City Mall in Mesa.

Tri-City Mall is not the same tired shopping facility some people will remember it as being. The place has been spruced up to be more contemporary, convenient and appealing.

Part of that change includes a discount movie theater, outside of which are a few food outlets, including Pita Stop.

I had received the Pita Stop menu some time back, along with the bill of fare from Nick Ligidakis' other restaurant, Golden Cuisine of Southern Europe, at 5024 E. McDowell Road in Phoenix.

It was the restaurant's menu at which I first took a gander. What a menu! Never have I seen such a varied and appetizing selection.

The Mesa outlet, however, is geared more toward the eat-and-run crowd. Most offerings are of the stuffed-into-a-large-thick-pita variety.

Getting past the display case of totally decadent and mouthwatering desserts to grab a menu takes a true showing of herculean strength.

Some of the selections screaming for attention include a cake dubbed After Death – a concoction of walnut meringue, white mousse, almond cream, almonds, buttermilk, cake, banana mousse, white chocolate frosting and hazelnuts at $3 a slice.

I know I will not have lived until I get a taste of Sweet Chocolate Death – chocolate meringue, chocolate mousse, chocolate cake, chocolate icing and almonds, also $3 a slice. Pita Stop does sell its homemade desserts by the slice or by the cake. Cakes are priced in the $20s. Also sold are a wide variety of salad dressings by the pint, with prices ranging from $4.25 for a feta cheese dressing to $2.55 for a vinegar and oil selection.

But we were here for the serious stuff this time, so we looked over an extensive menu of pitas, which range in price from $3.55 for the gyros to $4.95 for the mushroom steak pita.

Included on the menu are appetizers, four salads, a variety of dressings and 13 pitas. Also included is an item called Nick-A-Bob ($4.25), a spicy blend of ground lamb and beef topped with provolone cheese, lettuce, tomatoes, onions and yogurt sauce.

The gyro platter ($6.25) includes grilled gyro meat served over pita bread with yogurt sauce, feta cheese, kalamata olives, peperoncinis, red onions and tomatoes.

Among the more interesting selections were the deep-fried ravioli salad (deep-fried, cheese-stuffed ravioli, tossed in Romano and Parmesan cheeses, mixed with black olives, peppers, tomatoes, hearts of palm, red onions, salami, sugar peas and mustard vinaigrette dressing, $5.95); and the Reuben pita (pastrami and sauerkraut tossed in Thousand Island dressing and topped with Swiss cheese, $3.95).

We chose to split a Greek peasant salad ($4.95). For the main course, my spouse chose a gyro, while I ordered a Spartan pita ($3.95).

The wait for our order was not long, just 5 minutes. While the eating area had been fairly deserted when we arrived, the tables quickly filled up when Lamson College, located to the west of the eating area, let out.

Alcoholic beverages are not for sale in this food bazaar. At home, with a couple glasses of red wine, we unwrapped the generously proportioned dinner.

The salad was weighted down with feta cheese. A simple oil and vinegar dressing topped large chunks of tomato, slices of cucumber, thin-sliced red onion and green pepper rings, eight kalamata olives and just a bit of iceberg lettuce. Nothing in this salad had been sitting around. Everything was fresh.

Then came the pitas. My spouse could barely get his hands around the gyro, so much lamb had been packed into a fresh, pillowy pita. The slices of medium-cooked meat boasted a wonderful lamb flavor. My spouse thought the meat a bit on the dry side, I didn't. Both of us, however, found it very tender.

Included in the bulging pita was a homemade yogurt sauce – thin slices of red onion, tomato and shredded lettuce.

My Spartan pita could be likened to some of the very best pizza I've ever had. I like a thick crust, which the pita does resemble. Inside was a combination of grilled vegetables that included zucchini, green pepper, mushrooms, green olives and onions.

Artichokes and hearts of palm also were supposedly included in the mixture, which was tossed with Italian dressing. But the heavy melting of provolone cheese made most of the ingredients indistinguishable. But was it good.

What impressed me the most about Pita Stop is that the foods are fresh and great care is obviously taken. One doesn't usually find this caliber of food fare in a small mall outlet.

The Pita Stop's food deserves top marks. But the absence of honest-to-goodness service and ambiance precludes the awarding of a four-star rating.

The cost of the meal was $13.26.

Cox Arizona Publications Inc.

Friday, November 23, 1989

Restaurateur to feed 4,000 homeless

Cookbook proceeds help fund holiday goal

By Robert Perez
Tribune writer

Like countless others, Nick Ligidakis is going to be slaving over a hot stove today, except his Thanksgiving meal is going to feed about 4,000 people.

Ligidakis, owner of the Golden Cuisine of Southern Europe restaurant, is making his Thanksgiving statement by providing a hot meal for many of the county's homeless.

"I think we have about 6,000 homeless people in the Valley," he said. "I'll do 4,000 this year. Next year I'll do all 6,000. I made a commitment to myself that I would feed all the homeless in the Valley."

Ligidakis started making Thanksgiving dinner for the less fortunate four years ago, just a year after opening his Phoenix restaurant. That year, he provided 250 dinners to the Central Arizona Shelter Services – the Valley's only permanent homeless shelter.

"It felt so good, I said I'll do it again next year," he said. "When they came in the first year, I saw their eyes and it was like Christmas."

He did do it again, feeding 400 the second year. Last year, he made enough food for 1,400 people.

Ligidakis, whose restaurant is at 3903 W. Thomas Road, is a proud immigrant from Greece and a third-generation restaurateur. His restaurant, which he opened five years ago, is popular and has received some of the highest accolades from professional and amateur critics alike.

"I get up in the morning, and I get excited," he said. "I want people to appreciate not only me but other people in the industry who do a good job."

His humble upbringing, he said, is what has made him eager to help those in need.

"I grew up in a poor country with a lot of pride," he said. "I will never forget where I come from. Just because I made a little money in this country, it doesn't make a damn bit of difference."

But Ligidakis has made a difference.

Mary Orton, CASS executive director, said Ligidakis is a good example of what one person can accomplish.

"It's really important that people realize there is always something one person can do," she said. "It shows that one person can do a lot. His effort is from the heart, and he's helping a lot of people."

The cost of the meals, about $9,000 this year, is paid by proceeds from Ligidakis' cookbook, *Nick's Creative Cooking Made Easy*, and by proceeds from a $75-a-plate dinner. The dinner raised about $3,000, he said, and also elicited offers of help from other restaurateurs for next year.

Ligidakis' efforts in the past four years have made him somewhat of an unofficial expert on the homeless. In addition to providing dinner for the CASS shelter, he will supply St. Vincent de Paul Society, feeding centers in Surprise and Mesa, the Salvation Army and others. A total of 29 agencies will receive Ligidakis' fare.

"I'm not going to save the world," he said, "but at least for one day a year I bring them happiness."

The Valley's News and Arts Journal

1986

Best Pizza/East Phoenix
Golden Pizza
5024 East McDowell Road

"Substantial" hardly seems adequate to describe a Golden pizza (would you call William Gerry "pleasingly plump?"), but it's more than worth the extra calories. Made with a crisp, breadlike crust and ladled with thick tomato sauce (so flavorful it's surely been simmering on the back burner), then topped with your choice of fifty (that's what we said, FIFTY) ingredients and a ton of melted cheese, it looks a little like a casserole, tastes like something you'd get in an Italian home. We're pretty sure this is how the Refrigerator got started.

5024 E. McDowell

What the press is saying

SOUTHWEST ADVENTURES TO WRITE HOME ABOUT

Enchanted Victorian Garden

PHOENIX HOME & GARDEN

ARIZONA'S HOME MAGAZINE

OCTOBER 1995 $2.00

Golden Opportunity

Because Nick Ligidakis doesn`t forget what it was like to be new and poor in Phoenix, he`s cooked and served Thanksgiving dinner to the homeless of Phoenix for the past three years. In the past he`s raised funds for this project through profits from his cookbook (which he sells at his restaurant, Golden Cuisine), through donations and from his own pocket. Last year Ligidakis served more than a thousand people.

This year, because his plans are grander (he hopes to serve 4000 of the Valley`s homeless), he`s decided to open the project to the entire community.

Sunday, October 15, at 5 p.m., Ligidakis and some of his friends – all top Valley chefs – will host a special event to raise money for Nick Ligidakis` Fourth Annual Thanksgiving for the Homeless. Ligidakis, Erasmo Kamnitzer of Razz International Cuisine, Eddie Matney of KousKooz and other chefs will present a cooking demonstrationédin-

ner party at Golden Cuisine, located at Tower Plaza, Phoenix. The cost is $50 per person.

Each chef will prepare, cook and serve a favorite recipe that guests will be able to take home. After "class," everyone will gather for a gala dinner party.

"This will be a fun evening and a way of doing good," Ligidakis says. "I`ve contacted shelters in Phoenix, Glendale, Chandler, Scottsdale and Mesa, and everyone is enthusiastic about it."

Ligidakis`own story is the American Dream cooked up in gourmet style. His Golden Cuisine, a 7000-square-foot restaurant, is where he invents and prepares more than 250 made-from-scratch dishes. His 50-person dining room is booked at least a week in advance. The take-out menu, salad dressing he sells and pita stop menu are legendary. But when he came to Phoenix, the young Greek soccer-player-turned-chef only dreamed of such success.

"During one stretch, I had no money so I had to sleep in the kitchen," he recalls. "When I realized that we

were really going to make it, I told Karen, my wife, that I wanted to do something to give back to this community. The first year I called the Central Arizona Shelter and offered to prepare and deliver Thanksgiving dinner. I cooked 15 turkeys and I`ve been doing it ever since."

This year, because Ligidakis`own business has grown to impressive proportions, his plans for Thanksgiving are more grandiose. He intends to deliver 350 turkeys with all the trimmings to homeless shelters throughout the entire Valley.

"Everyone is excited about it," he adds. "Last year, my customers all volunteered to help," Ligidakis recalls. "I closed the dining room, cooked 24 hours straight through, and when we finished and delivered the food to the Phoenix shelter, many of them told me that it was the best Thanksgiving they had ever had."

If you are interested in attending the dinner or helping with this project, write to Nick Ligidakis at Golden Cuisine, 3903 E. Thomas Road, Phoenix, 85018.

PITA STOP

The good things are always worth waiting for – as long as you don't have to wait too long. In the case of Nick Ligidakis (who's fabulous *Golden Cuisine of Southern Europe* restaurant we reviewed both in our July 19th, 1985 and February 27th, 1987 issues), waiting the extra five weeks for his newest venture, *Pita Stop*, was an almost unbearable escalation of anticipation. This was especially true since I had acquired an advance copy of the menu, a listing that activated my salivary glands practically to the point of embarrassment.

Working with a fast food foreman, *Pita Stop* shares a commissary-style common seating area with a number of other operations on the newly-opened second floor of Tri-City Mall, next to the cinema. The tables and chairs are plain and functional, receiving some salvation from the green plants and umbrellas that help give the environs more of an outdoor feeling. If you want soft lights, quiet and privacy, this is not going to be your cup of tea. It is, however, great for people watching.

The menu is divided into appetizers, salads, pita specialties and desserts, with an additional listing of the homemade bottled dressing to take home. Many of the dishes are regularly available at *Golden Cuisine*, but several new ones have been added. Nick is not one to rest on his laurels.

Broccoli Melt ($3.75) consisted of five large, deep fried balls of a fluffy fusion of mild Cheddar cheese and chopped florets of the namesake veggie, coated with a wisp of a golden brown breading. They were delightfully light, similar in texture and taste to a fine souffle, only here contained in a thin shell, and enhanced with a rich Cheddar and bacon dipping sauce. Another strong contender for star status in the appetizer category (although it was listed under "salads," it easily contained enough to be an appetizer for four) was the Deep Fried Ravioli Salad ($5.95). Based on the snappy cheese-filled squares which were coated in grated Romano and Parmesan cheeses, it was augmented with black olives, green bell peppers, tomatoes, hearts of palm, red onions, salami and sugar peas, the entire salad then tossed in a piquant mustard vinaigrette dressing. The contrast of flavors and textures was magnificent. Unfortunately, we were not as enthusiastic about the true-flavored Potato Nuggets with tangy feta cheese sauce ($2.95). The latter, though very tasty, did not, in my opinion, make for a successful marriage with the rather conventional spud buds.

We tried a number of the pitas, and found almost all to be outstanding. One of the secrets of their success is in the bread itself, which Nick imports from a tiny bakery in Chicago. Of course he treats them differently, too. They are grilled ever so *slowly* in a mixture of olive, vegetable and coconut oils, so that they tan rather than brown and don't develop the crust that ordinary pita bread does. The Asparagus Chicken Pita was a take-off on a Marco Polo, with a tender, thick breast of chicken covered with smoky ham, crisp asparagus and melted zesty provolone cheese topped with mustard sauce in a folded, soft grilled pita cradle ($4.55). All the specialties in this section have the bread wrapped around them instead of being in a pocket, which Nick's pitas are purposefully lacking.

The Monte Cristo Pita is similar in ingredients to the famous sandwich, only here just the filling of ham and turkey is battered and grilled, then topped with melted Swiss cheese. I did miss the powdered sugar, however, to contrast to the nice smokiness of the ham and saltiness of the cheese. Nick makes his own *gyros*, a mixture of spiced ground beef and lamb that is vertically spit-roasted and thinly sliced. The Feta Gyros Pita combines a huge amount of meat with artichoke hearts and both feta cheese and feta sauce. This is a particularly messy sandwich, but licking your fingers is part of the fun (you certainly wouldn't want to waste any of this one anyway). The Nick-A-Bob had a huge oval ground beef and lamb patty on a bed of shredded lettuce, tomatoes and onions, topped with provolone cheese and yogurt sauce ($4.25). There must be some Greek in me somewhere, because I adore dishes made with lamb. Here its flavor was not masked by the other ingredients, and I especially loved it for that.

Other pitas that friends tried (and kept to themselves) were the Mushroom Steak, the Artichoke Chicken and the Bleu Roast Pita. Moans of delight ensued from the recipients of the first two, the latter complained of two much bleu cheese (but, without offering anyone else a bit, he managed to finish it with aplomb, so it most assuredly couldn't have been an unpleasant experience).

In addition to the usual beverages, they also have a range of natural flavored *Calistogas*, including cranberry, lemonade, mandarin orange and black currant, as well as *Baron's* ginseng ginger-ale and chocolate drinks.

All Nick's desserts are rich beyond imagination. At his *Golden Cuisine* restaurant, I almost always was so stuffed from his oversized portions of everything that I rarely had had room for these unique creations, though the descriptions had tantalized me on more than one occasion. Forget everything you ever thought about pudding and try his Jack Daniel's version ($2.50). With its bittersweet and semi-sweet chocolates, whipped cream, butter, eggs, rum and, of course, Jack Daniels whiskey amalgamated into one heavenly mixture, you know you'll be jogging for a week to work off all those calories. Unfortunately, this dessert, out of all the ones we tried, probably had the least of those fattening demons. The Cheesecake Brownie ($2.00) was creamy beyond belief. The Cinnamon Stick Cake had a base of a wonderfully tangy cheesecake with just a hint of cinnamon, topped with a honeyed walnut and pecan blend, then crowned with layers of golden, buttery filo pastry, a la baklava. If we thought eating that was a sinful act, we were ready to repeat when we finished the last gooey bit of the dark chocolate cake, white chocolate cream cake, raspberries and a Chambord (raspberry liqueur) almond crust that combined to comprise a cake called – you guessed it – A Sinful Act.

Undaunted, we proceeded on our orgy of indulgence to Sweet Chocolate Death, a layering of chocolate meringue, chocolate mousse, chocolate cake, chocolate icing and almonds. What a way to go! The only fitting sequitur, at this point, could be After Death. This is an original compilation containing strata of walnut meringue, white chocolate mousse, almond cream, almonds, buttermilk cake, banana mousse with bits of golden raisins, all bathed in a white chocolate frosting coated studded with a coat of chopped hazelnuts. It, too, was to die for!

Each of the cakes and pies are $2.50 to $3.00 per slice (whole cakes of impressive size, are $18.00 to $26.00 with 24 hours notice), except A Sinful Act which is $3.50 and $28.00 respectively. Generous cups of Italian espresso ($1.25) and cappuccino ($1.50) allow you to lazily linger for a little while longer – and think about all the wonderful dishes Nick makes that you're going to try tomorrow. After all, "tomorrow *is* another day."

FOOD: Excellent   ATMOSPHERE: Fair
VALUE: Excellent   SERVICE: Self
HYGIENE: Good

Tri-City Mall, Upper Level (Dobson and Main), Mesa, 564-9796. Hours: 10 AM 'til 9 PM, Monday thru Friday, Saturday and Sunday ' til 6 PM. No alcohol or credit cards.

Note: Nick's *Golden Cuisine of Southern Europe* on McDowell Road at 53rd Street in Phoenix should be open by about the third week of September, after some remodeling has been completed. Call 275-9223 for details.

**THE WESTERN EXPRESS
VOLUME VII NUMBER 20**

THE PHOENIX GAZETTE

MARQUEE

Week of April 28 - May 4, 1990

Greek feast

Golden Cuisine creates savory southern European meals

**Golden Cuisine
of Southern Europe**

3902 E. Thomas Road
Phone: 275-9223

Hours: 10 a.m. - midnight (light menu); 5-11 p.m. Wednesday-Saturday and 4-9 p.m. Sunday (regular menu)

Cuisine: Southern European

Atmosphere: Upscale casual
Children's menu: no

Price range: Moderate

Reservations: Recommended, even on weekdays

Marquee comment: A gem.

The success of Nick Ligidakis and his restaurant is one of those "sounds too good to be true" stories.

Ligidakis is, among other things, an immigrant, soccer hero, author and benefactor. He also owns and operates *Golden Cuisine of Southern Europe*, and it is in that area that he excels.

In less than a decade, he has elevated a former pizzeria to one of the best restaurants in the Valley. It began several years ago when he opened the *Golden Pizza* on McDowell Road and 52nd Street. A short time later, he changed the name to *Golden Pizzeria*; five years ago, he renamed it the *Golden Cuisine*; 18 months ago he moved the operation to Tower Plaza.

This is one of those places that definitely should *not* be judged from the outside. It sits between a cowboy nightclub and a saloon, and if you glance through the front window, it looks like a bakery.

But those who venture inside are well-rewarded with a pleasant dining experience.

The restaurant, which features southern European cuisine heavily influenced by recipes from Greece (Ligidakis' homeland) and Italy, has two menus. The light menu offers pizza, calzones, sandwiches and a few specialties.

The real treat, however, is the big menu. It lists 64 entrees from sun-dried sea bass to linguini pesce, private dinners, special Sunday dinners, a half-page of appetizers and desserts with names like "Fatal Obsession" (layered citrus cake), "A Sinful Act" (white and dark chocolate cake) and "After Death" (white mousse with walnuts).

This menu, offered on a limited basis, can be trying because deciding between Greco-Roman steak, Corinthian sea bass or veal melitzana can produce the anguish of "what if," as in "what if I get this but that's better?"

Ligidakis does all the food preparation himself. "Everything is made to order," he says. "I don't pre-cook anything." The kitchen directly faces the eating area so diners get to watch as Ligidakis creates.

And create he does. Most of his recipes are his own, and many of them are printed in a cookbook on sale at the front counter. All the proceeds from the book go toward an annual Thanksgiving feast he prepared for the Valley's homeless. Last year, he delivered 6,000 meals to 29 shelters.

Despite all that, the bottom line is, of course, the food.

Is it good?

It's excellent.

Although forewarned about getting full too early, we started our night there with spinach puffs and pepperoni tirato, which is about the size of a football. It was the first time we ever asked for a doggy bag for appetizers.

Everything on the big menu looks good, but we narrowed it down to steak Metaxa ($12.95) and tortellini romanolla ($9.95) and were well-satisfied with our selections, although both of us wished we'd skipped the appetizers when confronted with the size of the main course.

The service staff is small but knowledgeable and extremely helpful, and the fragrance of the desserts on display toward the front lingers long after the meal is completed.

The special Sunday and private dinners must be pre-ordered by the preceding Saturday night. Entrees range from leg of lamb to Bamia shrimp to Cornish game hen; prices range from $11.95 to $15.95.

One note of caution: The dining area is small, so reservations are highly recommended. But those willing to chance it usually will be seated in the bar and given a light menu.

Our bill came to $55.62, before tip and without drinks.

Marquee's restaurant reviewer prefers to remain anonymous in order to slip quietly in and out of Valley eateries. If you want to contact our reviewer, call 271-8651. We'll disguise our voice and call you back.

RECIPE FOR HIS SUCCESS

Hard work pays off for restaurateur

By Jean Novotny
The Arizona Republic

Nick Ligidakis has been in business for seven years, but he got his first paycheck only recently.

It has taken that long for the Phoenix restaurateur, owner of the *Golden Cuisine of Southern Europe*, to feel comfortable enough to take more from the business than just the amount he needs to live on.

That's how tough it is to make money these days in the food business. And it's getting tougher. The National Restaurant Association has projected there will be zero growth in real terms this year for restaurants.

What does it take to prosper in such a competitive climate?

Ligidakis has combined 100-hour work weeks with a willingness to diversify to develop his popular restaurant at 3903 E. Thomas Road in Tower Plaza Outlet Mall.

It's so popular that customers have to call two days in advance for reservations on the weekend.

Ligidakis' business actually has gotten better as the economy has gotten worse.

His secrets of success, however, are no secret to his customers.

One is hard work. Ligidakis said he's addicted to it. He puts in 90 to 100 hours a week, if not more, and takes only one day off a year, Christmas, which is also his birthday and his wedding anniversary.

Thanksgiving is the only other day he closes the place, and he spends that day cooking for the Valley's homeless. He prepared 5,000 meals last year and plans to do 7,000 this year.

The other element in Ligidakis' success formula is his expansion to such areas as cooking classes, a salad-dressing line, cookbooks, a dinner theater and sales of baked goods to other restaurants.

Those side businesses have helped push him closer to profitability.

Ligidakis expects to start making a profit, perhaps, $6,000 or $7,000 paying off debts he incurred when he moved to the 7,000-square-foot location in Tower Plaza two years ago.

When Ligidakis was getting the business started in 1984, he went for 1½ years without a day off and often slept on the floor of his tiny 38-seat restaurant, then located on McDowell Road.

"When I go back in my mind, I don't understand how I did it," said the 45-year-old Ligidakis, who grew up in Greece in a restaurant family.

"I think it was the customers who kept coming back, sometimes two or three times a week or sometimes every day. I felt obligated not just to them but to their friends who they told about the place.

"I could not let them down," he said. "For me, it was very important for the new people that the place was what it was built up to be."

Ligidakis said a restaurant must have consistency if its customer base is to be maintained.

"That is the No. 1 thing we want to achieve in our business," he said. "Customers can't be comfortable if the food tastes different each time. They need to get the same taste every time. That's why I'm always doing the cooking. If not, I'm supervising.

"I always know what's going on. My waiters say I can see through the walls."

And so at lunchtime and on Monday and Tuesday evenings, when he takes a little time off, the menu is reduced to basics so the consistency is not compromised.

The rest of the week, he holds court in his exhibition kitchen, and customers often line up to watch him meeting the challenge of preparing 30 or 40 dinners at once.

The former professional soccer player approaches that task as he would an athletic contest.

"I love it," Ligidakis said. "The more orders I get, the more I love it. I like to do what other people cannot do. It's impossible for other people to do what I do. It takes four people to do what I do. I push myself."

Consistency is a challenge because the menu is extensive and complex – there are more than 100 entrees, 85 toppings just for the pizza and more than 25 desserts – and because everything is prepared to order.

Most chefs prepare lasagna, for example, in bulk ahead of time. But not Ligidakis. The pasta is not cooked, nor is the dish assembled, before the order has been received.

Prospective employees learn quickly how important consistency is to Ligidakis.

"When I interview them, I tell them there is bad and there is good about this place," he said. "The good part is that they will make good money, our business doesn't slow down in the summertime, and they will always get compliments and raves from the customers.

"The bad part is me. I know what I want from them. I want them to know they can't make mistakes and repeat them over and over. They have to learn from me."

Ligidakis stresses quality and volume in his food. Because of this, he refuses to compromise when it comes to the ingredients he uses or the size of the portions served, as restaurant operators are tempted to do when money is tight.

Most customers, in fact, leave with doggie bags because *Golden Cuisine* portions are so large. He'd also like them to leave with other goodies from the restaurant's grocery and takeout section. The grocery center offers specialty ingredients for ethnic cooking, and the takeout area features fresh and frozen items for home preparation as well as baked goods.

The grocery and takeout section is just one of his attempts to diversify.

The *Golden Cuisine* does breads and desserts for other restaurants, such as Tomaso's, Raffaele's, Christo's and Milano's Restaurant, and his Golden Boy salad dressings are sold at groceries such as Euromarket, AJ's, Hilander Foods and Reay's Ranch Market.

Golden Cuisine also supplies food for a company called the Food Group, which employs people to go around to office buildings with baskets filled with muffins, sandwiches and salads for office workers.

Then there are the cooking classes every Saturday and the dinner-theater presentations in the back room on the weekends. A newsletter is in the works, and a dessert cookbook is ready to be printed.

"I want to do all this because I have the facilities," he said. "My overhead is too high, and I need other avenues to make money."

He said he also feels they are all things that will help him keep in touch with his customers.

"The only way to maintain my customer base is to make sure customers get what they came here to get," he said. "My bread and butter is my dining room, and I don't want to ignore that."

The Magazine of Wine, Food, Travel, & Fine Dining

WINE COUNTRY ®

I N T E R N A T I O N A L

FEBRUARY/MARCH 1990 $2.95

CHOICE CHEFS

Not long ago, Phoenix cuisine summoned up images of limp tacos and oversized steaks. Mexican food is still a specialty and cowboy steaks readily available, but thanks to some superb young chefs, the town's cuisine – like the legendary phoenix – has risen from its mesquite ashes.

Vincent Guerithault is credited with changing the face and taste of Phoenix. A classically trained French chef, thirty-six-year-old Guerithault was the first in Phoenix to combine Southwest ingredients with classic cuisine, inventing classics like duck tamales.

The first chef to receive a Citation of Excellence from the International Food & Wine Society, Vincent began his career at L'Oustau de Baumaniére, is Les Baux de Provence, where he worked alongside Wolfgang Puck. He arrived in Scottsdale in 1980 and quickly amassed a following. He opened his own restaurant, Vincent Guerithault on Camelback, to acclaim by food critics around the country.

Recently Vincent launched a private label wine, a delightful Chardonnay. Renowned artist Fritz Scholder created the art for the colorful label. The original painting now hangs in the restaurant.

Gourmands eagerly anticipated the opening in mid-December of Christopher Gross's long-awaited restaurant, Christopher's, at 24th and Camelback. Like Vincent, Chris Gross is a young, classically trained, inventive chef whose food is well presented but never pretentious, intriguing but not trendy. No doubt Christopher's will be hailed by critics, and devoted fans of Chris and Vincent will have difficulty choosing between them.

Several other chefs merit attention. Like Vincent and Chris, RoxSand began her career in Scottsdale, relocating in Biltmore Fashion Park a few years ago, where she repackaged her creative menu in a trendy interior. Spare, contemporary elegance is the hallmark of this setting, which features fine contemporary art and creative cuisine. Anything that RoxSand makes with blue corn is a winner and her salads go on forever.

Less posh, not nonetheless delicious, is the Coyote Café (no connection with the more famous Santa Fe, New Mexico, establishment) on Scottsdale Mall. Laurie Vaca is the young chef/owner. Guests may dine inside in a plain café atmosphere, or outside on the covered patio. Most everyone begins with an order of Laurie's black bean cakes and then works through the Southwest-inspired entrées, saving room for homemade ice cream and fresh-fruit desserts.

Purists rave about Nick Ligidakis's Golden Cuisine in Phoenix. Nick is a strapping, Greek ex-soccer player turned chef who crowds more than two hundred items on the menu, all homemade by him. His cuisine is a magical blend of Italian and Greek dishes, served in healthy portions, sans frills. In a world where presentation is everything, Nick presents his own way – in a simple, converted coffee shop. Despite the absence of ambiance, Saturday nights require a reservation weeks in advance.

New Times The Valley's News and Arts Journal **1990**

BEST MENU
Nick's Golden Cuisine
3903 East Thomas

I personally once counted every item on the dinner menu, and lost track in the 90s. Maybe it was the 70s. Maybe it was the 900s. And this was before I could factor in all the different pizza combinations, which probably increases the grand total by another couple of million. Anyway, Golden Cuisine head dervish Nick Ligidakis cooks everything to order, no matter what. Favorite menu items: the huge calzones. If you look carefully, you can see them on the TV weather pictures from outer space.

12,000 meals spark the spirit of Thanksgiving

by Sam Lowe

The Phoenix Gazette

Nov.

1991

Nick Ligidakis is a good interview. He's honest, straightforward, sincere and he answers the questions without hesitation and there's no reason to doubt any of what he says.

But still I wonder.

I wonder why a successful person who's never been poor or hungry would go to such lengths to help those who are.

What's in it for him?

So I put on my cynic's face.

"Why are you doing this?" I ask.

The answer is about what I expected. Ligidakis is honest, straightforward and sincere. He says he does it to help people. I should have known.

He speaks quietly, but with great passion, as he lists, once more, the reasons for his annual Thanksgiving feast. They're always the same. Last year. This year. Next year.

He says he enjoys helping people. He admits it gets rather expensive. He says he doesn't get discouraged, even though there are more hungry people every year instead of fewer.

His story is told frequently. It started six years ago. He'd had a good year and wanted to do something for the community, so he decided to put on a dinner for the homeless. He prepared meals for 250 people and delivered them to various agencies around the Valley.

"It was going to be a one-time deal," he says. "I cooked the food in my restaurant then delivered it. I figured that would be the end of it. But when they brought my pans back, they looked so happy. I thought if that's what it takes to make someone that happy, I'm ready to make a commitment."

Nick moved his restaurant to Tower Plaza and renamed it Nick's Golden Cuisine, and he's encountered financial problems (Chapter 11 proceedings and a dinner theater that didn't make it) but the project goes on.

Tuesday night, after he shuts down his restaurant, he'll start fixing turkey.

For 12,000.

That's not a misprint.

Twelve thousand.

"That's double what we had last year," he says. "The main reason we can help so many this year is that the Phoenix Valley Church of Christ is helping with food collections and raising money."

Ligidakis and his crew of 400 volunteers will prepare 450 turkeys, 80 cases of mashed potatoes, 100 cases of yams and 60 cases of cranberry sauce. They'll make equal amounts of bread, gravy and stuffing. On Thanksgiving, they'll deliver the meals to about 65 different agencies that serve the needy.

The church's involvement will reduce Ligidakis' share of the financial load, but he'll still put in a big chunk of his own money. Three years ago, it was $2,500. A reporter made a big deal out of it. He doesn't give out figures any more. Only that costs will be up about 20 percent.

Most of the money comes from the sale of a cookbook he wrote five years ago. He has sold more than 8,000 but Ligidakis says most of his friends and customers now have one, so sales have dropped off. He's planning three more.

"This doesn't get any easier," he says, still quietly, still passionately. "I'm amazed at how many homeless people there are. Twelve thousand this year. Can you imagine that? Twelve thousand! And there are some I can't get to. Thousands. When I started this, I thought I had it well-covered."

Although he's come to the realization that he'll never cure the problem, Ligidakis remains dedicated.

"Will it ever end?" he answers my question with one of his own, then answers it.

"No. As long as I live, I'll be doing this. If this restaurant doesn't make it, I'll go down the street and open up another one. this will continue."

The interview was over. He had been honest, straightforward and sincere.

But, having spent many of the last 35 years digging for ulterior motives, I still have a hard time believing that people do things for the reasons Ligidakis gives.

As we parted, I looked at the wall near the entry of Ligidakis' restaurant. It's covered with newspaper and magazine clippings about him, the restaurant and the Thanksgiving dinner, and for a second, I thought I had the answer:

He does it for the publicity.

But it's only a fleeting thought.

So the guy gets his name in the paper a lot.

Big deal.

On Thursday, 12,000 hungry people will get a good meal.

If I remember the "do unto others" rule correctly, that's what matters.

Nick's Cuisine of Southern Europe

3717 East Indian School, Phoenix
955-5225

by Howard Seftel

The menu at Nick's is so extensive that even an Evelyn Wood speed-reading graduate couldn't possibly get through it in less time than it takes to screen *Gone With the Wind*.

It's a good two feet long, almost as wide, and just a bit shorter than *A Tale of Two Cities*.

Cliff's Notes ought to add it to its inventory. I counted 38 appetizers (not including six kinds of stuffed potato skins and five versions of chicken wings), 13 salads and an astonishing 71 main-dish choices. The menu lists 80 pizza toppings, including sauerkraut, figs and oysters. After the 38 dessert options comes the staggering an-nouncement that there are "many more to come."

I wanted to scan the burgers, calzones, subs, pita specialties and breakfast items, but I promised my fifth-grader I'd be home before she finished law school.

Nick's is a pleasant place to do your reading. Now in its third Valley home, it features Mexican tile floors, gleaming stucco walls and obligatory posters of the whitewashed southern Mediterranean. Neatly stacked shelves of imported goods line the entryway.

No "less is more" philosophy from this kitchen. Portions here are firmly root-ed in practical Old World wisdom: "More is good, and a whole lot more is even better."

As you might expect, understatement, is not the hallmark of Nick's dishes. Goat shrimp, a house specialty, comes with some of the largest shrimp I've ever seen. These are what shrimp would look like, I imagine, if they pumped iron and took steroids. Four of these monsters get sautéed in garlic, olive oil and lemon, wrapped in a crisp slab of bacon, and sprinkled with sun-dried tomatoes and feta. Whew.

Veal melitzana seems to bring together all my favorite ingredients except hot-fudge sauce: two thin, tender pieces of breaded veal stuffed with a plateful of eggplant, artichokes and garlic in a chunky tomato sauce.

The pizzas have no short-comings, unless you're fool-ish enough to top them with pickled cauliflower and avo-cado. We chose hearts of palm and artichoke hearts, and got enough of them to satisfy even my craving for these costly treats.

Nick's calzones are simply outrageous. The stuffed, baked pockets of dough are mammoth, large enough to serve as a spare bedroom. They can easily feed three. Try the snow spago version, filled with crab meat, shrimp, asparagus, macadamia nuts, cashews and water chestnuts in a creamy cheese sauce with homemade pasta.

As the list of ingredients in the snow spago calzone indicates, Nick is a man who marches to his own culinary drummer. According to him, there are three ways to pre-pare a dish: the right way, the wrong way, and his way. You want it your way? Go to Burger King,. Nick will not alter his recipes or make sub-stitutions.

You won't want to change anything about dessert. The fig berry berry is fabulous, a buttery crust enfolding berries, figs and intense hunks of dark chocolate. Creamy cinnamon-stick cake, a cheesecake dotted with walnuts and pecans and drizzled with cinnamon syrup, is not far behind. And if you believe calories don't count, scarf up Final Addiction, a rich chestnut cake with coffee-laced white and dark chocolate.

Nick's extensive menu and friendly service make it an appealing place. Its seven-days-a-week late-night hours add to its charms. Except for slow readers and the terminally indecisive.

Putting the thanks back in Thanksgiving

by Bobbi Dugan
Echo Magazine
December, 1992

Seven years ago Nick Ligidakis looked around him and thought, "This is good. It's time to share." He had a home, a family, a successful restaurant. Ligidakis had come to America from Greece, 24 years before to play professional soccer. He stayed to become an upward-bound young entrepreneur living the Great American Dream.

Ligidakis had it all; including a small part of himself that really couldn't believe his good fortune. He had roots deep in European tradition. He had grown up in a post-war world that taught him many lessons about poverty, hunger and homelessness. Through hard work and stewardship he had gotten to a position of personal security, but he knew he could never enjoy his blessings while others around him went without. In this mood of introspection Ligidakis had an idea. He would invite a few of his less fortunate fellow citizens to Thanksgiving dinner.

So seven years ago, using his own money, his restaurant's kitchen, and the labor and encouragement of wife, children, friends and customers, Ligidakis put together a traditional turkey dinner for 250 people. "The next year it was 500." Nick says with raised eyebrow, as if he himself is astonished by the numbers, "and last year it was 12,000. Our goal is to feed 15,000 people this Thanksgiving."

Feeding 15,000 hungry would strain the abilities of many large organizations that exist for such purposes. Ligidakis and his crew of volunteers seem to do it with ease. Asked in early November if he as yet had enough donated money, food and help to bring off such an ambitious project, Ligidakis cheerfully replied, "No, but it will come in time. It always does."

Perhaps this is the confidence of someone who knows without a doubt he is doing the right thing, so it has to work.

What kind of folk does Ligidakis feed? "the homeless, the abused, the elderly, people with AIDS. It doesn't really matter. Anyone who is in need, we want to help," Nick says in his gracious manner. He talks at length about how much he gets personally out of the project . "It makes me feel so good when people write letters, or come to the restaurant to thank us," Ligidakis says. "Some of them hadn't eaten for days before the dinner." His voice gets soft, concerned. "Imagine having children

and watching them go days without food." Clearly Ligidakis cannot accept such a scenario. It's one of the reasons he does what he does

Another reason might be that Ligidakis loves food. He talks about cooking like some men talk about courting a beautiful woman. He seems endlessly fascinated with the creative possibilities presented by a loaf of bread, a jug of wine, and his own fertile imagination. "If you grow up in Europe, you grow up knowing good food," he explains, his Greek accent growing thicker as he remembers a different time and place, "You experience many varieties of food. You learn to create." Many of the succulent items on the menu at Nick's Cuisine of Southern Europe are marked "original," so that customers know they are Ligidakis' own invention. "Everything is made in house," Ligidakis states with pride, "Breads, pasta, everything. Each thing is made for you, the customer, personally."

Ligidakis' culinary offerings are as cosmopolitan as he himself. Greek, French, Italian and Spanish meals fill the menu.l The chef talks about each dish as if it were a beloved child; his creation that is first carefully prepared, then lovingly presented to the world. will his Thanksgiving dinner contain any special gourmet delights? "We serve turkey, dressing, potatoes, gravy, cranberry sauce," Ligidakis laughs, amused at his own answer, "It's a very traditional meal."

The turkey dinners are cooked at Ligidakis' restaurant, and delivered to various local social services who then distribute the food to their clientele. Salvation Army, St. Vincent de Paul, and others of their ilk are the recipients of Ligidakis' philanthropy.

It will take 450 turkeys this year to feed 15,000 people. As of this writing, Ligidakis doesn't have 450 turkeys. Before Thanksgiving rolls around he will need donations of food and money. He will rely on an army of volunteers to cook and deliver the meals. "It takes about 200 to prepare the food, and another 100 to deliver it," Ligidakis explains. The helpers represent every level of society; from school-children to the elderly, from the wealthy to the working class. Each seems to share Ligidakis' feelings about Thanksgiving. "I just couldn't sit down to a big dinner," he says very seriously, "knowing there are thousands of people out there with nothing to eat. I'm not going to save the world, but I know there are families who go hungry for days. It makes

me feel good to know this one day they will have enough to eat."

Ligidakis never went hungry as a child, but he grew up in a war-torn Europe with "lots of love and plenty of hard times." He looks around his beautiful restaurant, noisy with feeding customers and heavy with the scent of too much food, and seems almost surprised, "I am thankful to the community," he says. "I don't want to forget where I came from."

Still, organizing and expediting the feeding of 15,000 people is a very large payback, an enormous project, a terrific amount of work. "I don't think of it as work. It's so emotional. It's a high," Ligidakis says. He claims the many volunteers who help with the yearly event feel the same way, that the rewards of their efforts makes it all worthwhile. He has a hard time understanding why everyone doesn't reach out to their neighbor in need. "If you want to do something, just do it. Get involved." Ligidakis pauses and grins wickedly, his handsome Greek face lighting with mischief, "I'm tired of feeding all these thousands of people."

Ligidakis doesn't look like a man who ever gets tired. He exudes energy, health and vitality. Even during the interview for this story he was obviously aware of everything going on in the restaurant around him. He is stereotypically the American entrepreneur: Handsome, groomed, successful, charming. And, if his annual Thanksgiving charity is any indication, he's also a very nice person. Ligidakis seems almost too perfect. It is very tempting to be skeptical, to question his motives; tempting until a waitress, watching her boss walk away from the table at the end of the interview, sincerely asks, "Isn't he wonderful?"

Should any doubts about this remain, it is only necessary to linger at the bulletin board that stretches the length of the restaurant's foyer. Here are posted newspaper articles, citation, letters of appreciation from patrons and guests of past Thanksgiving feasts. Here also is a "thank you" note from that most sterling judge of character, a 7-year-old girl. "Dear Mr. Ligidakis," reads the clumsily-crafted missive. "Thanks for the food you gave us to eat. Happy Late Thanksgiving." You leave with the feeling that it is one of Nick Ligidakis' favorite pieces of correspondence.

Anybody wanting to volunteer or help out with this amazing Thanksgiving dinner project should call Nick's Golden Cuisine restaurant at 955-5225.

The Golden Age of Restaurants lives on, propped up considerably on the local scene by Golden Cuisine of Southern Europe, which serves wonderfully imaginative fare - worthy of gold medals, to be sure.

Sunday brunches, according to whichever pacesetter's list you are going by, may or may not be "in" this year. But, who cares about being trendy anyway? I, for one, feel that the big meal should come much later in the day so one can accomplish a few pleasant tasks at his leisure before being overcome by the inertia that sets in after stuffing one's face too full, an inevitable result of the many compelling temptations offered (and on the Sabbath, besides!) For my money, however, it's pretty hard to beat the old-fashioned Sunday dinner as *the* meal of the day , and it's even harder to beat the "Private Sunday dinners" offered by Nick Ligidakis at his recently transported *Golden Cuisine of Southern Europe.* this is a different approach to dining which results in a mood approaching that of eating at a friend's house. Nick only seats two tables an hour, and all the food from the special, more complicated menu, must be ordered at least 24 hours in advance. Needless to say, this day is by reservation only.

Having moved his entire restaurant from a space that was much smaller than his present kitchen is, Nick has now been able to greatly expand his operation to include a "Southern European Specialty Shop" of canned and packaged gourmet foods, another of his fast-food *Pita stop* sandwich and salad eateries, a "Sports Bar" (here, as well as in the restaurant, the walls are covered with pictures of Nick from his days as a professional player) with a liquor license pending, and, finally, a billion calorie area that features a carousel of sinful pastries and cases of "Di Rana" gelatos and other delectable frigid desserts, some even made with tofutti. Also, to be open soon, is a separate room for private parties.

As soon as we were seated, we were placated with a basketful of crisp, golden browned squares of pizza dough with a garlic, herb and butter filling, while waiting for our soups. This unusual bread course was totally addictive. The soups each were to be ordered for a minimum of two persons , so our quartet was able to sample only two varieties. The Baked White Bean Soup was absolutely incredible! Pottery ramekins held generous portions of white beans, carrots, ham, pork, chicken, sausages, onions and garlic (not to mention numerous herbs and spices, including the intriguing use of cloves) in a potage that would have been dense enough to stand your spoon in - even without the thick topping of melted white Cheddar cheese. A baked Eggplant Soup that also contained sweet peppers, garlic and Kasseri cheese was intensely flavored, though the cheese is naturally salty and Nick unfortunately got a little heavy-handed here with the salt shaker.

Each of the appetizers contained four average portions, so it was a snap to divide them all equally, though considerably more difficult to devour them all. In fact, it was impossible, considering we had to leave some room to at least have a taste of our entrees. The Garlic Press was full-bodied with the flavors of eggplant and garlic, sweet peppers and tomato, all pureed and formed into four fat pancakes, each about the diameter of a saucer, to be sauteed and laved with a hearty marinara sauce. In the Fried Onion Hearts, Nick used only the sweet and tender pale white cores of red onions and encrusted them with a cornmeal enriched batter that was gently cooked to a gloriously crunchy fare-thee-well. A hot tomato sauce was served alongside.

If those were great, the next two were fantastic! The Black Bean Pancakes were not pancakes at all, but a fusion of the beans with buck-wheat groats, chopped onion, garlic and olive oil, piled into a huge mound capped with a piquant tomato sauce swimming with sweet onions and peppers and a handful of Italian herbs. A clever and totally unexpected combination of spinach, cabbage, mushrooms, carrots and celery was sauteed with mint and garlic, then rolled in grape leaves, battered and fried to a crunchy perfection. The result was somewhat on the order of what egg rolls stuffed with *dolmades* stuffed with Vietnamese *cha gio* filling would be like. They were topped with a slick of savory marinara sauce and got rave reviews all around.

It's a funny thing, but sometimes the best reading dishes don't fare quite as well on the taste buds. The menu's description of the Mustard Green Fasoli Shells, for instance, had particularly tickled my fancy, and when one of my friends ordered it I must admit that I was a bit envious, even though we had all decided to do taste testing on each other's choices, and so I was guaranteed at least one bite. Large pasta shells, cooked perfectly *al dente*, were stuffed with a mixture of black, fava and Northern beans, lentils, minced ham, onions and garlic then smothered with a bacon and mustard greens tomato sauce. Really, I don't know why it didn't taste as heavenly as it sounded - perhaps there were just too many different flavors and textures battling for prominence. The Brochettes of plump, sweet Scallops sauteed with garlic and green onions, another story entirely, were terrific in their mantle of ultra-rich creamy wine sauce. They rested on a sturdy rice pilaf.

Another buddy's dish was absolutely ambrosial. A large foil pouch, also reposing on a toothsome pilaf, was opened to reveal its steamy insides - a wrapping of both beef and pork tenderloins encasing a slab

continued on next page

Golden Age of Restaurants Lives On…

co ntinued from previous page

of lamb which, itself, had been stuffed with garlic and Kasseri cheese. This delicious mass was surrounded by delicate baby onions and strongly influenced with fresh mint. Actually, I had reservations (no pun intended) about ordering the Kanel Duck because I can't ever remember having eaten that bird when it wasn't designed to have a crisp skin, one of its most noble attributes in my book. Having an unwavering faith in Nick's cooking, however, I decided to give his version a try. A falling-off-the-bone tender half-a-bird imbued with a melange of flavors ranging from rosemary (it had been simmered over several sprigs of this aromatic herb) to cinnamon to garlic to bay leaves to peppercorns was perched atop a large tangle of perfectly cooked fettuccini with a "sauce" made of slow-cooked onions and tomatoes in the duck's own juices, which were miraculously not at all fatty. It certainly made a believer of me!

We judiciously had chosen to have our salads after the entrees, and did manage to half-heartedly pick a little at a handsome platter full of Greek items that included tangy feta cheese, salty black kalamata olives, red ripe tomatoes, mild pepperocini, sweet green pepper and Bermuda onion slivers and peeled cucumber half-moons, all bound together with a light but titillating combination of virgin olive oil and red wine vinegar with a sprinkling of Mediterranean herbs. An alternative Dinner Salad is far from mundane with fresh veggies, olives and other goodies, in a choice of Nick's own dressings (which are all for sale in the gourmet shop): Cheddar Bacon, Yogurt, Feta, Mustard Vinaigrette and a few of the more usual ones.

Although we didn't have room for desserts this time, I would like to again share with you what I wrote about them last August 26th, when I reviewed the new *Pita Stop* in Mesa: "All Nick's desserts are rich beyond imagination. At his *Golden Cuisine* restaurant, I almost always was so stuffed from his oversized portions of everything that I rarely had had room for these unique creations,

though the descriptions had tantalized me on more than one occasion.

"Forget everything you ever thought about pudding and try his Jack Daniel's version ($2.50). With its bittersweet and semi-sweet chocolates, whipped cream, butter, eggs, rum and , of course, Jack Daniel's whiskey amalgamated into one heavenly mixture, you know you'll be jogging for a week to work off all those calorie3s. Unfortunately, this dessert, out of all the ones we tried, probably had the least of those fattening demons. The Cheesecake Brownie ($2.00) was creamy beyond belief. The Cinnamon Stick Cake had a base of a wonderfully tangy cheesecake with just a hint of cinnamon, topped with a honeyed walnut and pecan blend, then crowned with layers of golden, butter filo pastry, a la baklava. If we thought eating that was a sinful act, we were ready to repent when we finished the last gooey bit of the dark chocolate cake, white chocolate cream cake, raspberries and a Chambord (raspberry liqueur) almond crust that combined to comprise a cake called - you guessed it - a Sinful Act.

Undaunted, we proceeded on our orgy of indulgence to Sweet Chocolate Death, a layering of chocolate meringue, chocolate mousse, chocolate cake, chocolate icing and almonds. What a way to go! The only fitting dequitur, at this point, could be After Death. This is an original compilation containing strata of walnut meringue, white chocolate mousse, almond cream, almonds, buttermilk cake, banana mousse with bits of golden raisins, all bathed in a white chocolate frosting studded with a coat of chopped hazelnuts. It, too was to die for!

The portions here are huge, and, aside from the soups, about half of each appetizer and each entree was unable to be consumed by four professional gluttons - although God knows we tried hard - and had to be taken home. These "leftovers" were not only wrapped individually in foam cartons by the waitress, but even carefully labeled with the contents written on every one.

Most of the soups hover around the $3.50 range and the average

appetizer, which is larger than the customary entree in many other places, runs about $5.50, so you *can* have a first-class meal here and leave well satisfied while staying within our ten dollar budget. In addition, a selection of twenty entrees begins at $11.95, with only two exceeding, at $14.95. Those incredibly sinful desserts range from $2 to $3 - ambrosially delicious and an absolute steal - while more than a dozen and a half premium coffees are ground to order and brewed by the cup at a mere $1.25 per. Desserts (including homemade gelato and granita) and coffees are also served in the dining room nightly from 10 'til 1 AM.

One of the most special parts about *Golden Cuisine* is that Nick continually experiments in his spar time (I often wonder when that dynamo has a chance to sleep) to come up with delicious additional recipes of original dishes to add to his already enormous menu of well over 200 items, all of which he makes himself - to order, no less! Not satisfied to merely be a talented chef, he also wrote two cookbooks and last Christmas he again made over 500 complete turkey dinners with all the trimmings (at his own expense) to feed the homeless in Phoenix. Nick Ligidakis, we salute you and your fabulous *Golden Cuisine of Southern Europe!*

FOOD: Excellent
ATMOSPHERE: Fair/Good
VALUE: Excellent
SERVICE: Good
HYGIENE: Good

3903 East Thomas Road (at the east end of Tower Plaza), Phoenix, 275-9223. Hours: Lunch, 11 AM 'til 2PM, Monday thru Friday, 4 'til 11PM on Saturday. Private Dinners by reservation only on Sunday. Closed Monday and Tuesday. Cocktails (coming soon) and Credit Cards. Reservations practically mandatory for dinner, suggested for lunch. (*Pita Stop*, specialty shop and sports bar are open daily, call for hours of operation).

New Times

The Valley's News and Arts Journal

1992

BEST GYROS
Nick's Cuisine of Southern Europe
3717 East Indian School

You might think the key to a great gyro is a mound of fragrant beef and lamb. You might think it's hefty portions of lettuce, tomato and onions nestled in with the meat., You might think it's the fragrant yogurt sauce binding all the ingredients.

But if the bread's no good, the sandwich is no good.

At Nick's you get a hunk of grilled pita that you can sink your teeth into. Plus, it's stuffed with lots of juicy meat and some sharp onions.

By the time you finish, you'll have gyro juices all over your face, and if you're not careful, over your shirt, too. But don't bother cleaning it - just make it your permanent gyro outfit.

Nick's Cuisine and philosophy are both a delight

By Mark J. Scarp
Scottsdale Progress
Thursday, January 14, 1993

The dining area is far from romantic (they use fluorescent lights), but the reason the north wall of Nick's Cuisine of Southern Europe is filled with adoring newspaper and magazine clippings isn't the atmosphere.

It's the food. Big portions, cooked home-style and tasting authentic. And the selection? Heinz has 57 varieties. Nick's has 85.... and that's just your choice of pizza toppings.

The menu stretches out 24-by-32 inches, and both sides are covered with continental delights, the result of years of personal attention Nick Ligidakis and his family have devoted to the right combinations.

Along the bottom, Nick sprinkles quotations from Plato, Aristotle, Socrates and the *Bible*. Good ones, too.

The restaurant recently moved to a free-standing building on Indian School Road after several years under the name Golden Cuisine at Tower Plaza, next door to that country-Western mecca, Denim & Diamonds.

Companion and I started with a plateful of popcorn shrimp (our addition was lacking, as I counted 117 of them while Companion put the total at only 98). The appetizer was served with another plate brimming with small lightly baked bread squares dipped lightly in oil. *Abundanza!*

I enjoyed stuffed pasta shells *spinaci*, big and tender with seasoned spinach and at the bottom of it all, the essence of good tomato sauce. Companion dove into artichoke sole and pasta containing a steak of sole covered with artichokes, noodles and a full-bodied creamy sauce.

The menu contains a full column of items so specially prepared you have to order at least 24 hours in advance. There's a grocery featuring specialty and gourmet items for you to take home (I counted five different types of olive oil). And, no surprise, Nick caters.

Picky diners beware: There are no substitutions. House rules. They may do that kind of stuff at Subway, but not at Nick's. His own words on the menu (between a couple of philosophers) tells why: "Years of work and endless days of experimenting have gone on in order to perfect the tastes of each and every item."

Nick's is open from 7 a.m. to 1 a.m., so just about anytime is the best time to enjoy his breakfast, lunch and dinner offerings. Service is attentive and friendly. And with these portions, they stock lots of plastic foam take-home containers.

Where: 3717 E. Indian School Road
Phone: 955-5225
Price: Moderate
Cuisine: Continental
Ambiance: Comfortable

PERSPECTIVE

SECTION
C

SUNDAY
JUNE 27, 1993

THE ARIZONA REPUBLIC

ARIZONA
CORRESPONDENT
The Arizona Republic

Doing things Nick's Way

The restaurant is here because Nick Ligidakis wants it to be. His restaurant is his mission, and it's not for the fainthearted.

By Lisa Schnebly-Heidinger

It would never work as a franchise. In this world where radio stations, clothing stores and restaurants sell the same thing whether you're in Ahwatukee or Ajo, the familiar sells.

And then there's Nick's.

Actually, this pocket-sized restaurant on Indian School Road is Nick's Cuisine of Southern Europe.

You can tell when you walk in that no one here is tap-dancing, watching eagerly for your approval. Nick's is here because Nick Ligidakis wants it to be. His restaurant is his mission, and it's not for the fainthearted.

Fried hearts of palm?

You start with a menu about as big as the hood of your car. You peruse the sections, picking up speed as you realize you've read dozens of descriptions and are still in appetizers.

Fried hearts of palm? That probably hasn't been tried by a public that still seems to believe exotic vegetables come in frozen bags.

Or how about a tiger tail? That's lobster marinated in soy ginger, stuffed with chicken livers and wrapped in bacon.

Who comes up with this? Nick, of course, the man who also put a quote from Plato under the pasta, Sophocles with lobster meat pizza.

Nick wears his heart on his menu, offering his credos with his creations. Nick's Favorite pizza is our favorite now, but we wrinkled our noses when we first read it had potato, artichoke, feta cheese and bacon.

Like Mozart made music

Nick creates dishes the way Mozart made music: all in his head, able to picture the final result without writing it down or testing it first. With the only touch of arrogance I saw – or maybe it's just mischief _ Nick says sometimes he doesn't even taste a new dessert before he puts it on the menu.

Some of us find reading the dessert menu better than erotic poetry – white passion cake with macadamian cream filling mango mousse and kiwi chocolate; whipped cream cheesecake with pecans, walnuts, filo dough and cinnamon syrup; layered citrus cake with berry sauce, orange honey biscotti and creme de cafe mousse called Fatal Obsession.

Too much of this kind of talk and by the time you see Nick, his voice seems as rich and dark as Special Blend coffee, his eyes as large as shiny Greek olives.

Food from the man

There's no separating the food from the man, which wasn't always true. Nick came to the United States from Greece on a professional soccer contract that ran out of money practically the day he arrived from his homeland. Teaching himself English, he opened his first tiny restaurant on McDowell with $52.50.

"I slept in the back. I made it my universe," he says. In his 40s, tall and cinema handsome but with a weary walk from being backbone of the bistro, Nick doesn't sleep in the back, but "that's how I still treat all this...nonsense."

He tells about waking up at 3 a.m. recently with a new dessert recipe whirling around in his head. Driving down to the restaurant in the dark, more began percolating. By the time the sun was up and he was finished creating, a half-dozen desserts had joined his repertoire.

But dreaming is only half of it. Nick says the athlete's discipline he learned is what makes the restaurant work.

"No matter if you made it 1,000 times, you have to make a dish always the same," he says. "That is my challenge. I like challenges."

Dinners for homeless

That's why every Thanksgiving he gives a dinner for homeless that has swelled from less than a hundred to thousands, relying on customers' donations and assistance to feed the hungry.

He doesn't talk about it until I ask. That's just what you do, his shrug says. Feed the hungry.

But no one does it the way Nick does. Unless he can be cloned, he'll never start a chain.

"How do you franchise someone's feelings? Someone's character? This is chemistry; this is me."

Bad luck and landlords have caused him to move twice; he had to declare bankruptcy last time. But merchants trusted him, giving him equipment on faith to start again. Nick sounds like he was tempted not to, but customers' belief spurred him on. It was as if he wouldn't have taken failure personally, but since people counted on him to be an example of never giving up, he rose to it.

So Nick's is still using heavy starched tablecloths, staying open unbelievable hours and serving so many dishes the inventory must be heartbreaking.

It reminds me of a song Guy Clark sings: "You've got to sing like you don't need the money, love like you'll never get hurt, dance like nobody's watching; it's gotta come from the heart if you want it to work."

It does at Nick's.

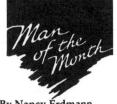

Man of the Month

Nick Ligidakis

By Nancy Erdmann
and Becky Kistler

That life is full for Nick Ligidakis is obvious. When entering his popular restaurant, **Nick's Cuisine of Southern Europe,** *customers are fascinated by the memorabilia covering the walls: posters from his homeland, Greece, and his tenure as a soccer player, and framed letters and editorial from politicians, Valley personalities, and his many satisfied customers. But then, ah then, the eyes fall upon the cases full of Nick's desserts!*

There are just too many choices here! The extensive menu lists over 200 carefully cooked-to-order Italian/Greek items, ensuring the restaurant's repeated presence on the "Valley's Best" lists. After one of Nick's exceptional dishes, the dessert choice brings customers up to view the cases two and three times. Eating at Nick's means never eating it all. Carry-home portions are the norm.

But it is owner/chef Ligidakis who is the real star of the establishment. He is an exceptional man. An author of several books, with at least two more in the works, Ligidakis has come to be known as the caring man who prepares (with the help of many, he is quick to point out) a Thanksgiving feast for Valley shelters, the homeless, and families in need.

Eight years ago at Thanksgiving, in an effort to return to the community all it has given him, Ligidakis fed approximately 250 persons. This year he will serve 15,000 less fortunate – all from his restaurant at 3717 E. Indian School Road in Phoenix and with the help of some 800 volunteers and staff.

He is just that way, a softspoken, compassionate, extraordinary chef working 18-hour days in a small kitchen within view of his customers. He seems always to be contemplating more ways to help others. His various charity involvements are too numerous to list.

Visit Nick's Cuisine, meet Nick, have at least a cup of coffee. Of course, there are over 50 coffee selections, so be prepared to make yet another difficult choice!

From where does your penchant

for hard work come?

Let me go back to when I opened my first restaurant a few years ago on East McDowell Road. That was about a 50 sq. ft. place. I was not known. I was trying to create this new cuisine which is a blend of several different cuisines, including Italian/Greek influenced by the French and the Spanish. Since I had no money and no customers to follow me, it was very difficult. I was determined to make it, worked for 18 months without a single day off, 16 to 18 hours a day, and slept in the storage room. I guess my drive comes from the fact that I'm self-taught and self-made, and what I possess here, my recipes and all the work I do, is created by me. It's very hard not to drive yourself and protect what you have created. Now our customers are there by the thousands.

You have an engineering degree. How did you get into the restaurant business?

Actually, when I came to America, I didn't come here to stay. I came to play on a professional soccer team. When the team went broke, being the proud and stubborn person that I am, instead of calling my parents to send me money for a ticket back, I got a job at a restaurant to earn my fare home. Then I met my first wife, and I think, still today, my kids are the only reason I stayed in this country.

What did you dream about becoming as a little boy?

I was never a dreamer. I was always realistic about what you can accomplish in life, what your limitations and capacities are. I had a great childhood and grew up with a lot of love, so I was always content with what I had. I never dreamed of being anything. I mean, I did want to be a great soccer player, that's just understood. The sport helped me tremendously by keeping my body and mind free of alcohol and drugs and anything that would clog my mind.

It's been said that despite your successes, you've never gotten rich because of your generous nature. If

money isn't of great importance to you, what brings you pleasure?

There are many things. Mainly the people that come here. I love my customers. They come here and think this is their home. I work hard for these people. That's my food, my work – I love it. I love to create things – a new dish, a new dessert. A lot of the items I make I don't even taste. I know in my head how they're going to taste because it's become second nature. I also have loyal employees, and I have a responsibility to them to keep my doors open.

Money has never been a friend of mine. I never liked money. If I liked money, I'd be a rich man by now. I think of money as a necessity of life, but it becomes an obsession with too many people. In fact, the more money I make, the more people I'm probably going to help. What I look for is spiritual fulfillment and I get that through my work and my contributions.

Where do you see yourself five years from now?

Probably doing the same thing. I'd like to write more books. I just finished my second book and have three more I'm working on. One will be a combination recipe and story-book about how I started and the recipes that I created along the way; another will be a tour of how the Greeks used to cook and how they ate, starting from 2500 B.C. to the Roman Empire to today; and the third book, which I'm calling *The Heroes of My Thoughts,* will be about my parents.

You have quite an extensive menu, offering 80 different pizza toppings alone! Do your customers have a difficult time choosing what to order?

Usually the first time they're here they do, but the wait staff helps them out. The repeat customers, and 90% of my customers are repeat customers, usually know what they want because everyone takes a little menu home. So before they come here they know what they want. Everything is made fresh – nothing is pre-made. We have zero waste

continued on next page

5024 E. McDowell

What the press is saying

Man of the month...

continued from previous page

because everything moves so fast.

Where do you get your recipe ideas?

They just come to me. A lot of times I'll wake up at three or four o'clock in the morning and they're in my head.

Have you ever taken a cooking class?

Never. Never went to school. Never took a cooking class. Was never taught by anyone.

What cookbooks have you written? Are these marketed nationally?

My first cookbook, *Nick's Creative Cooking Made Easy*, has been out six years and has sole more than 20,000 copies from this restaurant alone. That gives you an idea the kind of traffic we have. The second book will go national. It will be a beautiful book with lots of colors, pictures, and wonderful recipes. We also sell our dressings at A.J.'s, and I teach cooking classes at the restaurant.

Tell me about the charity work you do. How did you get started with your first "charity feast" in 1985?

I started eight years ago at Thanksgiving when I had the smaller restaurant. I felt I wanted to do something for the community, being thankful for my success. I called some of the shelters and asked if I could cook for them. I cooked for 250 people that first year. It was going to be a one-time thing. But the next day some of the homeless returned to thank me, and I will never forget the look on their faces. I've been doing it ever since. I honestly never thought it would mushroom into the 15,000 we will serve this year.

But I like challenges, and I like to draw attention to what we do and not to what we say. I also tried to motivate other restaurants to get involved, but most wanted to know what was in it for them. It's ridiculous that you can't just help someone, so I kind of gave up on that approach. So the last three to four years we've received a lot of publicity and now other restaurants are starting to do their own thing. We also share our Thanksgiving feast with poor families, the elderly, battered and abused women and children, AIDS patients, and homebound citizens. Last year we delivered to over 300 different locations.

I close my restaurant down for three days before Thanksgiving and cook, cook, cook. Volunteers help with everything, from collecting donations, publicity and the final delivery. I hear many heartwarming stories from the drivers about how grateful the people are. It's a wonderful feeling.

How do you fund this event?

Through proceeds from my cookbooks, my own bank account, and most of all from donations.

Last year you had an over-abundance of volunteers. What do you think you need this year to make the event even more successful?

Donations. Food or cash donations. They can bring the food here the Monday before Thanksgiving, or they can send the money to the restaurant.

What kind of food would you like people to donate?

Turkey, stuffing, potatoes, yams, cranberry sauce, vegetables, bread, pies, anything related to a traditional Thanksgiving dinner.

What are your aspirations and dreams for the future?

I want to write. I love writing. I may even write my autobiography some day. Then I'd like to open another place like a European pastry shot, a place where we'll play beautiful music and people can relax with coffee or tea and dessert. Desserts are very popular in this town. It would be different – very European. I'd like to do this because that kind of place can be franchised and profitable down the line. And in the distant future, I'd like to spend my retirement years in my country, in the Greek Islands where my family is.

Editor's note: If you would like to help fund the Thanksgiving program this year or volunteer your services, please call the restaurant at 955-5225.

New Times The Valley's News and Arts Journal **1993**

BEST LATE-NIGHT MEAL
Nick's Cuisine
of Southern Europe
3717 East Indian School

It's Sunday night at 11. The movie's over and the gang is hungry. Some crave pizza. Others want dessert. A dieter demands salad. And one guy who hasn't had a bite since lunch wants a full meal. Until now, this group had only three options.

1) Feast on a packet of ramen and microwave burros at home.

2) Move to New York City.

3) Wait until breakfast.

Fortunately, Nick Ligidakis has come to the rescue. He keeps his place, featuring the Valley's largest menu, open until midnight, seven nights per week.

Grab a pizza and choose from the 80 toppings. Or try calzone, burgers, pita sandwiches, salads, pastas, steaks, seafood or a specialty called "lamb and company in foil": lamb stuffed with kaseri cheese and garlic, along with beef and pork tenderloins, baked in foil with baby onions and mint.

There's also a monstrous dessert selection, including a wicked fig berry pie with raspberries and dark chocolate.

Phoenix is not yet the city that never sleeps. But thanks to Nick's at least it's no longer in bed by 10 p.m.

Valley chef celebrates big day

Despite setbacks, he's still cooking

By Scott C. Seckel
Special to Community

When Nick Ligidakis, a longtime Valley chef, declared bankruptcy, he lost his Thomas Road restaurant and east Valley fast food outlet. He also lost his home, his car and his wife.

"It's been a tough couple of years." Ligidakis said.

But today, Ligidakis will feed about 15,000 disadvantaged people. His is a seven-year tradition of providing a hot meal to the homeless, abused women and children, the elderly, and AIDS patients.

Ligidakis said his own recent spate of troubles didn't leave him as bad off as many.

"I'm still better off than most people. I'm not hungry. I still have food to eat and a place to sleep," he said. "You can always imagine how these people feel, but I'm not sleeping on the streets. If anything else, it made me stronger."

There are two reasons for his endurance: roots and hope.

"Psychologically they'll see me and say 'Look at this man. Over the years he has helped all these people and now he is down, he gave up,' " the 48-year-old Greek immigrant said. "So people give up hope. I want to give these people hope.

"These people are hungry throughout the year."

The Ligidakis family ran a restaurant in the small town of Kiaton, in Corinthia Province, Greece. Young Nick became a star on the youth squad of the Greek national soccer team.

"I don't want to forget what I came from - a poor country, a poor family," he said. "But we were never hungry.

"This is the greatest country in the world. And to see people digging out of garbage cans to eat...."

The first Thanksgiving Ligidakis gave something back, he fed 250 people. Last year he fed 12,000, putting in $5,000 he earned working 100-hour weeks in the kitchen. Total cost of the act of charity was $20,000.

This year his financial contribution will be between $3,000 and $4,000 plus proceeds from the sales of his cookbook and T-shirts, in addition to endless man-hours of labor.

Total cost this year will be about $30,000. Donations from friends and customers, as well as distributors who take a loss on the wholesale food Ligidakis buys, help shave costs.

St. Vincent de Paul and Central Arizona Shelter Services Inc. are helping with the effort.

Last week Ligidakis began cooking turkey, cranberry sauce, stuffing, gravy, yams, mashed potatoes, and bread. Helping him accomplish the act of charity are between 70 and 100 people.

"Mainly my loyal customers have been showing up," Ligidakis said. "They don't have to do that."

The operation is run out of his new restaurant, Nick's Cuisine, at 3717 E. Indian School. He said in the rush he frequently doesn't have the time to thank people for their needed donations of cash or time.

It's not ingratitude or forgetfulness: "They have to remember that we're not an organization that does that. We're just a restaurant with a few waitresses on the phone.

"If you work hard, if you treat people right, it you're sincere, it's going to work out."

Central Phoenix
COMMUNITY

10   The Arizona Republic/THE PHOENIX GAZETTE   Friday, April 19, 1996

Name: Nick's on Central
Address: San Carlos Hotel, 202 N. Central Ave., Phoenix.
Phone: 261-7899.
Reservations needed? Suggested but not always necessary.
Cuisine: Owner Nick Ligidakis calls it "cuisine of southern Europe," but if you can't find something you like on this menu, check to make sure you still have a pulse. There are literally dozens and dozens of choices. If you want a sandwich on pita, pick from 24 varieties. The basic gyros, $5.95, comes with a massive stack of meat – a seasoned blend of lamb and beef – topped with a tasty yogurt sauce. Save room for the desserts, baked on the premises from Nick's recipes. The cheesecakes are deliciously hefty, with a crust that's a treat on its own. If you need a real sugar fix, try the baklava.

Kid friendly? Booster seats are available, but you'll be most comfortable with older children or the best-behaved of the younger set.

Cost: Moderate. Lunch specialties, served until 4 p.m., are mostly $6.95 to $8.95. Dinner entrees run $12.95 to $16.95.

Service: Leisurely but attentive. If you order iced tea, available in several flavors, you'll get a carafe to take care of your refills.

Atmosphere: Set in the historic San Carlos Hotel, the restaurant has several eating areas: an outside patio; a formal dining room with mirrors and painting of Southwest scenes; and the front room with more of a cafe atmosphere. The eclectic decor includes a scattering of antiques, busts of musicians (Beethoven, not Bon Jovi) and framed pages from an ancient science text.

Comments: Check out the display of signed celebrity photos, including soccer legend Pelé, trumpeter-conductor Doc Severinsen and both Miss and Mrs. Arizona.

The restaurant is open daily from 6 a.m. until 11 p.m. Breakfast is served until 11 a.m. during the week and until 12:30 p.m. on Saturday and Sunday. The offerings, typical of the intriguing selections on the menu, include "cream toast" (white bread stuffed with cream cheese and walnuts, dipped in an egg batter, grilled, served with an apricot orange sauce).

— Kathleen Ingley

January 1996
$2.95

Food for Thought
by Nikki Buchanan

Nick Ligidakis has a great big heart and the soul of a Jewish mother. He simply can't bear the thought of anyone going hungry. That's why he closes his restaurant for four days every year and recruits something like 4,000 volunteers to help him serve 30,000 homeless people over the Thanksgiving holidays. And it goes a long way toward explaining why every day, in his new restaurant **Nick's on Central**, he feeds his customers to surfeit.

The man does nothing by halves, so it takes forever just to read his regular menu (twenty-seven appetizers, twenty salads... you get the idea), but the breakfast menu, offering a mere forty-five selections (including omelets, frittatas, pancakes and specialties) is considerably shorter. Of course, if you're a downtown drone with a time clock to punch or meetings to make, you'd probably rather cut right to the chase. So I recommend the Raspberry-stuffed Toast ($6.95), an impossibly florid assemblage composed of small round slices of white bread, stuffed with raspberries and cream cheese, dipped in egg batter and fried, then topped with an orange almond sauce. Considering the richness of the ingredients, you figure the kitchen will go easy on the portion size. But no. This is Nick's, where you'll get six slices and eat three, then buzz off to work with a sugar rush that'll get you through the entire morning.

Letters
January 4 - 10, 1996   New Times

St. Nick
After reading Marc Ramirez's article "no Fowl, Some Harm" (December 21), I am left with two questions: Is Nick Ligidakis responsible for repairing the tenuous community relations apparently created by the Garfield School District? Should he be held accountable for a failure to feed more than 32,000 people (needy or not-so-needy) when he stated a limit of 16,000?

Fear of liability discourages many businesses from generous acts; to that *New Times* is adding fear of a public flogging–proof that no good deed goes unpunished.
Jim Foley, Tempe

What on Earth prompted *New Times* to lambaste Nick Ligidakis for serving "only" 32,000 free Thanksgiving meals? Didn't the hit piece on Mother Teresa work out?
Chris Thomas, Phoenix

Marc Ramirez's article about Nick Ligidakis' Thanksgiving efforts was offensive to me and insulting to a Samaritan. Had a *New Times* reporter been on hand for Jesus Christ's miracle of the loaves, we might have read first about those who got nary a bite.

As one who knows firsthand the challenge of organizing volunteers during the holidays, I'm awed by the dedication of Ligidakis and his volunteers. Personally, I'd like to see *New Times* and reporter Marc Ramirez demonstrate their ability to do a better job of feeding the poor and hungry at holiday time before reading more petty cavil about a local "saint" Nick.
Glenn Michaels, Phoenix

Chef's story a lesson for all to digest

By David Leibowitz

So the guy went bankrupt. Big deal.

He took a chance, made a few lousy business decisions, and found himself eyeballs deep in ink the red of blood. It doesn't necessarily make him a bad person. You have to see the big picture, look at all he's done for the community, the lives he's touched. The guy has a heart, is worthy of emulation. I'm certainly glad to have met him.

And, nah, he's not named Fife Symington.

I'm talking instead about Nick Ligidakis, who owns a couple of restaurants in Phoenix, one on Indian School Road called Nick's Cuisine of Southern Europe, and another downtown, the new Nick's on Central.

Nick knows bankruptcy – he's still battling back from his second declaration of Chapter 11 in the last five years – but he also knows charity, which explains why his name's in the paper today. Instead of spending his time saying "I don't recall" 30,000 times at a bankruptcy court hearing, Nick's busy plotting his 10th consecutive Thanksgiving feast for 30,000 of the Valley's homeless, elderly, abused and flat-broke.

Wait, I mean 30,002. Seems if Fife and the missis aren't busy trading the family jewel collection back and forth come Turkey Day...

"Absolutely, they're invited," says Ligidakis. "But they're going to stand in line like everybody else. No privilege in my Thanksgiving."

Did I mention he has a sense of humor, too? He'd have to when you consider the loss he takes on this venture, which closes one restaurant down for five days of round-the-clock cheffing, and the other for two.

We're talking 30 grand, is his best guess.

Exactly, Nick, what are you, nuts? You're in the hole to the Internal Revenuers, you've barely got a laundry list of creditors paid off, and you're still playing Extremely Good Samaritan.

"I say I'm not crazy," he explains. "I believe. Beliefs are not what you say, it's what you do. I've made a commitment to myself and thousands of people. People look up to me and I can't let them down."

Like I said, worthy of emulation. I've heard you profess not to read the local rags, governor, but you could do worse than following Nick's lead, you know?

Anyway, the 50-year-old chef's largess dates back to 1985, when he still owned Nick's Golden Cuisine, his first venture, the one he worked 18 hours a day to get off the ground. He fed 250 folks that first year, then expanded a few thousand at a time, to the point where Phoenix alone reportedly plans to have 12,000 "dining guests" eat Nick's turkey and fixings this year.

"My businesses were a success," he recalls of that first year, "so I figured I'd give something back. That was going to be a one-time event...The next day, when the people in the shelter returned the pans, they stood there for like 10 minutes thanking me, I said, 'My God, is that all it takes to make people happy, a simple meal?'"

Of course, Nick learned the hard way that man can't live by bread alone. The lesson came in 1990, after some investors pulled out of a huge-and-improved version of Golden Cuisine. Nick ended up nearly $300,000 in the hole, he says, and had to declare bankruptcy. After cobbling together loans enough to open the Indian School location, he found himself another 230 grand in the red, and bankruptcy again.

Keep in mind, though, he chose Chapter 11, with its repayment option, and not the Symington route – Chapter 7 – wherein creditors are told go pound sand.

And now, Nick, after that year without a car, and the bust-up of your marriage due to stress?

"Three and a half years later, I have paid almost everyone," he says. "The only thing that keeps me in Chapter 11 is the IRS. We're in the process right now of making an agreement with them."

And in the process of coordinating for the feast, with its 2,300 donated turkeys and the 700 volunteers who deliver food across the region, and the assembly-line buffet to feed the homeless down on Monroe Street. Stop by if you're hungry, or send food beforehand if you're generous.

Whatever you do, though, please pay attention.

"My beliefs are I know there are ills in our society," says Nick Ligidakis. "I believe we need to be the doctors to fix it. If we touch two, three, five or six people in our life, it's going to multiply and society will get better."

Eating Out ... *Restaurant Reviews*

By Two Hungry Guys
September, 1996

Nestled in the lobby of Phoenix's historic San Carlos Hotel is one of the Valley's best kept secrets. The walls are lined with years of accolades from virtually every newspaper and magazine in print. And for good reason. Nick's On Central serves up some of the best food to be found in the Valley.

On entering, your attention automatically is riveted to the scrumptious desserts as you pass the six refrigerated cases it takes to contain all the Nick Ligidakis masterpieces. You can't help but peer through the glass to take in the spectacle, but don't forget to scan the jars of coffees and herb teas at eye level. Your waiter will want to know your favorite flavor to brew a pot of hot or a carafe of iced.

The simple, yet, elegant surroundings help to set the tone for the tour of southern European cuisine on which you are about to embark. The sophisticated and decidedly European song stylings of Edith Piaf and charles Aznavour add a touch of image to the ambiance.

If there is one flaw in the Nick's experience, it's the menu. There simply is too much from which to choose. Count them. 33 appetizers, 19 salads, 64 assorted pita sandwiches, burgers, subs and finger foods, 87 entrees, 27 different flavors of pizza and calzones (with more than 85 toppings to mix and match), and 44 desserts. Then there are the extensive breakfast and lunch menus. Whow!

For the purpose of this issue's review, we'll stick to the dinner menu – with one exception. There is no way one can review Nick's without mentioning his pizzas – the best pies this side of the Atlantic. For the traditionalists his Golden Pizza arrived topped with mounds of pepperoni, sausage, mushrooms, green peppers, onions and black olives. For those who choose to walk on the wild side, however, this is the place to get adventurous. Nick's Favorite immediately became ours. Heaps of artichokes, hearts of palm, bacon, feta and potatoes. The pies' toppings are stacked on Nick's patented "three-rise" dough with three types of cheese. They are to die for.

Our most recent dinner began with two soups. One, a cabbage and bacon creation, which, despite the high grade, smokey-yet-not-too-salty pork, was a little underseasoned. However the avgolemeno, a traditional egg-based Grecian formula with an unpresumptuous taste of lamb, had just the right amount of lemon to give it the zing of a sea breeze. They were a good start.

The appetizer listing contains many fried temptations, all of which spell fat with a capital "F". But, let's face it, you don't go to Nick's to diet. One of Nick's original "must dos" is the Feta Dill Fritters. How he can stuff them so full, yet keep them so light is beyond human comprehension. Or, start with a generous antipasto giardino salad. The portions are huge, but the wait staff come prepared with extra plates for everyone to sample.

The entrees – steaks, seafood pasta, poultry, pastas, seafood and veal – are all heavy courses. Most are original creations which hearken back to the traditional Old World cuisine, where one's food is meant to be savored. Many dishes come with freshly made pasta. Nick's home-made garlic bread accompaniment is made exactly the way the gods intended – every vampire's nightmare come true.

So, you think chicken is chicken? Nick's fowl dishes stand out because he tops the birds' double breasts with various combinations of sauces, meats, vegies and cheeses. Watching the waistline? Go grilled. Otherwise, most are sautéed (only after being pressed and rubbed with Nick's secret spices and herbs).

Our Salonika Chicken was smothered with slivers of hot Italian sausage, capers, pine nuts, fresh mushroom slices, peppercorns and a good helping of garlic, all tied together with an orange brandy and wine sauce that penetrated the accompanying toothsome fettucini. Memories are made of cuisine like this.

The Baked Cashew Seafood – promising a casserole filled with crab meat, shrimp and clams sautéed with celery, green onion, garlic, cashews and feta in a provolone sauce – caught our eye. We ordered. What we received, however, was an interesting variation of the traditional surf and turf. The Baked Seafood Steak, nonetheless, was a delight. Once we dived into the sautéed filet mignon covered with crab, shrimp, garlic, asparagus, and mushrooms, baked under an oozing layer of imported cheeses, the last thing we could do was let the waitress take it away!

Time for dessert? If you're thinking enough is enough already, our advice is to get up and leave the table and take ten laps around the dessert cases.

Awaiting us were Nick's specialties mere words cannot describe. With names like Last Act (strawberries, bananas and raspberries dipped in chocolate then baked in a white chocolate cake), Fatal Obsession (a layered citrus cake with berry sauce, orange honey biscotti, a berry chocolate mousse, creme de cafe mousse, topped with a bittersweet chocolate icing), they should all be Rated X and considered A Sinful Act. Need we say more?

Too stuffed to indulge in dessert? Then leave! Walk (don't run!) over to the Herberger, take in a play, then come back for pastries and coffee. It is the perfect evening out on the town. In fact, this is becoming so common among Nick's regulars we hear the county is building a downtown baseball stadium just to accommodate his overflow.

Planning an evening downtown is just that simple. We understand, however, that on nights with big events at the America West Arena and the Herberger, Nick's requires reservations. Be sure when you make dinner arrangements to allow about two hours to relax and enjoy your meal.

For the afternoon, Nick's has become very popular with the power lunch crowd. Call or fax ahead with your order to help speed things along.

Breakfast items seem a little pricier than the average, but this is breakfast with a different twist. And, the chef dishes out about all you can eat in a sitting. Morning still is a nice time to splurge.

Take-out is available on everything. However, it takes one-day advance notice for Nick to create that spectacular cake or pie to crown your private function.

Nick's on Central is located at 202 North Central Avenue in downtown Phoenix in the San Carlos Hotel. Dining is inside and outside on a misted patio. Dress is relaxed. Reservations are suggested, 261-7899.

Downtown

Dazzling Downtown Diners

By Donald Downes

Seems only newcomers and visitors to the Valley are unfamiliar, and then only briefly, with the food of Nick Ligidakis. Dazzling Phoenix diners since the mid-80s at various Valley locales, "standing room only" best describes the scene for the past three years at his Nick's Cuisine of Southern Europe, 3717 East Indian School. And SRO also characterizes the excitement of his newest venture in downtown Phoenix, Nick's on Central, in the historic San Carlos Hotel at 202 North Central.

Just prior to its early October debut, Nick – as he is known to his many fans and followers – took time from directing the remodeling of his restaurant to tell me about Nick's on Central and Nick's food.

"Gregory Melikian, the hotel's owner, asked me if I would be interested in coming down here," begins Nick, "and I said yes. The (Melikian) family has been eating in my restaurant for years. He came to me and said, 'A guy like you should go downtown. You will do well there.' I came and looked inside the hotel and I made my decision right then. I love this whole atmosphere. I love history. I love philosophy and culture. I'm a firm believer that we have to preserve our culture. You have a hotel that's been here since 1928," he says, gesturing at his surroundings. "The Acropolis has been there for 25 centuries. Whatever it is, it has an historical value and we need to preserve it. That's my main reason why I came down here."

In keeping with the hotel's period decor, the restaurant is outfitted with dated furnishings. Near Nick's signature display cases groaning with his famous cakes and other sweet sundries is a lobbylike area for afternoon tea or having a cup of coffee or a glass of wine while waiting to be seated. Prospective diners should plan how much room to leave for a wedge of cake.

Dining is in two areas: the step-down main dining room with a small alcove that Nick plans to use for intimate dinners, and a casual eating area banked by shelves of books and an active exhibition kitchen. Piped-in classical tunes share the air with wafting kitchen aromas.

Nick's signature food started about a dozen years ago with his first eatery, the trailer-size Golden Pizza on East McDowell. Nick says he spent about a year developing his style by reading and studying, finally deciding that the best cuisine for him would be the food of his native Greece and the Mediterranean. His hunch a winner, Nick moved into larger digs – Golden Cuisine of Southern Europe – at Thomas Mall in 1985. With room to move in the kitchen and more space for diners, Nick's sweet creations filled the restaurant's display cases while his signature savories packed the pages of the now notable extensive menu.

Those familiar with Nick's food and his current eight-page menu containing over 320 items are also aware of the gigantic portions. I once remarked that Nick's calzone could feed a small island nation. The pizzas too are enormous, ladened with toppings from a list of 85. It's really impossible to leave Nick's feeling hungry. In fact, most departing diners waddle out the door packing enough leftovers for another day's meals.

Realizing that many downtown businesspeople lack storage space for cartons of leftovers, Nick makes mini-versions of his calzones and pizzas at the downtown eatery, including a new jumbo shrimp pie with sun-dried tomatoes. A newly created lunch specialty menu ($6.95 to $9.95) is offered daily from 11 am to 4 pm; note, however, that portions are far from diminutive. Ready your fork for a midday meal like seafood tortellini with sauteed crab meat, shrimp, and mushrooms in a creamy sauce.

Have an early downtown meeting? Get your morning started with Nick's expanded breakfast menu featuring, among other specialties, his ham-stuffed pancakes with Swiss cheese.

And should business, the symphony, or the theater have you downtown at dinner time, drop into Nick's for new entree dishes like sliced lamb salad with eggplant, or scallops sauteed in olive oil and white wine with mushrooms, green onions, capers, artichokes, roasted red peppers, and garlic, tossed with cheese-filled spinach ravioli.

It's darn difficult to stroll by the dessert cases without eventually surrendering to a slice of one of Nick's celebrated sinful sweets – pick up a tidbit to chase away an afternoon's lull. With a couple of dozen cakes already to his credit, Nick has created still more. I'll wager that wedges of his new Symphony of Chocolate fly out the door; few will be able to resist a cake of dark, white, and chestnut chocolate veiled with an orange, cinnamon, white chocolate icing.

If you'd like to try your hand at a few of Nick's dazzling desserts, recipes are contained in his book, *My Golden Collection of Original Desserts*. Or try a main dish from a recipe in *Nick's Creative Cooking Made Easy*. The books are available at both restaurant locations, with proceeds from sales going toward Nick's annual charitable Thanksgiving feast that feeds many of the Valley's less fortunate. Now in its tenth year, the event is also sponsored by private donations as well as Nick's own funds. Over twenty thousand individuals are expected to be fed this holiday.

Though his charitable deeds are revered and his food admired by critics and customers alike, Nick remains a modest man for whom cooking and creating and giving are sources of joy.

"It's an honor to have so many people believe in the work you do. I say work, but to me it's an art. If I thought it was work I'd never go to work in the morning."

Some of the
Letters of appreciation...

Tumbleweed

December 8, 1989

 Golden Cuisine Restaurant
3903 E. Thomas Road
Phoenix, Arizona 85008

Dear Sirs:

On behalf of the Board of Directors, staff and clients at Tumbleweed, please accept our sincere thanks for your recent donation of "Thanksgiving Dinner" food.

It was much appreciated by our clients, and again, thank you for thinking of Tumbleweed.

Sincerely

JANET L. GARCIA
Executive Director

JLG:ls

915 North 5th Street • Phoenix. Arizona 85004 • (602) 271-9904

Chrysalis Shelter

A HOME OF RENEWAL FOR BATTERED WOMEN & CHILDREN

December 5, 1989

Mr. Nick Ligidakis
Golden Cuisine Restaurant
3903 E. Thomas Road
Phoenix, Arizona 85008

Dear Mr. Ligidakis & Staff:

We were deeply grateful for your very generous donations of 2
stuffed turkeys, bread, potatoes, yams, cranberries, and tea for
our Thanksgiving Dinner.

What a wonderful jesture of kindness, generosity, and good will you
have created in the community. Our b_ttered women and abused children
delighted in the feast.

I happened to see you on TV and marveled at what you were accomplishing.

Thank you for your kindness and may God bless you abundantly in the
wonderful Season of Christmas.

Sincerely,

CHRYSALIS SHELTER

Sister Michelle Dosch
Executive Director

/pk

PHOENIX SOUTH VETERANS PROGRAM
1041 WEST COLTER, #341
PHOENIX, AZ 85013
(602) 264-1792

Dear Sir,

First let me apologize for taking so long to get this to you. This letter needed to go out immediately after Thanksgiving.

On behalf of the staff and clients of the Phoenix South Veterans Program I would like to take this opportunity to thank you for the wonderful meal you provided on Thanksgiving Day. Your thoughtfulness is very much appreciated.

Our clients are homeless veterans, many of whom think their country has forgotten them after the sacrifices they made. Your action was a reminder that they still matter and are being remembered. You helped lift the veil of despair and let the light of hope shine through. Your generosity is a symbol of what is right with America at a time when others decry and deride the conditions under which the less fortunate must sometime live. You took the rare step of action, to do something, and not just look the other way.

Please pass on our thanks and wishes for a joyous holiday season to all who participated in your wonderful effort.

Sincerely,

Frank Cummings

Administrative Offices
(602) 257-9339

PHOENIX SOUTH
1424 South 7th Ave.
Phoenix, AZ 85007

Phoenix Lighthouse Ministries, Inc.

111 E. Southern
Phoenix, AZ 85040

Rev. Harold W. Kueneman
(602) 276-9409

November 29, 1990

Golden Cuisine Restaurant
3903 E. Thomas Rd.
Phoenix, Az. 85018
ATTN: Kathy Donhue

Dear Friends,

   We want to personally thank you for your generous
donation of Thanksgiving Dinner for the homeless families
here at Phoenix Lighthouse. Not only did we feed the
residents here, but almost one hundred homeless people
from the street were also fed. It is because of caring
and generous people like yourselves that we can continue
to feed and minister to homeless families. Enclosed
please find a brochure with more information about our
facility.

   Thanks again for your generous donation.

In His Service,

Harold W. Kueneman
Phoenix Lighthouse Ministries

For I was hungred, and ye gave me meat: I was thirsty, and ye gave me drink: I was a stranger, and ye took me in:
Naked, and ye clothed me: I was sick, and ye visited me: I was in prison, and ye came unto me:
MATTHEW 25:35 & 36

THE SALVATION ARMY
SOUTHWEST DIVISIONAL HEADQUARTERS

2707 East Van Buren Street, P.O. Box 52177
Phoenix, Arizona 85072
(602) 267-4100

November 29, 1990

Mr. Nick Ligidakis
The Golden Cuisine
3903 E. Thomas
Phoenix AZ   85018

Dear Mr. Ligidakis:

On behalf of The Salvation Army, I would like to express our sincere thanks for your generous donation of 500 Thanksgiving Dinners.   These were enjoyed by families in our shelter, adults in our Harbor Light Rehabilitation Program and seniors citizens.

Thank you again for your donation and for remembering The Salvation Army.

Sincerely,

Brenda Reichard

Brenda Reichard
Food Services Supervisor

BR/jrg

| WILLIAM BOOTH | COMMISSIONER PAUL A. RADER | MAJOR DONALD G. SATHER | EVA BURROWS |
| Founder | Territorial Commander | Divisional Commander | General |

5024 E. McDowell   314   Some of the Letters of Appreciation

HOMEWARD BOUND
Every Family Needs A Place To Call Home.

November 29, 1995

Mr. Nick Ligidakis
Nick's Cuisine Restaurant
3717 E. Indian School Rd.
Phoenix, AZ 85018

"NEVER DOUBT THAT A SMALL GROUP OF THOUGHTFUL COMMITTED CITIZENS CAN CHANGE THE WORLD; INDEED, IT'S THE ONLY THING THAT EVER DOES."

-Margaret Mead

Dear Nick:

With friends like you and your staff supporting our award-winning agency, we are indeed most blessed.

On behalf of the men, women and especially the children participating in the **Homeward Bound** program, heartfelt thanks for your generosity, kindness and support. Your donation of 70 Thanksgiving turkey dinners to our needy was greatly appreciated and truly enhanced **Homeward Bound's** efforts in assisting the families in our program during this special holiday. With your help, we fed everyone!

Each day our Case Managers and volunteer Sponsors are humbled by the complexity of issues facing today's family. Issues as simple as accessing food, shelter and water, and more complex issues like under-employment, lack of transportation, and poor access to health care.

Homeward Bound clients meet their many challenges with the support of two unique partners -- professional Case Manager and nurturing Sponsor. Success will continue to be measured on a case-by-case basis and in very human terms. Overall success is a family stabilizing and self-sufficient -- free of welfare programs, parenting well, healthy both mentally and physically, and hopeful about the future.

Again, thank you for your personal involvement in our effort which helps make this community we all serve a better place for all of us to live, work and play. I look forward to seeing you at our Sponsor Recognition Dinner next spring, where you will be our special guest.

Best wishes and kind regards,

P. David Bridger
Development Director

PDB:mg

Homeward Bound is a 501(c)(3) not-for-profit corporation. Tax ID #86-0660875.

29 WEST THOMAS • SUITE E • PHOENIX, AZ 85013-4492
602-263-7654
FAX: 602-265-4006

ST. VINCENT DE PAUL SOCIETY
PHOENIX DIOCESAN COUNCIL

Help Us Help Others

Programs & Services
Dining Room
119 S. 9th Ave.
Phoenix, AZ
258-5619

Medical/Dental Clinic
119 S. 9th Ave.
Phoenix, AZ
254-2919

Ministry to the Homeless
119 S. 9th Ave.
Phoenix, AZ
258-5619

Ministry to the Incarcerated
& Their Families
119 S. 9th Ave.
Phoenix, AZ
258-5619

Transient
Aid
Center (TAC)
2244 N. 12th St.
Phoenix, AZ
253-5326

Ozanam Manor/Housing
1730 E. Monroe
Phoenix, AZ
258-2018

Processing Center
& Food Bank
420 W. Watkins
Phoenix, AZ
254-3338

Stores
11518 Apache Trail
Apache Junction, AZ
986-1678

780 Marina
Bullhead City, AZ
758-5251

2109 E. Cedar
Flagstaff, AZ
779-4353

7018 N. 57th Ave.
Glendale, AZ
934-3249

1851 Commander
Lake Havasu, AZ
453-1776

13300 Central Ave.
Mayer, AZ
632-9521

2352 W. Main
Mesa, AZ
964-3925

Administration/
Training Center
420 W. Watkins
Phoenix, AZ
254-3338

Gary L. Brown
Executive Director

November 23, 1990

Mr. Nick Ligidakis
Golden Cuisine Restaurant
3903 East Thomas Road
Phoenix, AZ 85008

Dear Nick:

Our deepest thanks to you and to everyone on your staff who volunteered their time and energies so generously to provide Thanksgiving meals to the poor in Surprise and Peoria this year.

The Society, my staff, and I are well aware of the time and talents required by a donation of 1150 meals. Again, many, many thanks for sharing our commitment to fill a rapidly expanding need in the Valley of the Sun.

Cordially,

Christopher Becker
Director of Food Services

CB:rcj

P. O. Box 13600 • Phoenix, Arizona 85002
Telephone (602) 254-3338

PREHAB
OF ARIZONA

P.O. Drawer 5860 • Mesa, Arizona 85211-5860

(602) 969-4024

November 30, 1989

Mr. Nick Ligidakis
Golden Cuisine Restaurant
3903 E. Thomas Road
Phoenix, AZ 85008

Dear Mr. Ligidakis,

We, the staff and clients at Prehab's Autumn House, would
like to extend our deepest appreciation for the wonderful
Thanksgiving dinner that you prepared and provided for us.
It is heartwarming to know that people give of themselves
to such an extent and want to share with those who are less
fortunate.

Believe me, our clients thoroughly enjoyed every bite of
that delicious meal! At the end of the day, they felt
happy, full and nurtured. It's great to know someone
cares.

Once again, thank you for your generosity and support.

Sincerely,

Mellisa Womack
Director
Prehab's Autumn House

MW/sl

5024 E. McDowell   317   Some of the Letters of Appreciation

Arizona AIDS *Project Inc.*

919 *North First Street, Phoenix, Arizona* 85004-1902   602-420-9396

December 15, 1989

Nick Ligidakis
Golden Cuisine Restaurant
3903 East Thomas Road
Phoenix, Arizona 85008

Dear Nick and your wonderful volunteers;

What a wonderful way to express the true spirit of the
Holiday Season--to provide meals to people who are
infected with HIV disease. Too many people in our
society believe the way to find happiness and
fulfillment is through self indulgence. You, however,
have found the answer, in giving and doing for others.

Through your generosity we were able to deliver 84
Thanksgiving Dinners to clients, their caregiver, and
their families. I think it is important that you know
how many people you have touched through your time and
efforts and donations. You are to be commended for your
generosity.

I would like to extend to you an invitation to visit AAP
at your earliest convenience. I would love to show you
our agency.

Sincerely,

Sue Dodd

Sue Dodd, MSN
Executive Director

Scottsdale Community College

September 17, 1993

Mr. Nick Ligidakis
Nick's Cuisine Restaurant
3717 E. Indian School Road
Phoenix, AZ 85018

Dear Nick:

Well, you exceeded expectations on all counts! We were all impressed with your hard work, dedication and interest in the business. Your willingness to share your path to success opened a lot of student's eyes to the reality of an entrepreneur's life.

Everyone was truly amazed at how you put out your menu and some of your staffing insights. Your dedication to community service sets a standard for us all to look to for inspiration.

Thank you for coming to speak to our class and particularly for your candor and honesty. Good Luck to you.

Hospitably yours,

Lynn McGoff
Faculty
Hotel & Restaurant Program

JCPenney

GOLDEN · RULE
AWARD

JCPenney on behalf of the community commends
and thanks you for exceptional volunteer service.

Nick Ligidakis

Sally Sunderland
Chairman of Award Panel

Jim Order
JCPenney Manager

EMPACT - SPC

1232 E. Broadway Road, Ste. 120 • Tempe, AZ 85282 • Office (602) 784-1514 • FAX (602) 967-3528 • Crisis Line (602) 784-1500

Ilene L. Dode, Ph.D.	L. Jay A. Gray, Ph.D.	Steven Kalas, M.Th.
Executive Director	Clinical Director	Prevention Director

December 7, 1994

Mr. Nick Ligidakis
Nick's Cuisine
3717 East Indian School Road
Phoenix, Arizona 85018

Dear Mr. Ligidakis,

On behalf of Scottsdale EMPACT - SPC and our VISTA volunteers, I would like to extend our most sincere thanks to your organization for your generous support and assistance with your recent donation.

We were very pleased with the success of the Thanksgiving Celebration in our community. Thanks to your generosity several hundred people came together to enjoy a wonderful Thanksgiving feast.

Once again, we thank you for your continued support in serving the needs of our community. We look forward to working with you in the future.

With kind regards,

Alberto L. Esparza
Prevention Specialist
/lb

A non-profit agency certified by the American Association of Suicidology. A United Way Agency.
A member agency of: CODAMA.

Unived Way

Central Presbyterian Church
37 E. Indian School Rd.
Phoenix, AZ 85012
Rev. Joedd Miller, Pastor

November 30, 1994

Mr. Nick Ligidakis
Nick's Cuisine
3717 East Indian School Road
Phoenix, Arizona 85018

Dear Mr. Ligidakis,

I am writing to thank you for your generous attention to our community with the Thanksgiving dinners which you provided to so many people. Not many people who cook year-round and run a restaurant would want to take on such a gargantuan task as feeding so many people at a time when if possible a person wants to reduce work and enjoy family.

You effort to commitment has been inspiring and very helpful to many people.

May God continue to bless, challenge and nourish you throughout the holiday season and the New Year.

Sincerely,

Rev. Joedd Miller

JM/rb

November 29, 1993

Nick's Cuisine
3717 E. Indian School Road
Phoenix, Az.   85018

Dear Nick, Kathy and staff:

I wanted to send you a quick note of congratulations on a wonderful job regarding the THANKSGIVING FEAST. I'm certain that this generous act of giving has impacted many individuals across our community, many who will in turn reach out and make a difference for another person.

I wanted to let you know how much I enjoyed the opportunity to participate with this effort. It never ceases to amaze me at the generous and kind individuals that "migrate" to efforts such as this. Our organization has prospered because of the wonderful community and volunteer support we have received. I hope that our community will continue in its strong focus of giving and helping. We all benefit from the kindness and generosity of reaching out and helping one another.

Thanks again for your efforts. You can count on me for next year.

Sincerely,

Ted Rogers

2701 N. 16th St.
Suite 218
Phoenix, AZ 85006
602.264.9254

A
United Way
Agency

Sojourner Center
A safe haven.

January 3, 1995

Nick's Cuisine
3711 E. Indian School
Phoenix, AZ 85008

Dear Nick,

On behalf of the Sojourner Center and the women and children we serve, a most sincere thank you for your help in making this holiday season special for our community's battered women and children. The generosity of many caring people was a vivid illustration of the true meaning of Christmas and the spirit of giving.

Between our two Chirstmas Programs, Adopt-A-Family and Operation Santa, along with other miscellaneous donations, we were able to make this Christmas truly special for every woman and child in Sojourner Center's programs. This included providing gifts, parties, food and Christmas cheer to 17 women and 25 children in shelter as well as providing gifts, food and gift certificates to 41 families who are in the community.

Best wishes for a safe and happy new year. Again, thank you for your help.

Connie Phillips

Connie Phillips
Executive Director

P.O. Box 20156, Phoenix, Arizona 85036 ▪ (602) 244-0997 FAX (602) 244-8006
An Equal Opportunity Employer • Male/Female/Handicapped/Vietnam Veteran

ife Symington
Governor

Linda J. Blessing, DP.
Director

January, 1996

To All our Friends at Nick's Cuisine,

HAPPY NEW YEAR!!!

> "I don't know what your destiny will be but one thing I
> know, the only ones among you who will be really happy
> are those who have sought and found how to serve."
>   Albert Schweitzer

On behalf of the Division of Developmental Disabilities, we
sincerely thank you for your volunteer service in assisting
in our Holiday Adopt-A-Family Program.

Many of our families have additional financial stress due to
the sometimes enormous costs of caring for a family member
who is disabled. The extra assistance during the holidays
does make a difference.

Again, thank you! We deeply appreciate your generosity and
caring. Have a great New Year!

Sincerely,

Randi Rummage

Randi Rummage
Volunteer Services Coordinator
DES/DDD District I

Faith McLoone

Faith McLoone
Volunteer Services Coordinator
DES/DDD District I

Thank you so
much for all of
your wonderful meals
for our clients this
Thanksgiving!! Our
families really appreciated
your generosity. Thank You!
Randi Rummage

City of Phoenix
HUMAN SERVICES DEPARTMENT
SENIOR SERVICES DIVISION

November 30, 1994

Nick's Cuisine
3717 East Indian School Road
Phx., Az. 85018

Dear Nick,

Many thanks for your help in serving a Thanksgiving meal to the needy individuals who participate in City Of Phoenix programs. Telephones have been ringing off the hook all week with people calling to express appreciation for the excellent meal.

I must admit that I had a few tense moments after promising 2,500 people that they would get a meal, knowing that you were collecting turkeys right up to the last minute. Kathy really has nerves of steel!! She did an excellent job of coordinating this extraordinary effort-particularly just before her wedding!

Thank you Nick for your hard work, and the work of your employees . You gave many people something very special to celebrate this year!

Best wishes for a happy holiday season!

Sincerely,

Cathy Maiden
Cathy Maiden
Senior Services Coordinator

City of Phoenix
HUMAN SERVICES DEPARTMENT
SENIOR SERVICES DIVISION

January 8, 1996

To Whom It May Concern:

This letter is written to confirm that on December 14, 1995, Nick Ligidakis of Nick's Cuisine was awarded the 1995 Business Award at the City of Phoenix, Community Recognition Dinner. This special recogntion was granted to Mr. Ligidakis because of his humanitarian effort in feeding the hungry on Thanksgiving Day. Each year the City's Human Services Department recognizes special individuals and organizations in the community who perform outstanding community service. Nick's Cuisine certainly fits the bill!

If more individuals in private industry performed community service with the committment that Mr. Ligidakis does, the world would be a better place!

Sincerely,

Cathy Maiden

Cathy Maiden
Senior Programs Coordinator

5024 E. McDowell   327   Some of the Letters of Appreciation

City of Phoenix
HUMAN SERVICES DEPARTMENT
EDUCATION DIVISION

December 7, 1994

Nick's Cuisine
3717 E. Indian School Rd.
Phoenix, AZ 85008

ATTN. Nick Ligidakis

Dear Mr. Ligidakis:

I would like to take this opportunity to express appreciation on behalf of Phoenix Human Services Department Head Start Families for the Thanksgiving dinners, form Nicks Cuisine.

The families expressed that they really enjoyed the delicious dinner.   Your example of sharing has truly given meaning to Thanksgiving Day.

Again, on behalf of Head Start Families, I sincerely extend a sincere thank you and best wishes to you and your staff.

Sincerely,

Hiram Carroll
Head Start Caseworker III

HC:eh

c: Karen B. Easley
        Ellen O'Kelly

NEW CASA DE AMIGAS

303 West Portland • Phoenix, Arizona 85003

December 5, 1991

Mr. Nick Ligidakis
Nick's Golden Cuisine
3903 E. Thomas Road
Phoenux, Az. 85008

Dear Mr. Ligidakis:

    May we take this opportunity to express our appreciation
for your kind thoughtfulness, concern, and support for the
clients of the Casa de Amigas that we are serving.

    Turning troubled lives into responsible human beings is
an expensive proposition. Your contribution will help us in
helping people to help themselves, and we share with you in
the joy of knowing that in love and respect you have
participated in the rehabilitation of others.

    Your donation is tax exempt under our status as provided
in I.R.S. code, section 170 of 501 (c)(3). Tax ID 86-0185416.

                                        Sincerely,

                                        Joan B. French
                                        Executive Director

The following information is available for our mutual benefit
in record-keeping:

TYPE OF CONTRIBUTION :   Thanksgiving Dinner for 30

VALUE : $300.00

JBF:jrr

A home of recovery for the women with a drinking problem.
Casa De Amigas receives public funds from the Arizona Department of Health Services, thru CODAMA.

Osborn School District No. 8

"Over a Century of Excellence in Public Education"

Founded 1879

1226 West Osborn Road
Phoenix, Arizona 85013
Telephone (602) 234-3366
FAX (602) 265-1583

December 9, 1992

Nick's Cuisine
3717 East Indian School Road
Phoenix, Arizona 85018

Dear Nick,

As I watched the human interest story on the evening news Tuesday night, I was so impressed with the restaurateur who gave so much of himself for others. Little did I know you would reach out to our families the very next day with some of your turkey dinners.

Your kindness will have a long lasting effect on many lives. We thank you for your generosity in a time of great need in our community.

Sincerely,

Joanne L. Talazus,
Principal-Longview

April 22, 1993

Mr. Nick Ligidakis
3717 East Indian School Road
Phoenix, Arizona   85018

Dear Nick:

Congratulations for being a JCPenney Golden Rule Award Finalist!

Each year at Thanksgiving time, I deeply appreciate all your efforts when you see that the more than 400 homeless men, women, and children we serve receive a hot meal. I know that you have also greatly expanded your efforts and serve even more than our guests. I feel it is only appropriate that you be recognized for your efforts to help those that are less fortunate.

Thank you, too, for designating CASS as the recipient of the contribution of $250.

I look forward to seeing you at the luncheon on May 19th.

Sincerely,

Mary Orton
Executive Director

MO\aj\gen\nick.493

UNITED WAY

City of Phoenix
HUMAN SERVICES DEPARTMENT
SENIOR SERVICES DIVISION

November 30, 1994

Nick Ligidakis
Nick's Cuisine
3717 E. Indian School
Phoenix, Arizona 85018

Dear Nick,

Westside Senior Center thanks you immensely for your generous
donation. Thanks to you and your staff we were able to feed
approximately 200 Seniors, who other wise might not have had a
Thanksgiving Dinner.

May you and the staff at Nick's Cuisine have a Happy and Safe
Holiday Season.

Thanks Again,
Westside Senior Center
4343 W. Thomas
Phoenix Arizona 85031

5024 E. McDowell

Some of the Letters of Appreciation

 **Cystic Fibrosis Foundation**

June 23, 1994

Carey Sweet
NICK'S CUISINE
3717 E. Indian School Rd.
Phoenix, AZ 85018

Dear Carey:

Thank you for your generous contribution to our Moonlight Magic Event. Donations from companies such as yours enable us to offer a first-rate silent auction to our guests. Accordingly, we are able to raise money which brings us closer to our goal in finding a cure to this terrible disease.

I look forward to working with your company in the future. We appreciate all you've done to support Cystic Fibrosis.

Very truly yours,

Amy R. Post

Amy R. Post
Director of Special Events

Arizona Chapter
2345 E. Thomas Rd., Suite 420   Phoenix, Arizona 85016
(602) 224-0068   Fax (602) 224-0432

SPRING HAVEN

*A residential treatment center for
girls who are victims of sexual abuse.*

November 21, 1991

Nick Ligadakis
Golden Cuisine
3903 E. Thomas Road
Phoenix, Arizona 85008

Dear Mr. Ligadakis,

Enclosed is a certificate expressing our appreciation for your donating to the girls at Spring Haven West.

I was sorry you were unable to attend the volunteer recognition luncheon to thank you personally. I had full intentions of coming to you to thank you and to give you this certificate but I see a month has already passed and I haven't been able to get to you.

The staff and the residents of Spring Haven thank you for your consideration and generosity throughout the year. Again, I am sorry not to meet you personally.

Sincerely,

Margaret Rand

Margaret Rand, M.Ed.
Director
Spring Haven West

MR:pmw

Enclosure

*A program of Catholic Social Service Phoenix,
a division of Catholic Family and Community Services*

1825 W. Northern Avenue • Phoenix, Arizona 85021 • 997-6105

5024 E. McDowell   334   Some of the Letters of Appreciation

A Division of
Foodmaker, Inc.
4239 South 43rd Place
Phoenix, AZ 85040
602/437-1346

May 13, 1994

Nick Ligidakis
3717 E. Indian School Rd.
Phoenix, AZ 85018

Dear Nick:

Congratulations! We at JACK IN THE BOX restaurants are pleased to declare you a
local **HERO.**

More than one hundred Valley residents were nominated, reflecting as many
outstanding stories of courage and heroism. Our panel of judges selected you as
on of the very best. Being named as one of the ten local heroes is an
accomplishment of which you can justifiably be proud.

In recognition of your heroism, please accept the enclosed Heros Certificate.

Again, congratulations on your willingness to share your talents with others.

Sincerely,

Chrissa M. Wurm
Regional Marketing Manager
JACK IN THE BOX restaurants

Enclosure

CW/ap

SHELTER FOR HOMELESS FAMILIES
WITH THEIR CHILDREN -
SHELTER FOR HOMELESS COUPLES
AND SINGLES -
HOMES FOR THE HANDICAPPED -
TRANSITIONAL AND LOW-COST
HOUSING -
FUTURE INTERNATIONAL RESEARCH
EXCHANGE IN LIFE SPAN STUDIES
WE ARE NOT A GRANT-AWARDING
FOUNDATION-

November 16, 1991

TO: Nick Ligidakis
    Golden Cuisine
    3903 E. Thomas Rd.
    Phoenix, Arizona 85018

Dear Mr. Ligidakis,

We are writing to express our thanks for your thoughtful kindness.

Bud Gleave informed us that he told you about our Homeless Ministry
and of your extremely generous offer to include us for Thanksgiving
dinner meals.

We are most grateful for your offer to not only include but to deliver
a Thanksgiving dinner for our homeless families, couples, singles, and
mentally handicapped. Enclosed is our information sheet. Remember, for
delivery, take either Thomas, or McDowell, or Van Buren or Washington
to 15th Ave. We are a half block north of Van Buren. Look for sign
Capitol Square Apartments. This is the site of the Whole Life shelter.

We enjoyed reading your excellent newsletter. How I personally wish I
could attend your cooking classes, but I could not pay for it because
until we are funded, we seldom have enough money to buy food to feed
our people three times daily, seven days per week. We always depend on
God's grace through donated food to make up for what I cannot purchase.
Would you consider taking a tax writeoff for cooking classes for me?

God bleass you for your offer.

Sincerely,

Isabel McMahel
Isabel McMahel
President

(602) 256-2828   (602) 254-6553
338 NORTH 15TH AVE. • PHOENIX, AZ 85007
(On Site of Capital Square Apartments)
MAILING ADDRESS:
P.O. BOX 13207 • PHOENIX, AZ 85002

1300 W. Queen Creek Road
Chandler, Arizona 85248
(602) 899-3113

December 13, 1993

Nick's Cuisine
3717 E. Indian School Road
Phoenix, AZ 85018

Re: Thanksgiving Donations

Dear Sir/Madam:

On behalf of all Sunburst clients and staff, I would like to thank you for your generosity. Your donations have been much appreciated by all of us and have made our Thanksgiving a very special day.

Sincerely,

Carolyn G. Haynes, Executive Director

Index

Notes & Personal Recipes

Notes & Personal Recipes

Notes & Personal Recipes

ORDER FORM

Coming in August, 1997:

Nick's new exciting inspirational book presented by Inkwell Productions:

"The Heroes Of My Thoughts"

True heroes will make you believe in yourself. They will inspire your mind with confidence to be the best you can be. And through their examples will infuse your heart with courage to overcome the difficulties in your life.

This new book is a travel of the mind to the past to find the ones who have touched our lives and have motivated us to be who we are, and a journey into the future to find solutions to inspire the ones we love and help them be sensitive to our social problems and kind to themselves.

This new book includes 36 chapters filled with stories and thoughts from Nick's childhood to the present. This book is a tribute to his parents, whom he considers to be his two biggest heroes.

To reserve a copy of this book, fill in the bottom of this form and return to Inkwell Productions, P.O. Box 388, Phoenix, Arizona 85001

If you would like to reserve a copy of Nick's new book, *"The Heroes Of My Thoughts,"* please check the box below. No money is necessary at this time. You will be notified by mail when the book is published by August, 1997.

☐ *The Heroes Of My Thoughts*

If you would like to order any of the following books, please check the box next to the titles and send this form with your check or money order for the appropriate amount. No shipping or handling charges are added to the cost.

☐ *Nick's Creative Cooking Made Easy* $15.95

☐ *My Golden Collection of Original Desserts* $21.95

☐ *5024 E. McDowell* $25.95

Mail this form with your check or money order to:
Inkwell Productions
P.O. Box 388
Phoenix, Arizona 85001

For more information call (602) 262-2610 or FAX (602) 252-4929